MERTON & THE PROTESTANT TRADITION

MERTON & THE PROTESTANT TRADITION

Edited by William Oliver Paulsell

FONS VITAE

The Fons Vitae Thomas Merton Series

Merton & Sufism: The Untold Story, 1999
Merton & Hesychasm: The Prayer of the Heart, 2003
Merton & Judaism: Holiness in Words, 2003
Merton & Buddhism: Wisdom, Emptiness, and Everyday Mind, 2007
Merton & The Tao: Dialogues with John C. H. Wu and the Ancient Sages, 2013
Merton & The Protestant Tradition, 2016

Fons Vitae is deeply grateful to Anne Ogden, Jeannie Younger, and Emma Proietti for their proofreading.

First published in 2016 by
Fons Vitae
49 Mockingbird Valley Drive
Louisville, KY 40207
http://www.fonsvitae.com

Library of Congress Control Number: 2016954484

ISBN 978-1891785-740

Cover photograph of Martin Luther King, Jr.

This book was typeset by Neville Blakemore, Jr.

Printed in Canada

To Sally, Stephanie, and Diane

The sponsorship of this volume is offered in honor of my father, Owsley Brown II. His example of a life in faith is the most profound of gifts to me. The Protestant tradition was the rock upon which he stood to admire the gifts of life. His hopes of being always generous in spirit, as well as loving and kind at heart, are the model upon which I base my life today.

Owsley Brown III

CONTENTS

Contents, continued

THE FONS VITAE THOMAS MERTON SERIES

Professional theologians and lay readers, scholars, and spiritual seekers in a broad spectrum of religious practice regard the Cistercian monk Thomas Merton (1915-1968) as one of the most important spiritual writers of the last half of the twentieth century. The writing impelled by his monastic life's interests in the world's religious traditions are recognized as a seminal and continuing catalyst for inter-religious dialogue in the twenty-first century.

Ewert Cousins, a distinguished Professor of Religion and the General Editor of both the World Spirituality Series and the Classics of Western Spirituality Series of Paulist Press, has called Merton an "axial figure" who bridges, within his own experience and theological work, the contemporary estrangements between religious and secular perspectives. Dr. Cousins has publicly shared his opinion that Thomas Merton means almost more today to many than he actually did in his lifetime. He is becoming an iconic figure who models inter-religious dialogue for those who are seeking a common ground of respect for the varied ways in which human beings realize the sacred in their lives. Merton's life and writing, especially when it focuses on the contemplative practices common to the world's major religions, have indeed become a forum, or a bridge in Cousins' term, upon which those engaged in inter-religious dialogue can meet and engage one another.

In his reaching out to living representatives of the world's various religious traditions by correspondence, and by his immersing himself in the study of religious traditions other than his own Roman Catholicism, Merton models the inclusivity of intellect and heart necessary for fruitful inter-religious dialogue. His personal journal for April 28, 1957, witnesses to his zeal for a unity of learning and living as a method of personal "inner work" for ensuring communication and respect among religious persons:

> If I can unite in myself, in my own spiritual life, the thought of the East and the West, of the Greek and Latin Fathers, I will create in myself a reunion of the divided Church, and from that

> unity in myself can come the exterior and visible unity of the church. For, if we want to bring together East and West, we cannot do it by imposing one upon the other. We must contain both in ourselves and transcend them both in Christ.

The Fons Vitae publishing project for the study of world religions through the lens of Thomas Merton's life and writing brings Merton's timeless vision of all persons united in a "hidden ground of Love" to a contemporary audience. The first five volumes of the Fons Vitae Thomas Merton Series—*Merton & Sufism, Merton & Hesychasm, Merton & Judaism, Merton & Buddhism,* and *Merton & The Tao*— featured essays by international scholars who gathered in three academic conferences in Louisville, Kentucky to assess the value of Merton's contributions to inter-religious dialogue. Each volume includes Merton's own writing across various genres: essays, poetry, and transcriptions of his lectures to the novices at Gethsemani that highlighted Merton's interest in contemplative traditions other than his own.

This sixth volume in the Fons Vitae Thomas Merton series, *Merton & The Protestant Tradition*, engages Merton's hospitality to the entire Christian experience particularly mediated to him through his close reading of Protestant thinkers and theologians, and then his subsequent use of their ideas and experiences in his own books and general writing. More importantly, the Protestant tradition informed Merton's personal meditations and prayers. Merton's openness to the Protestant tradition extended beyond his personal study and prayer. He was the first monk of Gethsemani to dialogue and meet with groups of neighboring Protestant teachers and their students from Louisville and Lexington, Kentucky. The first part of this volume is a scholar's report on Merton's evolving attitude toward the Protestant tradition as evidenced by his books, correspondence and private journals.

Celebrating the centenary of Merton's birth in 2015, Fons Vitae published *We Are Already One: Thomas Merton's Message of Hope*. Over one hundred contributors reflected on their first encounters with Merton's writing and then on the continuing influence that Thomas Merton's life and witness has continually exerted on their lives. The second part of this new volume continues this celebration of Merton's importance in the lives of contemporary Protestants. These personal essays demonstrate that the monk's dialogue with the Protestant tradition continues into the twenty-first century.

The forthcoming volume in this series will present studies by anthropologists, sociologists, and first nation scholars and theologians edited and collected under the title *Merton & Indigenous World Wisdom*. We hope that the Fons Vitae Thomas Merton series will find a place in the libraries of those who promote the study and practice of contemplative religious traditions.

Jonathan Montaldo and Gray Henry
General Editors
for the Fons Vitae Thomas Merton Series

THOMAS MERTON'S PRAYER

The following prayer was offered by Thomas Merton at the First Spiritual Summit Conference in Calcutta. It appears as part of Appendix V in *The Asian Journal of Thomas Merton.* We offer it again here as the context from which this book arose and in which it has been prepared for publication.

> Oh God, we are one with You. You have made us one with You. You have taught us that if we are open to one another, You dwell in us. Help us to preserve this openness and to fight for it with all our hearts. Help us to realize that there can be no understanding where there is mutual rejection. Oh God, in accepting one another wholeheartedly, fully, completely, we accept You, and we thank You, and we adore You, and we love You with our whole being, because our being is in Your being, our spirit is rooted in Your spirit. Fill us then with love, and let us be bound together with love as we go our diverse ways, united in this one spirit which makes You present in the world, and which makes You witness to the ultimate reality that is love. Love has overcome. Love is victorious. Amen.

PREFACE

Brother Paul Quenon, of the Abbey of Gethsemani, had talked to me several times about putting together a book on Thomas Merton and Protestants. As a Protestant minister and a frequent visitor and retreatant at Gethsemani, I was interested, but kept putting him off because of other projects in which I was involved. We were very pleased when Fons Vitae, a publisher well known to Merton readers for its high quality publications, expressed an interest in the project. Brother Paul began to suggest writers and I began research.

When I was a seminarian and graduate student at Vanderbilt University, I had the opportunity to visit Gethsemani five times in a group of young aspirants to the Protestant ministry. On two of those occasions Thomas Merton met with us. The first time I had no idea who Merton was, although a few of my fellow students did know. As soon as that session was over I went to the bookstore in the old gatehouse and bought a paperback copy of *The Seven Storey Mountain*. Like many others, I was greatly influenced by it and was ultimately led to reading of almost all the Merton corpus. This, in turn, generated an academic interest in Cistercian history and participation in annual Cistercian history conferences at Western Michigan University. Merton and the Cistercians have been a significant influence on not just me, but my whole family. My wife and I make annual retreats at Gethsemani, and when our daughters come to our home in Lexington they always want to visit the monastery. One daughter is now an associate of an Episcopal monastery in upstate New York. The other teaches courses on spirituality at Harvard Divinity School. I realize that this book represents the culmination of many fine experiences we have had with monks whose hospitality is always warm and gracious.

Many thanks to Brothers Paul Quenon and Patrick Hart, as well as Fathers Matthew Kelty and Michael Casagram, and a series of Gethsemani Guest Masters, who, over the years, have contributed so much to my own spiritual development.

This book will have two parts. The first part will be a reporting on Merton's evolving attitude toward Protestants found in his books, letters, and journals. The second part will consist of articles by Protestants who describe the kinds of influence Merton has had on them. I am grateful to all who contributed.

William Oliver Paulsell
July 1, 2016

PART I
PROTESTANTISM IN MERTON'S WRITINGS

INTRODUCTION

William Oliver Paulsell

The general contours of Thomas Merton's life are well known to those with an interest in spirituality. Born in 1915 in Prades, France, he was the child of artists who met while studying art in Paris. Three years later a brother, John Paul, was born. Unfortunately, Merton's mother, Ruth Jenkins, died of stomach cancer when he was only six years old. John Paul moved in with his grandparents in New York, and Thomas traveled about with his father who wanted to paint in a variety of locations. They eventually settled in St. Antonin in France, where he received some basic schooling.

After they moved to England, his father died of brain cancer. Thomas was 16 years old. He was taken in by a friend of his father, Thomas Bennett, a London physician, who saw to it that Merton completed his education. Receiving a scholarship, Merton enrolled in Clare College, Cambridge, supposedly to study languages. Before entering Cambridge he made a trip to Rome where he was impressed with the churches, particularly the Eastern Orthodox and their iconography. Religious feelings began to stir, but they did not last.

The year in Cambridge was a disaster. Exercising his new freedom, Merton decided to sample every dissolute pleasure he could find, especially those that included sex and alcohol. When Merton went to New York to visit his grandparents during the summer, a disgusted Bennett wrote him a letter suggesting that it would be best if he did not return to England.

Merton enrolled in Columbia University where he became heavily involved in campus life. He joined a fraternity, flirted with communism, worked on the humor magazine and the campus annual, and joined the track team, among other things. He developed some friendships which would be important to his writing career later, including a fellow student who would later publish his early autobiography.

Two professors were major influences on Merton: Mark Van

Doren and Dan Walsh. Merton encountered Van Doren by accident. He was looking for a history course for which he had registered, but realized he was in the wrong classroom. For some reason he decided to stay where he was and discovered Van Doren's course on Shakespeare was scheduled for that room. Later Merton said, "It was the best course I ever had in college." It was here that he heard about "life, death, time, love, sorrow, fear, wisdom, suffering, eternity."[1]

Walsh was not a regular faculty member but taught two days a week on Duns Scotus and Thomas Aquinas. He knew Etienne Gilson, whose book on *The Spirit of Medieval Philosophy* was an important influence on Merton's conversion. He was also a friend of Jacques Maritain with whom Merton would develop a friendship and who would later visit him at Gethsemani. Merton liked Walsh because he rose above different points of view and saw Catholic philosophy "in its wholeness."[2] Under these kinds of inspirations, and others, Merton began to develop a more serious interest in religion, specifically Roman Catholicism. Gilson's *The Spirit of Medieval Philosophy* helped him see God in a different way. He received instruction in the Catholic faith and was baptized and confirmed in 1938.

After graduation in 1938 he began work on a Master's degree, writing a thesis on William Blake. He had an intention to study for a Ph.D. but did not complete it.

He now began to see a vocation in the priesthood as a possibility for him, and applied to become a Franciscan. However, he was told that his previous life at Cambridge indicated he probably did not have a vocation. That was a major disappointment for Merton. He bought a breviary and began to pray the offices regularly, thinking that if he could not become a monk he would at least try to live like one.

Merton had been teaching extension courses for Columbia, but finally found a position in the English Department at St. Bonaventure College. He enjoyed his teaching and was comfortable in the Franciscan atmosphere of the school. However, he did not see this as his life's work.

In the summer of 1940 Merton visited Cuba, a popular vacation

---

1. Thomas Merton, *The Seven Storey Mountain*. New York: Harcourt Inc., 1948, p. 197.

2. *Seven Storey Mountain*, p. 241.

spot for Americans. He visited a number of churches and had what many would call a mystical experience in a Franciscan church. Still, he complained that he had not yet developed the prayer life that he wanted.

Dan Walsh had once mentioned the Abbey of Gethsemani to Merton, and he decided to spend Holy Week there. He was now twenty-seven years old. The retreat experience was powerful. After a brief time working with Catherine Doherty serving the poor in Harlem, he decided that he needed a situation where he would have time to write. On December 10, 1941, he entered Gethsemani. The rest, as they say, is history.

He became a novice, a Junior with temporary vows, and finally solemnly professed. In 1949 he was ordained a priest. During his lifetime he published over fifty books, and many more appeared after his death including five volumes of letters, seven volumes of his journal, and several unpublished manuscripts. His early autobiography, *The Seven Storey Mountain*, was a best seller and has influenced hundreds of thousands, probably millions, of readers. Doctoral dissertations have been written about him, and the celebration of his centennial in 2015 stimulated even more publication.

In the monastery he served as Master of Scholastics and, later, Master of Novices. From time to time he felt the urge to join the Carthusians or the Camaldolese, which were hermit orders. He even made plans to move to Mexico, Chile, and Nicaragua. Nothing came of them. However, Abbot James Fox had a small hermitage built where Merton could spend afternoons, then an occasional day, then a few overnights, and finally he was allowed to make a permanent move. He spent the last three years of his life as a full-time hermit. He died in an accident in Thailand in 1968 while attending a meeting of Asian abbots.

Throughout his life he remained a faithful Catholic. He had to endure the decisions of censors of his writings, he was told by the Trappist authorities that he had to stop writing about peace issues, and he often chaffed under monastic traditions that he thought were out of date. His writings were orthodox, but his letters and journals reveal struggles with theological issues about which he could not publish. Those who have studied his whole life saw the evolution in his thinking about many issues. Some scholars distinguish between the early Merton and the late Merton. One element of that evolution was his growing appreciation of non-Catholic Christianity and the other major religions of the world. What was his attitude toward the Protestant tradition in this evolution? To that issue we now turn.

BOOKS

THE SEVEN STOREY MOUNTAIN

William Shannon, who was one of the foremost Merton scholars, noted that Merton converted to Catholicism at the height of Catholic triumphalism. The Church was still responding to the Protestant Reformation, and refused to open itself to questions. It believed that it alone had the truth, and all other churches and religions were wrong. Merton bought into this outlook, and the *Seven Story Mountain* reflects an attitude about Protestant inferiority. Shannon quoted a young woman who said, "Why is he so vituperative about Protestants? Are they really that bad?"[1]

Merton's maternal grandparents were Protestants. Although they contributed financially to Zion Episcopal Church, they never attended. There was a general attitude in the family of opposition to Jews and Catholics. His grandmother was attracted to Christian Science and read the books of Mary Baker Eddy. That was, Merton said, "the closest she got to religion." His grandfather's hatred and suspicion of Catholics "really took root in my mind, and became part of my mental attitude." Merton said that as a child he went to Sunday School a few times, but found it so boring that he went to play in the woods rather than go back.[2]

His mother, Ruth Jenkins Merton, attended Quaker meetings. "This was the only kind of religion for which she had any use."[3] Merton reported that he attended a Quaker meeting with his father when his mother was in the hospital. Father explained that Quakers just sat quietly until the Holy Spirit prompted someone to speak.

His father was the organist at an Episcopal church. Merton said that he gave thought to becoming a Catholic, but knew such a move would be a problem in the family. However, Merton later concluded that his father always understood art as contemplation, and "that it involved the action of the highest faculties of man."[4]

1. *Seven Storey Mountain*, p. xxi.
2. *Seven Storey Mountain*, pp. 27-30.
3. *Seven Storey Mountain*, p. 11.
4. *Seven Storey Mountain*, p. 222.

Later, when Owen Merton was dying from brain cancer in a London hospital, Thomas realized that his father was the only one in the family who had any kind of faith. During his suffering, Thomas believed, Owen's intelligence and will were turned to God and communed with God. His suffering was used to perfect his soul. "It was a great soul, large, full of natural charity," Merton wrote, "and his terrible affliction was not destroying him."[5]

Merton occasionally attended the Episcopal Church where his father played the organ. He was impressed with the processional and liked the stained glass windows, especially the one with an anchor in it. As a child Merton said he had dreams of going to sea and seeing the world. There was an American flag, and "one of those little boards they have in Protestant churches, on which the numbers of the hymns to be sung are indicated by black and white cards." Merton wrote that he "came out of church with a kind of comfortable feeling that something had been done that needed to be done." He added, "I see that it was very good that I should have got at least that much of religion in my childhood."[6]

When Merton and his father returned to France, Owen Merton wanted Thomas to have some religious instruction, although he was not enthusiastic about French Protestantism. At the Lycée Thomas attended, a "fat Protestant minister" explained Jesus' parables, such as the Good Samaritan and the Pharisee and the Publican as moral lessons. Merton's evaluation: "it was practically useless."[7]

While at school in England at Ripley Court Merton was exposed to Anglicanism, which he described as "a class religion, the cult of a special society and group, not even of a whole nation but of the ruling minority of a nation."[8] It seemed to him that there was no doctrinal unity, the people did not really believe in the sacraments, and there was no mystical bond between people. He complained about "its lack of vital contact with the Mystical Body of the True Church, the social injustice and the class oppression on which it is based."[9]

He described a sermon given by the chaplain at Ripley Court on I Corinthians 13. "Charity," in this sermon meant being a gentleman.

5. *Seven Storey Mountain*, p. 92.
6. *Seven Storey Mountain*, p. 14.
7. *Seven Storey Mountain*, p. 59.
8. *Seven Storey Mountain*, p. 72.
9. *Seven Storey Mountain*, p. 73.

He suggested to the boys that in this chapter they substitute 'gentleman' for 'charity.' Merton mused that Paul's famous statement about faith, hope, and love, could be changed to "faith, hope, and being a gentleman, but the greatest of these is being a gentleman." Merton doubted that Christ died on the cross in order that these boys all might become gentlemen.

While Owen Merton was dying, Thomas Bennett, who would become Merton's guardian, sent him to Strasbourg for the Christmas holidays to stay in a Protestant pension in an attempt to improve his knowledge of French and German. Merton was impressed by a theologian, Professor Hering. He described Hering as "one of the few Protestants I have ever met who struck one as being at all holy: that is, he professed a certain profound interior peace, which he probably got from his contact with the Fathers of the Church, for he was a teacher of theology."[10] Merton's impression was that he saw various religious forms of belief as manifestations of a human instinct. This helped to confirm Merton's evaluation that "Protestant theology does, in certain circumstances, amount to little more than a combination of sociology and religious history."[11]

Experiences in America did not help his attitude. Back in New York with his grandparents, Merton attended Zion Episcopal Church on Easter, but was irritated with the whole experience. "I used to walk around the house or sit at the dinner table telling everybody what a terrible place Zion Church was, and condemning everything that it stood for."[12]

He tried visiting a Quaker meeting house where his mother had once attended. There was nothing there that was different from any other Protestant church except that people sat in silence until the Holy Ghost inspired someone to speak. Finally a woman stood to speak. She began, "When I was in Switzerland I took this snapshot of the Lion of Lucerne." Merton concluded, "They are like all the rest. In other churches it is the minister who hands out the commonplaces, and here it is liable to be just anybody."[13] The Quakers, he said, are just what their name says, a Society of Friends.

While home, Merton visited the World's Fair in Chicago. He picked up a few pamphlets on Mormonism, but was not convinced

---

10. *Seven Storey Mountain*, p. 92.
11. *Seven Storey Mountain*, p. 93.
12. *Seven Storey Mountain*, p. 127
13. *Seven Storey Mountain*, p. 128.

by the story of the discovery of the Book of Mormon.

One day while looking in the window at Scribner's New York bookstore, he saw Etienne Gilson's classic book, *The Spirit of Medieval Philosophy*. He had just signed up for a course in French Medieval Literature, so he bought the book. Returning home on the Long Island train, he began to look at it. When he saw the Latin words Nihil Obstat and Imprimatur he realized he had bought a Catholic book. He said that he was tempted to throw it off the train. His family's anti-Catholicism had influenced him. However, he did begin to read it, and it became very important in his formation. It taught him to think of God as Being Itself, which has no cause. He had never had an adequate comprehension of what Christians had meant by God, but Gilson had given him a new understanding.

Merton now had a new desire to go to church so he tried Zion Episcopal again. The priest, however, had a love for literature and that was the focus of his preaching. Merton was looking for something more. He thought that the priest, who doubted most Christian doctrines, did not know what his vocation was. Once again, Protestantism had failed him.

While a student at Columbia he had an occasion to meet a Hindu monk from India, Bramachari. Merton liked him and was drawn to his religious life. Bramachari was struck by how often Protestant ministers would ask him if India had been converted to their form of Christianity. Bramachari told him that Christian missionaries would never convert anyone because they lived on a higher social level than the people they were trying to convert. They lived too comfortably and in such a way that Hindus could never regard them as holy. Protestant missionaries did not know what asceticism meant. Hindus wanted to know if Christians had any saints to send them.

Merton was still exploring and thought he might try the Quakers again. However, the reality was that he was being inexorably drawn to the Catholic Church.

The criticism of Protestantism that has thus far been mentioned reflects his thinking in the late 1940s when he was writing *The Seven Storey Mountain*. The book appeared in 1948. While he will always be a Catholic, his views on Protestantism will evolve. He will become more open to it, although he will always see it as lacking much of what Catholicism has to offer.

CONJECTURES OF A GUILTY BYSTANDER

This book is often cited as Merton's most ecumenical book, even though he stated in the Preface that "this is not a book of professional ecumenism." There was no effort, he wrote, to show areas of agreement or disagreement or seeking any kind of mutual understanding. In fact, Merton had no use for organized ecumenical institutions. He did find theologians and ideas in the Protestant tradition that interested him which he found "relevant and stimulating." [14] This particular book was published in 1966, near the end of his life, and represents the near conclusion of a long process of evolution. He did say, however, that if the Catholic Church, as a result of Vatican II, is going to turn toward the modern world and other Christian traditions, it is important that some contemplative and monastic theologians participate in the conversation. For Merton, ecumenism was an interior matter. He wrote, "If we want to bring together what is divided, we cannot do so by imposing one division upon another or absorbing one division into the other. But if we do this, the union is not Christian. It is political and doomed to further conflict. We must contain all divided worlds within ourselves and transcend them in Christ." [15]

Merton complained about a theological conference held in the Monastic Chapter about the certitude of faith. He said that they did not pay enough attention to the ecumenical movement and just wanted to prove that Protestants are wrong. He took note of the usual Protestant critique that the Catholic Church operated on authority, not freedom. However, he claimed that it was in Christ where true freedom was to be found. The hope for spiritual, interior, and personal freedom was also found in other branches of Christianity. While Catholics believed they had received the Spirit of God, of Sonship, which makes them free, Protestants made the same claim. Merton was not ready to say that the Protestants were wrong. "How do I know what grace God can and does give to sincere evangelical Christians who follow Christ?" [16] Merton was sure that Protestants would be better off in the Catholic Church, but they don't see it that way for reasons neither side can understand. Merton called for the effort to understand them, but each

---

14. Thomas Merton, *Conjectures of a Guilty Bystander*. Garden City, NY: Doubleday, 1966, p. vi.

15. *Conjectures*, p. 12.

16. *Conjectures*, p. 76.

should continue its own way.

One of the groups in which Merton seemed to have a particular interest was the Shakers. There had been a flourishing Shaker community not far from Gethsemani, and Merton was interested in the preservation of the buildings that were no longer occupied. Shaker communities included men and women, but celibacy was the norm. Obviously, the group would eventually die out.

Merton mentioned receiving a letter from one of the few remaining Shaker elderesses in New Hampshire. The elderess said that they were not concerned about extinction; they had done what the Lord had asked them to do. Merton commented that, "The Shakers have been something of a sign, a mystery, a strange attempt at utter honesty which, in trying to be too ideally pure was nevertheless pure—with moments of absurdity."[17] Their vision, unfortunately, led nowhere. However, Merton said that their impressive craftsmanship resulted from the reality of their vision.

He wondered why the Shakers were so hated at first. People were disturbed at the idea of celibate men and women living in the same community. Because of the strict discipline, people in New England called them "Catholics."[18]

In *Conjectures* Merton made two ecumenical statements which were often repeated in his writings. "If I do not have unity in myself, how can I even think, let alone speak, of unity among Christians? Yet, of course, in seeking unity for all Christians, I also attain unity within myself."[19] Later he added, "I will be a better Catholic, not if I can refute every shade of Protestantism, but if I can affirm the truth in it and still go further."[20] He broadened this idea by suggesting, "If I affirm myself as a Catholic merely by denying all that is Muslim, Jewish, Protestant, Hindu, Buddhist, etc, in the end I will find that there is not much left for me to affirm as a Catholic and certainly no breath of the Spirit with which to affirm it."[21]

Merton believed that the genius of Protestantism was to be found in its struggling with the theology of justification by faith. In this context he mentioned the problem of conversion. How does

---

17. *Conjectures*, pp. 118-119.
18. *Conjectures*, p. 310.
19. *Conjectures*, p. 128.
20. *Conjectures*, p. 129.
21. *Conjectures*, p. 129.

one convert the good who see no need of it?[22]

The tension between conservatives and progressives at Vatican II was a frustration for Merton. He saw them as more and more closed to each other. This caused him to have doubts about the new openness to non-Catholics. "An ecumenism that does not begin with charity within one's own Church remains questionable." He called for "friendship, spontaneity, and spiritual liberty," adding that "too much emphasis on organization can be stupefying."[23]

In *The Seven Storey Mountain* Merton complained about his childhood frustrations with Anglicanism. In *Conjectures* he made some of the same criticisms. He was exasperated with its priests who praised the developments of modern society: airplanes, radios, and other wonders. He said, "It was this famous "joy-of-living" view of Anglican religion that made me want to become a Roman Catholic."[24] He was not able to find anything very new in the new secularity.

Later, in *Conjectures,* he wrote a more positive word. He was impressed with a history of Anglican religious orders, *Silent Rebellion,* by A. M. Allchin, an Anglican scholar and writer. He later became a good friend of Merton and visited Gethsemani three times. Allchin had wide scholarly interests, and was one of the founding leaders of the Merton Society in Great Britain and Ireland.[25] Merton said that there is a "special monastic quality" in Anglican monasticism which was a witness against what he called the "torpor" of nineteenth century Anglicanism. Merton concluded, "The book is interesting and disturbing, and one cannot get away from a certain ambiguity in Anglican religious orders. I am glad I came all the way to Rome."[26]

THE COLLECTED POEMS

In "A Letter to Pablo Antonio Cuadra Concerning Giants," Merton suggested that Christ can be found in unexpected persons. This is a long prose poem with eight sections. In Section 4 Merton said that

---

22. *Conjectures*, p. 151.

23. *Conjectures*, pp. 287-288.

24. *Conjectures*, p. 293.

25. See entry of Allchin in *The Thomas Merton Encyclopedia*. Edited by William H. Shannon, Christine M. Bochen, and Patrick F. O'Connell. Maryknoll NY: Orbis Books, 2002, p. 6.

26. *Conjectures*, pp. 307-308.

the greatest sin of the West, which he calls the European-Russian-American complex, is "its unmitigated arrogance toward the rest of the human race." This arrogance failed to recognize that God is present in all people, and each person is to be treated as Christ.

He was critical of both missionaries and colonizers for not being able to see that the people they conquered were basically equal to themselves and in some cases superior. Where missionaries failed was in their inability to see Christ present in South American Indians, Hindus, and the Chinese. Some of the early church fathers, he said, believed that some of the ancient philosophers had been "precursors of Christ."[27] Missionaries did not hear the voice of Christ in the Indians as Clement had heard it in the pre-Socratic philosophers.

In Section 5 of the poem Merton made a statement similar to those he made in his comments on ecumenicity: "If I insist on giving you my truth and never stop to receive your truth in return, then there can be no truth between us."[28] He added, ". . . no man knows that the stranger he meets coming out of the forest in a new country is not already an invisible member of Christ." We must accept the reality that God speaks in unpredictable ways.

SEEDS OF DESTRUCTION

Merton could, from time to time, be critical of his own Church. In an essay in *Seeds of Destruction,* Merton mentioned that Pope Paul VI called for self-examination. This call came two weeks after four African-American little girls were killed in the bombing of a Baptist Church in Birmingham, Alabama. On the same day, Merton reported that a white Eagle Scout had killed a young African American boy simply because the boy was black. Merton said that this was not done by a Catholic, but Catholics in that same region had identified themselves with racial segregation and the denial of civil rights to Negroes.[29]

Merton admired Martin Luther King, Jr. but believed that as far as the civil rights movement was concerned, both Catholics and Protestants were confused in their sympathies.

---

27. *The Collected Poems of Thomas Merton.* New York: New Directions Books, 1977, p. 381.

28. *Collected Poems*, p. 383.

29. Thomas Merton, *Seeds of Destruction.* New York: Farrar, Straus and Giroux, 1964, p. 12.

CONTEMPLATION IN A WORLD OF ACTION

In an article that first appeared in the Journal of Ecumenical Studies[30] on Protestant Monasticism, Merton referred to the monastery of Taizé, an ecumenical community in France. It was founded by Roger Schutz who bought a house near Cluny in southeastern France, using it to shelter refugees and Jews during World War II and later taking in German prisoners of war. After the war it became a monastery. The monks took their first vows in 1949. All were Protestants from a variety of backgrounds. Roman Catholics began to join in 1969. Schutz's goal was to overcome divisions among Christians. During the summers Taizé attracts thousands of young people, and the monastery has established small communities in various parts of the world. The focus is on the inner life and human solidarity. Taizé music and forms of worship are sometimes used in Protestant churches.

As he often did in his writings, Merton pointed out the importance of Martin Luther's crisis of faith for Catholic monks. Luther was an Augustinian canon and technically not a monk, but he lived the life of a monk. His crisis was, according to Merton, a "decisive point in the Reformation." His belief in *fides sola*, faith alone, led to his repudiation of monasticism. Merton wrote, "He challenged the whole monastic ethos, dominated by the monastic order as reformed and incorporated into the cultural and political life of Europe and Charlemagne."[31] He believed that Luther's experience has relevance for Catholic monks who want to renew their monastic lives. His repudiation of what seemed to be a false and formalistic monastic life "struck a blow for monastic truth." One can have Luther's kind of experience and still remain a monk, not necessarily to reform the rules, but to have a renewal in the Spirit, to recover the meaning and hope of the life. Merton's Journals and Letters reveal his dissatisfaction with some of the life of Gethsemani, but he also believed that renewal must be more than legislative changes or expedients. "It has to be a kind of a miracle of water in the desert."[32]

Merton called for ecumenical openness on the part of monasteries. This has to be more than allowing Protestant seminarians to

30. *Journal of Ecumenical Studies*. Vol. 5, No. 2, 1968.

31. Thomas Merton, *Contemplation in a World of Action*. Garden City, NY: Doubleday, 1971, p. 181.

32. *Contemplation*, p. 186.

come "to view a living diorama of Church history." He believed that there should be enough flexibility to allow the rise of ecumenical monastic communities. Non-Catholics and unbelievers should be allowed to participate seriously in a monastic community, at least temporarily.

Merton wanted the monastic life to acquire an ecumenical relevance. There should be an openness which provided for discussion of creedal or sectarian differences "with polite detachment" that would involve risks at the deepest level. "And this certainly," he said, "will mean more than sharing gripes about the stupidities of one's ecclesiastical establishment."[33] He was not interested in the latest clichés or conversations about relics and indulgences which have already been "laid to rest."[34]

Responding to Luther's faith alone theme, Merton said that the works of the monk, while not a means to justify him, should enable him to celebrate and explain the witness of faith.

As an aside, Merton suggested that in the geographical area of Gethsemani, Central Kentucky, the purest sort of monastic witness to work had been the Shaker communities. Shaker craftsmanship, he said, "is the most authentic, tangible, and impressive fruit of the monastic and mystical experience in America." He added, "The Shaker spirit is entirely monastic in its celibacy, its poverty, its humility, simplicity, faith, pacifism, gentleness and in its combination of otherworldliness with a profound respect for materials and for their proper use in everyday human existence."[35] Merton made several trips to Shakertown and took many photographs of the abandoned buildings whose architecture he believed had a kind of purity about it.

He raised a question about vows and suggested that their nature needed to be reexamined. Did Luther think that monastic vows and a legalistic existence were the same thing? Is a monastic life without vows possible? He reminded us that there were no vows in desert monasticism. Merton, writing in the late 1960s, noted that there was an "enormous number of professed religious seeking dispensation from their vows" as well as others leaving without any permission.[36] Knowing that structures are necessary for any

---

33. *Contemplation*, p. 187.
34. *Contemplation*, p. 193.
35. *Contemplation*, p. 189.
36. *Contemplation*, p. 192.

community life, he suggested taking vows might be appropriate for a minority of monks, while others might take up the life for a limited amount of time, such as two or three years for training and retreat. He even proposed the possibility of married people temporarily living the life.

Merton saw the Reformation as now taking the form of ecumenism. Thus, Luther's experience could be seen as the focus for monastic renewal on the ecumenical level. Authentic monasticism can contribute to an ongoing Reformation. True ecumenism, Merton said, "enables the Catholic to find himself by discovering what the Reformation means to him and for him, and the Protestant to rediscover in and for himself the relevance that Catholicism has never ceased to have for him."[37] The experience of the Reformation, Merton wrote, was "the discovery of a more immediate and radical commitment to God's unfailing promises in faith."[38]

In *Mystics and Zen Masters*[39] Merton had another article on "Protestant Monasticism." Here he also mentioned the importance of Luther's monastic experience. Merton believed that Luther's theology was shaped by his revolt against the religious life he was living which, in Merton's opinion, had serious deficiencies, if it was not totally corrupt. Luther's frustrations, as enumerated by Merton, included "sterile devotionalism, attachment to trivial outward forms, forgetfulness of the essentials of Christian faith, and obsession with accidentals."[40] The works that, in Luther's mind, did not justify the monk were monastic observances that were supposed to bring about a state of perfection in the life of vows. In light of justification by faith, monastic vows were invalid.

Yet, Protestant monasticism does exists. In the United States there are Episcopal houses for both women and men, and the ecumenical monastery of Taizé in France is well known and appreciated by Protestants. In this particular article Merton focused on Protestant monasteries in France, Germany, and Switzerland. Some of the qualities of the communities for Merton were freedom, flexibility, and a lack of stereotypical institutional ways. The Taizé

37. *Contemplation*, p. 194.

38. *Contemplation*, p. 196.

39. Thomas, Merton, *Mystics and Zen Masters*. New York: Dell Publishing Co., 1961, pp. 188-202.

40. *Mystics and Zen Masters*, p. 188.

emphasis is on "simplicity, openness, and vitality."[41] It is ironic that the Reformation which tried to destroy the monastic life theologically is now showing signs of renewing it.

Merton did have a critique of Taizé. When two monks from there visited Merton, he was put off by their concern to clear everything with Catholic officials. They seemed to need Catholic support and Merton wondered whether perhaps the Catholics needed them. Merton called this absurd. "What is the good of being Protestants if they abdicate their freedom?" The Taizé brothers said that this was necessary for the ecumenical movement.[42]

---

41. *Mystics and Zen Masters*, p. 191

42. *Learning to Love.* Ed. by Christine M. Bochen. HarperSanFrancisco, 1997, pp. 250-251. June 12, 1967.

JOURNALS

RUN TO THE MOUNTAIN: THE STORY OF A VOCATION

Volume 1

The first volume of the journals covers the years 1939-1941. Merton did not enter Gethsemani until December 10, 1941. The early harshness of his attitude toward Protestantism moderated to some degree, but he is still a long way from the appreciative comments he will make later. As a new convert he accepted without question the superiority of the Catholic Church and had little appreciation for the "separated brethren."

One of the continuing issues in the Catholic Church is the value of priestly celibacy. Efforts to allow a married clergy have gone nowhere. Merton supported priestly celibacy and wrote, "to argue against the vow of chastity is to argue against religion." Religions that have married priests have wasted away and all but denied God. Protestantism, with its married clergy, has ceased to be a religion. Protestant churches are locked up except for one hour on Sunday. Anglicans keep their churches open but nobody comes.[1] Merton believed that the metaphysics of Thomas Aquinas was necessary to Christian thought then and for the future. Luther, who eventually married, had no metaphysics, and as a result Protestantism had no theology and no religion.[2]

Merton was also critical of the Protestant attitude toward the crucifixion. For one thing, Protestants had taken away the *Stabat Mater Dolorosa.* They do not like blood and see Jesus as a martyr.[3]

In a May 13, 1941, entry, while still at St. Bonaventure, Merton reflected on the many pointless arguments in which he had been engaged and how foolish he was. He quoted several passages from the letter of James which, he noted, Luther called the Epistle of Straw. Luther was convinced he had the truth, more convinced,

---

1. *Run to the Mountain.* Ed. by Patrick Hart OCSO. HarperSanFrancisco, 1995, p. 48. October 9, 1939.

2. *Run to the Mountain*, p. 84. November 2, 1939.

3. *Run to the Mountain*, p. 200. April 1940.

Merton said, than he was in all his arguments for God, faith, and Church. One of the quotations was 3:6, "The tongue is a fire. The tongue is placed among our members as a world of iniquity; it stains the whole body, sets on fire the cycle of nature, and is itself set on fire by hell." (NRSV) Merton wrote, "It has just for the first time occurred to me that my opinions, judgments, arguments, defending the highest things I believe in may all be foolish." He called his self-justification "stupid."[4]

He also mused on a time in 1933 when he was with his grandparents in Douglaston. He had been to Rome and felt religious stirrings within him. However, as these began to fade he said that he tried "in an obscure and proud and protestant way" to love God. He prayed "in shame and secret," tried to read the Bible in the hope that no one saw him, and tried to be good "in some way." However, he said that at the same time he was reading D. H. Lawrence and thought about how little he had really known of life compared to what he thought he knew. "I found out, I suppose," at Cambridge.[5]

A few days later, in 1941, he thought back to 1937, the year before his conversion to the Catholic Church. He had begun to attend the Episcopal Church in Douglaston. He even attended a mid-week service. He would return home (to his grandparents) and feel pleased with himself. He kidded about it with the family but admitted that he was actually happy about it.

The minister of the church had been asked by parishioners to preach about controversies in the early church. He talked about the Pelagians, the Manicheans, and others and treated each one as a struggle for liberty against dogmatism, rather than explaining Christian doctrine. Merton wanted to hear about doctrine, about what he was supposed to believe.[6]

When Merton and his father lived in St. Antonin there was what he called a sort of Calvinist cenacle. It was at the edge of town, had a whitewashed interior, and looked like a courtroom. They attended once, but it was too grim for his father, and Merton did not mind when they never went back.

Merton remembered how cold it was in the Protestant chapel in the Lycée he attended. The students huddled around the stove and the chaplain taught them the parables of Jesus. He said that

4. *Run to the Mountain*, p. 365. May 13, 1941.

5. *Run to the Mountain,* p. 371. May, 1941.

6. *Run to the Mountain,* pp. 373-374. May 18, 1941.

they all nearly froze to death.[7]

While he was a student at Ripley Court in England the students attended the village church. Merton called it "a very good affair." On Sunday evenings the students would listen to Ms. Onslow read from Pilgrim's Progress, and he liked that, too.

On one occasion he went to a Christian Science service, probably at the urging of his grandmother, who read Mary Baker Eddy's books. However, he could not make much sense of it. He remembered liking a church in Rye (NY), a Lutheran Church in Strasbourg, the chapel at Oakham, the Quaker Meeting House in Flushing, and in England, Ealing and the churches at West Horsley and Brooke. He also liked a little church in Scotland where a man named Houghton officiated and his tenants prayed. Merton wondered if he was actually ordained. All of this, he said, was very different from what he experienced at Catholic churches in New York and Havana and Olean.[8]

In another pre-Gethsemani comment, Merton warned against mistaking a flourishing Christian culture for the flourishing of the Church. He believed that the only way to measure a church is by the number of saints it has, for sainthood is independent of culture. He added that the decadence of a Christian culture does not mean that the Church is decadent "as Protestants, Communists, and so on, believe."[9]

ENTERING THE SILENCE: BECOMING A MONK AND WRITER

VOLUME 2

The first part of this volume is The Novitiate Journal beginning with Merton's acceptance as a postulant on December 13, 1941, and ending with Good Friday, April 3, 1942. It consists of a few reflections on his experience and seven poems he authored. He made a reference to Augustine's comment that you do not understand scripture unless you live its meaning in your own life.[10]

Second is A Journal Memoir: Dom Frederic Dunne. It is a

---

7. *Run to the Mountain*, p. 374. May 18, 1941.

8. *Run to the Mountain,* pp. 373-375. May 18, 1941.

9. *Run to the Mountain*, p. 442. October 18, 1941.

10. *Entering the Silence*. Ed. by Jonathan Montaldo. HarperSanFrancisco, 1996, p. 8. February 1, 1942.

memoir Merton wrote on his abbot for whom he had great affection. When he found out that another monk, Father Raymond Flanagan, was writing his own memoir of Dom Frederick, which became *The Less Traveled Road,* (1953), he gave it to him.

Third, when he completed the *Seven Storey Mountain* in 1946, Merton began a new journal, much of which would later be published as *The Sign of Jonas.* Jonathan Montaldo, the editor of *Entering the Silence*, this volume of the journals, used the first working, but not final title, The Whale and the Ivy. The final version of the title was *The Sign of Jonas.* This is one of Merton's most popular books. It contains the famous statement from a censor of the *Seven Storey Mountain* that Merton was not capable of writing such a book with "his present literary equipment," and suggested that Merton take a correspondence course in grammar. [11]

This volume had few references to Protestantism since Merton's evolution on this subject had barely begun. The first mention of anything Protestant in this journal is a critique of Calvinists and pantheists who find an interior peace and have a strong sense of union with God. However, Merton believed that this could be "purely natural and aesthetic" and probably an expression of one's own spirituality rather than an experimental knowledge of God. For him, it was important not to seek experiences and "not to stop at the aesthetic sense of anything." [12]

A month later, he affirmed that Catholics have the only true sacrament which "orders human love to an eternal and mystical and Divine end." [13] In January, 1949, he complained about a Georgia priest being married in a civil ceremony and a former Anglican priest, then Catholic, going back to Anglicanism because Catholic doctrine was too rigid.[14] However, several months later he expressed appreciation for a Parkminister Carthusian, Dom Humphrey, for his interest in non-Catholic mystics.[15] At the end of the year, while seeing some sights in Louisville, he commented on a Protestant church that had the word Mass on its sign. They offered it on Sundays as if, Merton said, "they had caught some rare creature and had it in a cage for men to come and view." This church, as Merton saw it,

11. *Entering*, p. 63, April 16, 1947.
12. *Entering*, pp. 80-81, May 31, 1947.
13. *Entering*, p. 83. June 13, 1947.
14. *Entering*, p. 271. January 20, 1949.
15. *Entering*, p. 311. May 15, 1949.

was a meeting house. For him the term Church meant "house of God," not the home of a congregation.[16]

A SEARCH FOR SOLITUDE: PURSUING THE MONK'S TRUE LIFE

VOLUME 3

The third volume of Merton's journals contains his well-known experience at Fourth and Walnut in Louisville. Standing on that corner he realized, "that I love all the people and that none of them were, or, could be totally alien to me." He characterized the experience as waking from a dream that he had a "special vocation" to be different and in a special category. The fact was, he wrote, that he was "still a member of the human race," which was important because "the Word was made flesh" and became a member of the human race. He said, "I have the immense joy of being a man!"[17] This experience no doubt contributed to Merton's growing openness to other people and other religious traditions.

Merton believed that Catholicism lacked the medieval spirit of "broadness, universality, compassion, joy," in its understanding of human nature, a cosmic outlook, eschatology, asceticism, mysticism, and poetry. Yes, Catholicism had its asceticism, but it was "Protestant, self-disciplined, dour, individualistic, and puritanical."[18]

He added a whole list of Protestant features of Catholic life:

> Distrust of emotional symbolism in art, poetry, and contemplation.
>
> Distrust of what is interior, joyful, and happy.
>
> Efficiency, productivity, and prosperity as a sign of election.
>
> A stern and legalistic approach to the divine will.
>
> It is harsh and aggressive.
>
> A separation of body and soul with a contempt for the flesh.
>
> Appreciation of comfort and ease along with self-discipline.
>
> The primacy of economics.

---

16. *Entering*, p. 447. December 13, 1950.

17. *A Search for Solitude.* Edited by Lawrence S. Cunningham. HarperSanFrancisco, 1996, p. 234.

18. *Search*, p. 234. January 20, 1959.

He concluded, "We are much more akin to those new Puritans, the Communists, than to our Catholic forefathers."

Merton devoted a January 20, 1959, journal entry to ecumenism. He complained about pamphleteering about church unity in which he found an "idiotic lack of tact—lack of any sense of what church unity means: union in love." He wrote that seeing church unity as a matter of submitting to papal authority is "pitifully absurd." He was bothered by a pamphlet by Pére Jugie, who said that the Orthodox Church was also absurd because it was unable to define new doctrines. Therefore, it should submit to Rome on doctrinal matters. The Church, Merton said, is not going to be united by "therefores." Unfortunately, he believed Christianity has too many people who are authorities on what is wrong with different Christian groups. He quoted Jesus, "Do you think that when I come I shall find faith, or love, on earth?"

Merton suggested, "Wouldn't it be a little simpler and more honest to stop and look at what is right in different views of Christianity?" Catholics don't have to deny their faith in papal authority, but he admitted that Roman authority had done things to antagonize some other Christians uselessly and uncharitably.[19]

Once again Merton mentioned Shakertown. He had a great interest in that historical community. Perhaps it was on his mind so much because the abandoned community was just a short distance from Gethsemani. It would eventually be restored and become a popular historical site for tourists and historians, their dining room being especially popular.

The official name of the Shakers was The United Society of Believers in Christ's Second Appearing. The group was founded in England in 1747. Eventually, led by Mother Ann Lee, it founded several communities of men and women in America, including one in Kentucky not far from Gethsemani. Because they practiced celibacy they eventually died out, although there are still a few individual Shakers in the United States. Their name refers to their worship practices which caused them to shake while in a mood of spiritual exaltation. They were also known for their simplicity of life and their craftsmanship.

Merton saw Shakertown in light of his own vocation, for he believed the two communities had much in common. He thought that if Shakertown had survived it would have evolved as Geth-

19. *Search*, pp. 248-249. January 20, 1959.

semani evolved. The women would now be driving tractors; the men would be advertising bread and cheese. "And all would have struggled with guilt."[20]

In one other Protestant reference, Merton received two letters from Meg Chatham, a Protestant minister's wife. He described both of them as remarkable. He commented, "The work of grace in their hearts is wonderful or so it seems to me."[21]

TURNING TOWARD THE WORLD: THE PIVOTAL YEARS

VOLUME 4

By the 1960s Merton's attitude toward Protestants had become much more open and less critical. Indeed, he showed real enthusiasm for ecumenism. He quoted a French writer who said that saints such as St. Seraphim and St. Francis of Assisi brought about the union of churches in their time. Merton said, "That is exactly my ideal and my desire." He noted that among the Martyrs of Uganda were two or three Protestants. All of the martyrs, Catholic and Protestant, were one in their sanctity and their witness. "A great sign," said Merton.[22]

An occasional problem in the monastic life is that some parents did not want their sons to become monks. In 1960 Merton reported having a conversation with a monk's Protestant mother. She had brought her son up from Texas, but did not want him to enter Gethsemani.[23] If some Protestants are suspicious of the Catholic Church, some are even more suspicious of monks.

Merton's ecumenical influence was having an impact on Gethsemani. Father Killian McDonnell, an important Benedictine Catholic ecumenist from St. John's monastery in Collegeville, Minnesota, came to Gethsemani to talk to the novices about the ecumenical movement.

Point of personal privilege: I participated in an ongoing Roman Catholic-Disciples of Christ ecumenical dialogue in Cambridge, England, many years ago. Father McDonnell was one of the Catho-

---

20. *Search,* p. 287. June 7, 1959.

21. *Search*, p. 386. April 29, 1960.

22. *Turning Toward the World.* Ed. by Victor A Kramer. HarperSanFrancisco, 1996, p. 9. June 6, 1960.

23. *Turning,* p. 41. September 4, 1960.

lic representatives. That dialogue has been going on for well over a quarter of a century. The topic of discussion was the Eucharist. It was not easy to find common ground on that subject, but Father McDonnell was a calm and reasonable voice in that conversation.

In April, 1961, Merton reported a visit from John Beecher and his wife, a visit that included lunch in their small trailer. Beecher was an English professor at Arizona State University who resigned his position in order to participate in a long Peace March from San Francisco. He left the march in Chicago because the young people had no discipline. They constantly bickered and had no peace in themselves. Beecher said that everywhere they went they were often welcomed by Protestant ministers, but there were no contacts with Catholics, especially priests.[24]

Merton heard that Abbot James Fox referred to "my ecumenism," and was "really keen" on it, although he said little to Merton about it. Merton was concerned that it was becoming "some kind of silly, organized racket to bring publicity to Gethsemani." Merton had no interest in that. He only wanted the good that comes from "simple and charitable conversation." No publicity needed. If left that way it will give glory to God.[25]

There are numerous references to Protestant theologians and visits with Protestant seminary students in this volume. Those items will be covered in later chapters.

DANCING IN THE WATER OF LIFE: SEEKING PEACE IN THE HERMITAGE

Volume 5

One of the Anglicans with whom Merton was most impressed was A. M. Allchin. He was the priest and the librarian at Pusey House in Oxford, as well as chaplain to students. Later, he became a canon at Canterbury Cathedral and eventually a university professor in Wales. His first contact with Merton was in 1963, visiting Gethsemani after attending the ecumenical Faith and Order Conference in Montreal. Merton described him as "a nice person very interested in monasticism," and liked his book on Anglican monasticism. Merton wrote in his journal, he "thinks American Protestant theology is lovely, which it is." He was impressed with Allchin's "dear sweet

24. *Turning*, p. 111. April 23, 1961.

25. *Turning*, p. 55. October 2, 1960.

Anglican spirituality" which stimulated an interest in reading some of the Anglican divines.[26] There would be two other visits with Merton in 1967 and 1968.

Allchin recommended Augustine Baker's *Inner Life of Dame Gertrude More*, an English Benedictine. Merton appreciated the book, especially a chapter of Divine Inspiration which led to some introspection. He realized he had focused too much attention on publishing, contacts, and an active life. Silence and interior life, he concluded, had to come first.[27] This led to a comment 10 days later, "Cut down on the more superficial types of ecumenical contacts and especially on time consuming palaver and many visits."[28]

In September of 1963 Merton found himself in the hospital in Louisville attempting to deal with the effects of a cervical disk problem. Under the heading "Some reflection," he thought about the future. He realized that health problems would continue, that in his writing and contacts he wanted to focus on poetry and poets, that the most important thing was to deepen his knowledge of spiritual reality, and, finally, to reduce superficial ecumenical contacts and many visits.[29]

As already noted, mention of the Shakers appears off and on in his journals. His admiration of them continued to be very strong. In an October 23, 1963 journal entry, he gave thought to why the Shakers were originally hated so much. Probably their celibacy was the issue. Men living chastely with women was unnatural in the minds of pioneers, and there might have been a fear of the loss of virility.[30]

Another Protestant group that attracted Merton's attention was the Bruderhof movement. One of the more controversial groups in the Protestant Reformation was the Anabaptists. They were not interested in reforming the church; they wanted to go back to the pre-Constantinian church and restore early Christianity. As a result, they were continually persecuted. Some found asylum in Moravia, where Jacob Hutter established communities based on the common ownership of property. Out of this came the Bruderhof group which

---

26. *Dancing in the Water of Life*. Ed. by Robert E. Daggy. HarperSanFrancisco, 1997.

27. *Dancing*, p. 16. September 10, 1963.

28. *Dancing*, p. 18. September 20, 1963

29. *Dancing*, p. 18. September 20, 1962.

30. *Dancing*, p. 26. October 24, 1963.

wanted to continue the tradition of common ownership.[31]

Merton read a book on the history of the Bruderhof movement and was impressed that the group wanted to dismantle all of its power. They said that the power and authority of God in Jesus Christ through the Holy Spirit will be the only thing that counts among them.

In a January 30, 1965 entry, Merton reflected on his time at Gethsemani. He said it provided some of his happiest moments, especially in the woods and fields, but also with the novices. There had been terrible moments. "But good moments too with Protestants coming here."[32]

Merton was no longer just the triumphalist Catholic. His vision was broader, and he had developed a respect and appreciation for Protestants while still seeing himself fundamentally as a Catholic.

LEARNING TO LOVE: EXPLORING SOLITUDE AND FREEDOM

Volume 6

Volume Six of Merton's published journals, *Learning to Love*, tells us about his 1966 love affair with a student nurse. As he reflected on the relationship which was both exhilarating because of their love and painful because he knew that his life would always be at Gethsemani, he thought about Martin Luther's distinction between God's "alien work," which reveals who we are by suffering and humiliation, and God's "own work," whereby God heals by his love. In this affair, Merton said, "I have seen a lot of both—and she has too."[33]

When Abbot James Fox was told about the relationship by another monk, he told Merton he must make a clean break. As he and Merton talked about it, a partial solution evolved that Merton would do more ecumenical work in the retreat house as a cure for loneliness. Merton decided that "constructive contacts" would be good for him, and the Abbot favored the idea of Merton talking to ecumenical groups including "Protestants, Buddhists, etc."[34]

As ecumenical relationships became a more important part of

---

31. *Dancing*, p. 108. June 2, 1964.
32. *Dancing*, p. 199. January 30, 1965.
33. *Learning to Love*, p. 96. July 15, 1966.
34. *Learning to Love*, p. 82. June 14, 1966. .

Merton's life, he wondered about the purity of his own faith. Was he willing to risk theological compromises? In the midst of all of this he affirmed, "I have no hesitation in firmly desiring and intending to be a Catholic and to hold with all my heart to the true faith of the living God manifested in Christ and his Church. Whatever I seek in other traditions is only the truth of Christ expressed in other terms, rejecting all that is really contrary to His truth."[35]

In a June 12, 1967 entry, Merton reported a visit from two brothers of Taizé from a mission in Chicago. They claimed that in order to maintain their important place in the ecumenical movement they needed a good relationship with Rome. They believed that they must clear everything they were doing with Rome because they needed Catholic support. Merton called this "absurd." "What is the good of being Protestants if they abdicate their freedom and get into this ludicrous tangle of telephone wire and red tape." The brothers insisted that this was necessary for the ecumenical movement.[36]

At the end of Volume Six of the journals, the editor, Christine M. Bochen, added three Appendices. One is titled "Some Personal Notes." After this struggle with his love for the young nurse, designated simply as M, Merton reflected on the purity of his own faith. His ecumenical contacts had had a serious impact on him. He raised the question of his willingness to risk compromises in doctrinal issues. Now, in 1966, he reaffirmed his Catholic faith, the true faith in God which is manifested in Christ and the Church. Whatever he sought in other traditions was only "the truth of Christ expressed in other terms," but rejecting anything contrary to "His Truth."[37]

THE OTHER SIDE OF THE MOUNTAIN: THE END OF THE JOURNEY

VOLUME 7

In November, 1967, Merton was contacted by the Quakers' American Friends Service Committee asking him to be part of a peace team that would meet with representatives of the Viet Cong in the hope of developing some peace proposals for Washington. Merton very much wanted to do it, but was sure that the abbot would disapprove. Merton said, "It really raises the question of my staying

35. *Learning to Love*, p. 358. February 4, 1966.
36. *Learning to Love*, p. 251. June 12, 1967.
37. *Learning to Love*, p. 359. February 4, 1966.

here." However, he saw no real alternative to Gethsemani and his hermitage. He did add, "In any case, being here, I have forfeited all freedom to do things that perhaps I should do—and this is a real problem." He trusted that there would be some solution that would take him by surprise as the hermitage situation did.[38]

Four days later he mentioned that he was working on an article for the *Journal of Ecumenical Studies* on ecumenism and the monastic life. This article later appeared in *Contemplation and a World of Action.*[39]

There are a number of brief, sudden ecumenical references that are a bit surprising. For example, in a December, 1967 entry, Merton mentioned that in a Mass for a group of nuns on retreat at Gethsemani, he substituted a prayer by Lancelot Andrewes for the Confiteor. Andrewes was a seventeenth century Anglican Bishop and one of the translators of the King James Version of the Bible published in 1611. He put together a book of Private Devotions, which was Merton's source, for use in his personal prayer life. It was later published. Merton added that when he had coffee with the nuns after Mass he used another Andrewes prayer.[40] Later he wrote that he received a Christmas card from a Shaker elderess in Canterbury, New Hampshire and appreciated the message.[41] Such ecumenical news seemed normal and commonplace by 1967.

The rest of this volume is devoted to his Asian Journal. There are no Protestant contacts, but his understanding of Eastern religions deepened.

38. *The Other Side of Silence.* Ed. by Patrick Hart. HarperSanFrancisco, 1998, p. 12. November 18, 1967.

39. *The Other Side of Silence,* p. 14. November 22, 1967.

40. *The Other Side of Silence,* p. 21. December 7, 1967.

41. *The Other Side of Silence,* p. 27. December 19, 1967

LETTERS

THE HIDDEN GROUND OF LOVE: LETTERS ON RELIGIOUS EXPERIENCE AND SOCIAL CONCERN

One is able to trace the chronology of Merton's ecumenical evolution through the journals because the entries are in chronological order. However, such an effort is more awkward when working through the published letters as they are grouped topically and by addressees. Sorting that out would be confusing, and a violation of the integrity of the editors of the volumes. There is value in seeing correspondence to individuals in one place.

Merton was an indefatigable correspondent. He wrote to people all over the world: some intellectuals, some poets, some scholars and writers, some theologians, some ordinary people who asked for advice about their religious lives. These same people wrote to Merton. They ranged from Boris Pasternak to a laywoman who was finding it hard to believe in God.

One of his important non-Catholic correspondents was the Anglican, A. M. Allchin, previously mentioned as a priest, a librarian, a canon, and a professor. Allchin wrote to Merton in October, 1963, asking him to write an introduction for a book on Isaac of Stella, a twelfth century Cistercian monk. Merton agreed to do it and thanked Allchin for the book he had sent. Merton said he would like to have something on the Cambridge Platonists and the Anglican William Law, and reported that he had been reading Dame Gertrude More.[1]

A few months later, April 25, 1964, Merton thanked Allchin for a Thomas Traherne book and mentioned that it would be helpful to him if he decided to write a book about Anglican mystics. He also thanked Allchin for a series of essays by Anglicans on the Virgin Mary, and reported that he was reading Thornton's *English Spirituality*, Stranks's *Anglican Doctrine,* and McAdoo's *Moral*

1. *The Hidden Ground of Love: Letters of Thomas Merton on Religious Experience and Social Concerns.* Ed. by William H. Shannon. New York: Farrar, Straus and Giroux, 1985, p. 25.

Theologians. Merton said, "the best of Anglicanism is unexcelled, but that there are few who have the refinement of spirit to see and embrace the best, and so many fall off into the dreariest rationalism." Merton believed it was very important for Catholics who are now beginning to use the vernacular in worship to have an appreciation of the Anglican tradition.[2]

Allchin asked Merton to write an article for his journal *Sobornost.* Although Merton received these kinds of requests all the time and usually turned them down, he agreed to do something. Merton also reported that he had an article on contemplation and ecumenism coming out in a small Dominican journal. He also mentioned that he had been using the Anglican Lancelot Andrewes's *Preces Privatae,* usually translated Private Devotions, at night in the hermitage.[3]

A month later he told Allchin that he would have permission to see him when he was in the United States since he would still be involved in ecumenical meetings.[4] Allchin arrived in January, 1967, to teach for a semester at the Episcopal seminary, General Theological Seminary in New York. Merton encouraged him to come to Gethsemani any time after Easter. He noted that Allchin opined that church life seemed to be in a general turmoil. Merton agreed and feared that Catholics were experiencing the same confusion as Protestants "with anyone and everyone rushing about in all directions." He suggested that "the old monolithic business was too rigid," but that some agreements on basic truth would be good.[5] Allchin did make his second visit with Merton in early April, 1967.

On September 15, 1967, Merton responded to two of Allchin's letters. One was about a planned visit the next year, which Merton encouraged. The other was about Allchin's plan to spend a sabbatical year in Crawley Down, an Anglican monastery. Once again, Merton affirmed his belief that one of the important functions of monasteries should be to host people who want to live the monastic life for a limited time, perhaps a year or two. There should be permanent members who might be more active, but others who would be contemplatives. Having everyone make solemn vows was no

2. *Hidden Ground,* p. 26. April 25, 1964.
3. *Hidden Ground* p. 27. May 22, 1965
4. *Hidden Ground,* p. 27. June 26, 1966.
5. *Hidden Ground,* p. 28. January 14, 1967

longer workable. There are many people, Merton believed, who might have "monastic vocations of a modified kind."[6]

Merton wrote to Allchin on March 24, 1968, about what would be his final visit. Merton was excited about the possibility of spending an entire day exploring Shakertown with him. On the way back to Gethsemani they heard about the assassination of Martin Luther King, Jr. on the car radio. They drove to a restaurant in Bardstown operated by an African-American friend of Merton. A picture was taken of Colonel Hawks, the owner, Allchin, and Merton with a picture of John F. Kennedy on the table.[7]

There are several letters to Edward Deming Andrews. Andrews was a scholar of Shaker studies. He wrote *The People Called Shakers* and *Shaker Furniture*, which Merton regarded as his best books. *The Hidden Ground of Love* contains seven letters to Andrews, several of which are unusually long for Merton, and one to Andrews's widow.

Merton and Shirley Burden had discussed writing a book together about the Shakers. Merton's part would be on Shaker spirit and mysticism as seen in their lives and their craftsmanship. He saw great significance in their integration of the spiritual and the physical in the work they did. "There is no question in my mind," Merton wrote, "that one of the finest and most genuine religious expressions of the nineteenth century is in the silent eloquence of Shaker craftsmanship." Merton thought about how similar the Shakers and the Cistercians were, yet there was no contact between them. The letter Merton received from Andrews inspired him to pursue further studies of the Shakers. He concluded the letters requesting more books on the Shakers and some reproductions of Shaker paintings he would like to use in a book on religious art that he was planning.[8]

In a January 17, 1961, letter to Andrews, Merton mentioned that some people were hoping to buy Shakertown and restore it. At this point it was just a group of empty buildings. The owners had put a high price on them, and Merton hoped that he could interest Barry Bingham, the owner of the Louisville *Courier-Journal,* in the project. On August 22 of that year he wrote to Andrews that "It is very certain that the Shakers preserved many many (sic) deeply

6. *Hidden Ground*, p. 29. September 15, 1967.
7. *Hidden Ground,* p. 30. March 24, 1968.
8. *Hidden Ground*, p. 32. December 12, 1960.

important religious symbols and lived out some of the most basic religious myths in their Christian and gnostic setting. I cannot help feeling also that the very existence of the Shakers at that particular moment in history has a very special significance, a sort of 'prophetic' function in relation to what has come since."[9]

In a letter written on December 21, 1961, which the editor William Shannon designated Cold War Letter 12, he affirmed that the Shakers witnessed to the fact that humility is what keeps one in "communion" with the truth, which is one's inner truth. It is a truth known without knowing, which was true of the Shakers.[10]

Merton enjoyed Shaker music and described some of their songs as naïve and honest. His favorite was "Decisive Work" which he said was more than just a "pious song." It contained great power. In another letter he wrote that the Shakers "saw that their work as a cooperation in the same will that framed and governed the cosmos and more governs history."[11]

One of the contributors to this book is Professor James Baker, a Baptist, who wrote his Ph.D. dissertation at Florida State University on Merton. He had been part of a student group from Southern Baptist Theological Seminary in Louisville that had visited Gethsemani where Merton spent some time speaking with the group. Later, at Merton's invitation, Baker visited him on September 4, 1968. Soon after that visit Merton began his journey to Asia. The dissertation was later published under the title *Thomas Merton Social Critic*.[12] In two letters Merton thanked Baker for his work which Merton said provided him some insights into his own writing. Merton said that he was struck by how much he had said that was "premature, provisional, and in many ways inadequate." He realized that much of the appreciation for his work has come from Protestants, and that the first dissertation on him was by a Baptist. Merton was concerned that within the Catholic community people were "either too uncritical or too critical." He said, "I appreciate the more objective and balanced view of my work that is sometimes taken by those outside the Catholic Church. Inside it, I seem to get

---

9. *Hidden Ground,* p. 35. August 22, 1961.

10. *Hidden Ground,* p. 36. December 21, 1961.

11. *Hidden Ground,* p. 37-38. December 28, 1961.

12. *The Letters of Thomas Merton and Victor and Carolyn Hammer.* Ed. by E. Douglas Scutchfield and Paul Evans Holbrook, Jr. Lexington: University of Kentucky Press, 1971.

either total adulation or total rejection."[13]

Merton sent Baker a few minor things he had written and suggested that he seek out writings that had been published in fairly obscure places: *Motive*, a controversial magazine intended for Methodist college students that was later closed down, the *Catholic Worker,* a newspaper published by Dorothy Day and Peter Maurin, mimeographed items that Merton sent around to friends and others, a pamphlet on Camus's The Plague, an article on sacred art in *Jubilee*, and one in *Katallagete* published by two professors at Berea College. Finally, he suggested that Baker explore material in the Merton Center at Bellarmine College, now Bellarmine University.

Merton's final judgment on the dissertation:

> You certainly did a lot of work on it and went through a lot of material which I think you have summarized objectively and fairly. Naturally such an account has to be a very simplified one and I sometimes feel a bit oversimplified. But that is probably partly my own fault too, as I never manage to say fully all that I want to say. There is always something overlooked, some other aspect that needs to be remembered. I certainly did not find you too critical: you are most benign, and I think your work does help to get a real understanding and perspective of what I am trying to do.[14]

Merton kept up a correspondence for over eight years with Etta Gullick, a British Anglican, who taught at an Anglican theological school in Oxford and later was a lecturer on various spiritual writers. Merton referred to her as "my most real contact with England."[15] He especially appreciated her because she wrote about England, whereas his other British correspondents only referenced issues in which they were interested. Merton thought of her as almost a sister which helped fill his lack of having a real sister.

In one letter Merton responded to Gullick's concern that she might be a heretic. He said, ". . . personally I have long since given up attaching importance to that sort of thing." He had no idea of who she was in the eyes of God, "and that is what counts." Merton believed that the two of them were one in Christ and the presence

13. *Hidden Ground*, p. 69. June 11, 1968.
14. *Hidden Ground*, p. 70. June 25, 1968.
15. *Hidden Ground*, p. 353. June 14, 1962.

of "some material heresy" did not make much difference to him.[16] Three months later he did say to her, however, "I believe that the Roman Church is the only one that can claim to say the last word."[17] The open minded and liberal Merton would always remain a faithful Catholic, just as he told his brothers when he left for Asia that he would always be a monk of Gethsemani. In one letter of January 7, 1964, Merton complained of all the people who want to consult him. "I refuse to become a one man ecumenical movement, which would be silly."[18]

Still, Merton had a change in attitude toward the Anglican tradition. He wrote about the favorable climate of the Anglican Church, and said that the job of that Church was to keep alive its "spiritual simplicity and honesty quite apart from all fuss and works." He was concerned, however, that the Catholic Church was becoming more hostile to contemplative prayer.[19]

Gullick was "anguished" that there was little hope of Anglicans and Roman Catholics ever achieving institutional or sacramental union. Merton replied that he was not "terribly anguished," and believed that such ecumenical hope was bound to be illusory. The kind of unity that interested him was unity in love and in the Holy Spirit. "Prayer is the thing, and union with the suffering Lord on his cross."[20]

Another of Merton's ecumenical correspondents was John C. Heidbrink, a Presbyterian minister. He had been a Presbyterian chaplain at the University of Oklahoma, where he participated in a sit-in. Later he became acquainted with Martin Luther King, Jr. He joined the Fellowship of Reconciliation (FOR) in 1960 and served as secretary for church relations at the group's headquarters in Nyack, New York. At a peace conference in Prague he worked with Daniel Berrigan and Jim Forest to set up the Catholic Peace Fellowship. Later he arranged for Thich Nhat Hanh to visit Merton at Gethsemani. Merton had an extensive correspondence with Heidbrink.

In October, 1961, Merton wrote to Heidbrink, "I am very anxious to be in touch with any one who is working for peace at this

16. *Hidden Ground*, p. 358. March 24, 1963.
17. *Hidden Ground*, p. 358. March 24, 1963.
18. *Hidden Ground*, p. 364. January 7, 1964.
19. *Hidden Ground*, p. 368. September 12, 1964.
20. *Hidden Ground*, p. 377-378. November 24, 1966.

hour."[21] Merton was concerned that Catholics just did not realize what the situation really is. He believed that it is the obligation of every Christian to find some way to avoid the annihilation of the human race and abolish war. Two months later Merton admitted that he was glad to know more about the Fellowship of Reconciliation. He had never heard of it, although it is one of the leading peace organizations in the country. Merton invited Heidbrink and others in the FOR to come to Gethsemani and discuss the important issues. He referenced "Bridges of Faith," an article by Heidbrink, and wrote that the article represented what Merton believed about Christian unity. He specifically called for dialogue with Christians behind the Iron Curtain.

Apparently Heidbrink had encouraged Merton to become more ecumenically involved. Merton said that there was no way he could be active in any kind of organization. He wrote that whatever ecumenical work he did at Gethsemani was just talks to groups that come and conversations with visitors. He said "I have in no sense whatever any mandate or approval or mission in the Church to work for ecumenism." What he did, however, was tolerated and approved by the Cistercians with certain limits. So, Heidbrink should not say anything about Merton's belonging to any institution, although "I assume it is legal to say that I am a Catholic."[22]

On September 25, 1962, Merton sent in his application for membership in the Fellowship of Reconciliation. William Shannon, the editor of *Hidden Ground,* pointed out in a footnote that the FOR was regarded as a Protestant organization which Catholics did not join. Merton's action was "unusual and ahead of his time."[23] He urged Heidbrink not to publicize it.

Merton began to think about a peace retreat with some of the "key" people in the peace movement. He wrote to Paul Peachey about the idea and sent a copy of the letter to Heidbrink. The idea was that a group of around ten people would spend three days at Gethsemani under the aegis of Merton to discuss and exchange ideas. The Abbot said there should be no publicity of the event. In a May 20, 1963 letter to Heidbrink, Merton wrote, "The chief thing would be the atmosphere of recollection and thought, and the

21. *Hidden Ground* p. 402. October 30, 1961.
22. *Hidden Ground,* p. 407. February 15, 1962.
23. *Hidden Ground,* p. 410. September 26, 1962. See footnote.

exchange of ideas."[24]

In a May 9, 1964, letter to Heidbrink Merton began to express some second thoughts. He saw a need to reduce the number of groups that come to Gethsemani. A formal session with planned topics was just not something that Gethsemani did. "We are not geared for it," Merton wrote. He suggested just an informal visit with a few people rather than an organized meeting.

There followed letters about trying to set a date, always a difficulty for busy people. He did offer the hermitage as a site for conversations. The retreat was actually held on November 18-20, 1964. Heidbrink was unable to attend as he was having surgery, and Merton invited him to come for a visit later.

In 1965 and 1967 The Center for the Study of Democratic Institutions sponsored two conferences on Pope John's encyclical on Peace on Earth (*Pacem in Terris*). Merton indicated that there was no way he could participate, and he lamented the absence of any Catholics "with any kind of recognizable status."[25]

In a letter to Heidbrink on November 20, 1965, Merton resigned from the Catholic Peace Fellowship. The self-immolation of Roger La Porte and the highly publicized burning of draft cards left Merton very uncomfortable and ambiguous, but he did not see his resignation as a betrayal of the peace movement.

However, in a December 4, 1965 letter, Merton repented of his decision. "I recognize very clearly the wrong I did all of you with my telegram and first letter." He agreed to remain a sponsor of the Catholic Peace Fellowship with the understanding that in political and other matters he would remain "independent and autonomous." Nevertheless, he told Heidbrink, "I am morally and spiritually with you, I back the stated claims of the CPF, especially the moral and pastoral ones."[26] Actually, Heidbrink left the FOR in 1967.

On March 5, 1967, Merton responded to a request that he read a manuscript of a book on mysticism by Heidbrink. Merton indicated that he had received many manuscripts that people wanted him to read, but he would try to read at least some of it by the next time Heidbrink visited. For Merton, it was a very important topic. Mysticism, Merton thought, was very much under attack, especially by the new Catholic theologians. He believed that the main source for

24. *Hidden Ground,* p. 412. May 20, 1963.
25. *Hidden Ground,* p. 418. January 22, 1965.
26. *Hidden Ground,* pp. 425-426. December 4, 1965.

support would come from non-Catholics. In a letter to E. I. Watkins, a former Protestant who later became a Catholic and entered Downside Abbey in England, Merton wrote, "There is no question that the mystics are the ones who have kept Christianity going if anyone has."[27]

There is a bit of interesting correspondence with an Anglican nun, Sister Penelope Lawson. She had been a teacher and a librarian, and had written *The Wood: An Outline of Christianity* and other books. Some felt that her best work was her translations which included Athanasius, Origen, Bernard of Clairvaux, and William of St. Thierry. Her correspondence with Merton concerned her translation of Isaac of Stella, an early Cistercian father.

Merton's critique of her translation of Isaac was very thorough, indicating that Merton was a careful reader of Latin texts and was sensitive to passages that reflected ideas of interest to moderns such as existentialism, Jungian psychology, and Platonism, which he saw in Isaac. Some of his comments were grammatical, others related to vocabulary matters. He suggested words that should be substantives rather than adjectival, the deeper meaning of several terms which he is not sure she quite expressed clearly enough, and that she avoid the use of phrases that might be distasteful to the modern mind such as "vices being nests of snakes and cradles of death." That was more "Luther's kind of thing" Merton wrote. He suggested possible translations of words for her.[28]

In his next letter he told her that his response was the result of black coffee at five in the morning, and when he drinks black coffee he gets very enthusiastic about things. He said, "I am sure that you stood up to the tidal wave, and your letter shows no bad results. Still, of course, all I said is to be taken with reservations."[29]

In the last letter in this series he told her that she had done an "excellent job," expressed regret that the book had been turned down by Herder, and suggested that she might publish parts of it in *Cistercian Studies.* He also indicated that he had completed an introduction for her book.[30] It is worth noting that Merton took very seriously the scholarship of an Anglican on a Cistercian subject.

There are several letters in *Hidden Ground* to Pope John

27. *Hidden Ground*, p. 583. May 7, 1963
28. *Hidden Ground*, pp. 478-479. October 17, 1965.
29. *Hidden Ground*, p. 480. November 2, 1965.
30. *Hidden Ground*, pp. 480-481. July 27, 1966.

XXIII. They expressed abundant enthusiasm for the new Pope, but Merton also took the opportunity to explain his hope to establish a monastic foundation somewhere in Latin America which would receive special groups of people such as writers and intellectuals for discussions and retreats. Merton admitted that "the time has not yet come" for such a project, but he had hoped the Pope might have an interest in the idea.[31]

It never came to fruition. However, a few months later Merton reported to the Pope that he had received permission to have a series of small retreats for specialized and elite groups, such as theologians, the heads of Protestant seminaries, professors at a Catholic university, psychiatrists, writers, artists, and poets. The goal would be to gather together people highly qualified in their fields who would have an interest in the spiritual life.[32]

Two months later, April 11, 1960, Merton thanked the Pope for his interest in the retreat project. He mentioned that he had recently spoken to over fifty Protestant seminarians and pastors at Gethsemani. He saw them as people of good will, sincere, and open. He spoke to them not as a critic of their errors, but as one who understood their desire to seek God. They asked Merton if the Catholic Church was really interested in them, and he replied that the desire was to understand each other better.[33]

June J. Yungblut was a Quaker correspondent with Merton. She and her husband John had worked in South Africa with the American Friends Service Committee. They contacted Merton when they were directing Quaker House in Atlanta. John attempted to arrange a visit at Gethsemani for Martin Luther King, Jr., but King was assassinated before it could happen. June organized a tribute to King at the Liturgical Conference in Washington in August, 1960. At this event and on television Freedom Songs, for which Merton had written the words, were performed.

On June 22, 1967, Merton wrote to June about a book John was writing, *Rediscovering Christ,* later published in 1974. Merton questioned John's Christology, and said, "I am still hung up in a very traditional Christology myself." Although he said John's chapter sounded as plausible as other moderns, he could not see Christ simply as a mystic among others. Merton said he was influenced

31. *Hidden Ground,* pp. 482-483. November 10, 1958.
32. *Hidden Ground,* p. 484. February 11, 1960.
33. *Hidden Ground,* pp. 485-486. April 11, 1960.

by the Christ of Byzantine ikons and Transfiguration mysticism on Mount Athos. He just could not see Christ receiving a little flash of light like all the other mystics. But, he concluded, "I am not a good judge of this chapter."[34]

THE ROAD TO JOY: LETTERS TO NEW AND OLD FRIENDS

On December 1, 1963 Merton wrote a letter to one of his Anglican aunts in New Zealand, Agnes Stonehewer, known affectionately as Aunt Kit. After giving her some news about his life in the hermitage, he responded to her concerns about her faith. Merton urged her not to get too philosophical about it. He told her it was better to have a simple faith and leave the rest to God. "We can only say that we believe and that we really don't know."[35]

Two and a half years later he wrote a letter to her that revealed how far the evolution of his religious thinking had come. He told her that he was not doing any ecumenical work at the moment. He was now living in his hermitage, and the abbot thought that Merton should not be doing any active work with people. He was not anxious about it, but, he wrote, if he lived in New Zealand he would think that ecumenical work would be "quite important." He mentioned his many Anglican contacts in England and Boston, all of whom were "High Churchy." Merton confessed, "I am a pretty liberal bloke myself, if not radical." He felt at home with the Church of England except when people were "stuffy and insular" about it. He claimed that he had not been and will not ever be "aggressively Roman" and opined that it would be impossible for him to "go too far with a really 'popish' outlook. We are all too hard-headed and independent."[36]

Stonehewer drowned in a ferry accident in New Zealand when the lifeboat she was in capsized. John Merton, the older brother of Merton's father, wrote to tell about the death. Merton responded with a letter indicating that he wanted to stay in touch with the family in New Zealand. He mentioned that he had a number of Anglican friends, including A. M. Allchin. Merton wrote, "I think of myself very much as an English Catholic though Roman. Anyway all that

34. *Hidden Ground*, p. 637. January 22, 1967.

35. *The Road to Joy: Letters to New and Old Friends.* Ed. by Robert E. Daggy. HarperSanFrancisco, 1993, p. 60.

36. *Road to Joy,* p. 75. June 1, 1966.

is very much in evolution these days."[37]

In 1930, when Merton was only 15, he spent the Christmas holidays in a large Protestant pension in Strasbourg. This was at the suggestion of Thomas Bennett, who was Merton's guardian. The hope was that this experience might assist Merton in improving his French and German. A Protestant university professor, Jean Hering, took an interest in Merton. In *The Seven Storey Mountain,* Merton wrote that Hering was "one of the few Protestants I have ever met who struck one as being at all holy: that is, he possessed a certain profound interior peace, which he probably got from his contact with the Fathers of the Church, for he was a teacher of theology."[38]

Merton tried to revive the relationship by writing a letter in 1963, but that letter no longer exists. On April 6, 1964, he wrote again in response to a letter from Hering. He expressed regret at not being able to find a periodical Hering recommended, but said that he had "contacts with all the Protestant seminaries in this area and have been able to obtain several of your articles and your commentary on First Corinthians."[39]

In 1967, after many years of no communication, Merton received a Christmas card from an uncle, Harold Brewster Jenkins, his mother's brother. Jenkins expressed the hope that Merton would write to his wife as she had thought highly of him and John Paul. Merton responded with a letter to both. He wrote about his life in the hermitage and friends from Columbia days and others with whom he still keeps in touch. He added, "Otherwise I see a lot of ministers and others on an 'ecumenical' basis. My main interest in that line is keeping up with Buddhists, especially Zen people."[40]

The Road to Joy includes a number of circular letters intended for people who asked about his life and writings. In one written in 1963 he said that he became a monk as a way of "finding the true significance of my life, and my right place in God's creation." He added, "I have no criticism of anyone who seeks truth elsewhere. There are all kinds of ways to God, and ours is only one among many. But it seems to be the one for me, and it is the one I have chosen and accepted as God's will."[41]

---

37. *Road to Joy,* p. 87. June 17, 1968.
38. *Seven Storey Mountain*, p. 92.
39. *Road to Joy*, p. 61. April 6, 1964.
40. *Road to Joy*, p. 83. December 31, 1967.
41. *Road to Joy,* p. 89. 1963.

In Easter, 1967, Merton recommended a new English journal, *Theoria to Theory*, edited by Anglicans. Its purpose was to generate a dialogue between theologians and contemplatives and scientists, as well as philosophers and humanists. He called it "the most promising new venture of its kind I have seen." It was, he said, "promising and free-wheeling," compared to new Catholic publications which he called "too formal and still a bit triumphalist."[42]

In his Pentecost 1967 letter, Merton mentioned Pentecostal movements which "do not restrict themselves to far-out Protestant groups." There is, he believed, a hunger for the Spirit in ways that can be experienced. When asked about his opinion of these movements, Merton said, "the phenomenon represents a real spiritual hunger." For himself, Merton wrote, he is drawn to the desert and wilderness existence which is not looking for particular kinds of experiences.[43]

In a Midsummer 1967 circular letter, Merton noted that some people wanted to send him gifts. There was nothing they could send that he really needed, and he suggested instead that people send help for the refugees of the Arab-Israeli war. He recommended supporting a Quaker agency: The Friends Band of Missions, in Richmond, Indiana.

One of Merton's close friends at Columbia was Seymour Freedgood who later became an editor at *Fortune* magazine. While trying to set a date for Freedgood to visit him at Gethsemani, Merton said, "I have a tendency to get enmeshed in a group of Ecumenical folks from various places around here like Vanderbilt (University) and this eats into the time that is necessary for me to tie my shoes and think and rather not think. Later when they have evaporated I can think twice about the signal (to visit)."[44]

Sister Therese Lentfoehr was one of the important people in Merton's life. They had a long correspondence that began in 1939 and ended in 1968, a few weeks before Merton's death. In addition to correspondence she typed manuscripts for him. She assembled the largest private collections of Mertoniana which, after her death, eventually found its way to Columbia University. They finally had a proper visit in 1967 at a Gethsemani picnic.

Their correspondence covered a variety of subjects, but poetry,

42. *Road to Joy,* p. 101. Easter, 1967.

43. *Road to Joy,* p. 102. Pentecost, 1967.

44. *Road to Joy,* pp. 124-125. January 2, 1964.

prayer, and writing were frequent ones. She sent him books, relics, and other gifts. She was disappointed that she was not allowed to attend Merton's ordination.

Merton made frequent references to Protestants in this correspondence. On July 15, 1949, he described some hostile letters he received from a priest about *The Seven Storey Mountain* and *Seeds of Contemplation.* He complained, "They were more extremely bitter and savage than any criticism I have ever got from Protestants or unbelievers."[45] In a May 6, 1950 letter, he expressed frustration over the publication of *What Are These Wounds?*, a book about Saint Lutgarde. He tried to stop publication. It was a book he did not want to write, but the abbot asked. Merton said that the sale of his other books dropped as a result, and he warned that "the book is just wrong for the non-Catholic reader in this country."[46]

During the 1960s Merton's meetings with Protestants increased. He mentioned to Sister Lentfoehr in a May 10, 1961 letter, "Mostly I am busy with class and with Protestants."[47] A few months later he complained about his time being consumed with other responsibilities "as I am now seeing quite a lot of the various retreatants, particularly Protestants still."[48] In an April 1, 1964 letter, he told the sister about a visit with a Czechoslovakian Protestant theologian, Jan Lochman. Merton described him as "a very fine person, quite young," and said that they had a "very moving quiet conversation one evening after he had heard Compline." He added, "I had the impression of talking to someone out of the Acts of the Apostles."[49]

It appears that Sister Lentfoehr was also getting involved ecumenically. Merton told her on March 27, 1965, that "There is a blessing on every attempt at ecumenism that is simple and sincere, and your desire to do this is not for your own sake but for God and the Church and for them."[50] He added that he was not currently doing any ecumenical work because the Abbot wanted him to withdraw from it. He was now focusing his attention on life in his hermitage. However, on February 21, 1968, he wrote that he

45. *Road to Joy,* p. 194. January 15 1949.
46. *Road to Joy,* p. 202. May 6, 1950.
47. *Road to Joy*, p. 238. May 10, 1961.
48. *Road to Joy,* p. 238. September 19, 1961.
49. *Road to Joy*, p. 248. April 1 1964.
50. *Road to Joy*, p. 250. May 27, 1965.

would have liked to spend the whole of Lent on retreat, but said he has some appointments, "mostly ecumenical."[51]

In 1968, Philip Cascia, a high school junior, wrote to Merton concerning a term paper he was writing on ecumenism. Merton responded on April 10, 1968, "In a general way I'd say that the ecumenical movement is certainly an excellent thing, and it has meant new life for all Christians. Of course it is something of a fad in some places . . . . But basically, is a good thing."[52]

THE SCHOOL OF CHARITY: LETTERS ON RELIGIOUS RENEWAL AND SPIRITUAL DIRECTION

On January 2, 1942, Merton, at the request of Abbot Frederick Dunne, wrote a little statement about his life. He said that he had no memory of a Protestant baptism, although it was "barely possible." He described his father as a "just, prayerful, and devout man," who died "a good Anglican." Young Merton attended an Anglican school in England, but he thought the religion he received there was too liberal and without substance. Assuming this was true of all churches, he progressed from being anti-clerical to "a complete unbeliever." The result in his life was "disastrous."[53]

In *The School of Charity* there is a series of letters to Father Killian McDonnell, a Benedictine monk of St. John's Abbey in Collegeville, Minnesota, who was very involved in the ecumenical movement. In a May 31, 1960 letter to him, Merton suggested that he and one or two other monks from St. John's come to Gethsemani for a visit and retreat. He indicated that he had received permission to have some small retreats for discussion of things important to the Church. Merton mentioned Protestant theology professors, professors from Bellarmine College in Louisville, some Negro artists and perhaps a few beatnik writers. The retreats would be informal and not considered a movement, rather a personal visit. "So far," Merton wrote, "it has been going nicely."[54]

Three years later Merton wrote to Father McDonnell, "I am beginning to think that my vocation is not ecumenical." Still, he

---

51. *Road to Joy,* p. 261. February 21, 1968.

52. *Road to Joy,* p. 266. April 19, 1968.

53. *The School of Charity*. Ed. by Brother Patrick Hart. New York: Farrar, Strauss, and Giroux, 1990, p. 5. January 2, 1942.

54. *School of Charity,* p. 133. May 31, 1960.

said, he would keep up his ecumenical activity, "when it seems to make the most sense." He complained, however, that Protestant theology discounts nature and the fact that man is made in the image of God. The theological seriousness of American Protestantism is "not high." He saw it as a combination of religious pragmatism and sociology. He did say that Karl Barth "is almost the one among theologians alive today that I like best." However, since Merton realized that he is not "a Curial-Marian type," Protestants "just tend to sit and listen and listen passively and to accept almost anything." Nevertheless, he affirmed that there are "some good men at the Baptist Seminary in Louisville and at Vanderbilt."[55] This letter was written in what Brother Patrick Hart called the "Middle Formative Years" when Merton was meeting with Baptist, Disciples of Christ, Presbyterian, and Episcopalian seminary students in the area.[56]

Merton continued to have correspondence with Anglican nuns in England. To Mother Mary Margaret, an Anglican abbess, he wrote that he hoped some day to write on Anglican spirituality. In the meantime he sent her a mimeographed essay he had written on English mystics. He suggested that he might write a little meditation for her on the spirit of ecumenism "or some such thing." He said that practical ecumenism is a matter of working at small things when possible and praying together "as best we can."[57]

Merton's interest in the Shakers continued to appear in his letters. He corresponded with Sister Prisca, OSB, a cloistered nun in Bethlehem, Connecticut, thanking her for sending information about a Shaker community at Sabbathday Lake. He had thought that the only surviving community was at Canterbury with half a dozen elderly women. He was surprised to learn that some of the sisters as Sabbathday Lake were "relatively young" and saw that as a hopeful sign. He wrote to Sister Prisca, "I have always been very impressed by their eschatological spirit, their sense of themselves as a sign of the last days and the new creation."[58]

Father Peter Minard, a French Benedictine, came to the United States to found a small contemplative community near Oxford, North Carolina, sometime in the 1960s. He discovered he had cancer and returned to France where he died in 1988. The little monastery

55. *School of Charity*, p. 189. December 20, 1963.
56. *School of Charity*, p. xi.
57. *School of Charity*, p. 197. January 16, 1964.
58. *School of Charity*, p. 197. February 10, 1964.

was taken over by Gethsemani. Father Matthew Kelty gave leadership to it, and I personally made a number of retreats there during his tenure, as did others from nearby colleges and universities. Father Matthew was a welcoming host. He eventually left to become a hermit in Papua, New Guinea, and the community was taken over by monks from St. Joseph's Abbey in Spencer, Massachusetts. The same kind of hospitality prevailed.

On January 9, 1965, Merton wrote to Father Minard at the beginning of the project a long letter of encouragement. Oxford was a simple, rather primitive set-up. The individual cabins or cells were constructed of 2x4s and plywood. The chapel was plain and simple. Part of the letter was devoted to Merton's thoughts about the hermit life. Father Minard was all alone in what he called a monastic diaspora. After the Cistercians took it over, Oxford never had more than three or four resident monks, so it was always a semi-hermit community. A number of Protestants made retreats there and developed friendships with Father Matthew.

Merton told Father Minard about his ecumenical contacts. Specifically, he described his sessions with students from Southern Baptist Theological Seminary in Louisville. They were interested in Gethsemani and the monastic life, and Merton said he had "very interesting talks with them." He told Father Minard that they were attracted to mental prayer and contemplation "which had hitherto been unknown to them." Merton believed that among Protestants in general there was a new interest in solitary prayer. "The idea of *lectio, oratio, contemplatio* (reading, prayer, contemplation) is in fact quite congenial to them, minus the Latin." [59]

Merton was always curious about other forms of community life. On July 4, 1964, he wrote to an anonymous Brother H., a member of a Bruderhof community in the United States. The Brother had sent him some books, one of them about Eberhard Arnold, the founder of the movement. Merton wrote, "There is no question that there is a similarity of spirit between your Brotherhood and our Monastic Order," and said they should be in touch with each other. Merton invited the Brother to visit Gethsemani. He also discussed some of the problems of community life, but added, "Let me assure you that your 'rightness' and your faithfulness are evident. Never fear, your joy has eternal foundations." [60]

---

59. *School of Charity*, pp. 262-263. January 9, 1965.
60. *School of Charity*, p. 220. July 4, 1969.

The original purpose of Merton's hermitage was ecumenical. A letter to Dom André Louf (April 6, 1963) contains a long discussion of the hermit life. However, Merton mentions that originally the hermitage was intended as a place where Merton could meet with non-Catholic retreatants in a quiet setting apart from the monastery. "Since then," Merton wrote, "the visits of the retreatants have stopped; I have spent more than afternoons, as much free time as I could get, and finally, since last October I have been sleeping here."[61]

On April 29, 1965, Merton resumed his correspondence with his Anglican friend, Mother Mary Margaret. They had earlier corresponded about his writing a little ecumenical meditation which he encouraged her to edit. He mentioned that he had used a Protestant translation of the Bible by James Moffatt but was open to using the King James Version, a product of the English Reformation. He did not like modernizing the Biblical text. As a result of Vatican II the Catholic Church was experiencing many changes on the local level that concerned Merton. He advised Mother Mary Margaret "to maintain traditions that we are now eagerly throwing overboard (Latin, Gregorian chant, etc.) in monastic communities."[62]

Merton had an extensive correspondence with Dame Marcella Van Bruyn, a Benedictine now living a solitary life. He thanked her for her translation of Raïssa Maritain. At the end of the letter he said that he was convinced that there was "much triviality under the guise of ecumenism." He did not think anyone should feel obligated "to get involved in every little ecumenical picnic—or to be enthusiastic about such things."[63]

A month later, Merton wrote to Father Gerard Bryan, a Gethsemani monk, who was studying for a doctorate in Rome and writing a dissertation on Bernard of Clairvaux and Teilhard de Chardin. He inquired about the Vatican Council and whether it was going to impact Gethsemani. He said, "I seem to have heard strange mutterings at one time or other about something called ecumenical dialogue, but of course that must be something perilous and communistic."[64]

---

61. *School of Charity*, p. 276. April 26, 1965.
62. *School of Charity*, p. 279. April 29, 1965.
63. *School of Charity*, p. 302. April 17, 1966.
64. *School of Charity,* p. 304. May 27, 1966.

THE COURAGE FOR TRUTH: LETTERS TO WRITERS

One of Merton's projects was to publish a book of selections from the Desert Fathers. He wanted to include an introductory essay by D. T. Suzuki on the Fathers who, in Merton's opinion, resembled Zen masters. The censors rejected the idea, but Merton did receive permission from the Father General of the Cistercians, Dom Gabriel Sortais, to publish essays by himself and Suzuki separately. He thought of inviting Eric Fromm and "a Protestant such as Paul Tillich" to join in that conversation. However, Dom Gabriel objected to dialogue between Cistercians and Buddhists, Protestants, and Jews in one book. Such a book would be published by a non-Catholic, James Laughlin at New Directions press.[65]

Merton wrote a letter about the project to Jacques Maritain, a Catholic theologian, asking for his opinion about it. Maritain replied, and Merton sent the letter on to the Father General. However, the Father General had decided that this material should not be published in book form. Merton thanked Maritain for "considering the matter."[66]

In another letter to Maritain, Merton repeated what he had said to others about the purpose of his hermitage. He told Maritain that a small house was about to be built where he could have dialogue with Non-Catholics and intellectuals. When there are no meetings, he could be there alone and enjoy the solitude.[67] In a later letter Merton complained to Maritain that there was real hostility to an "inner, silent, recollected, wordless form of prayer." He concluded, "I feel personally that what I have to say now is much more for those who are not in the Church than for those that are in it."[68]

Merton had a lengthy correspondence with Czelaw Milosz, a Polish poet who had joined the Polish resistance during World War II. He later worked for the Polish diplomatic service in New York, Washington, and Paris. He published poetry and a number of novels while in Paris. Eventually, he found his way to the United States and became a professor at the University at California at Berkley. Merton wrote a number of long letters to Milosz as they

65. *The Courage for Truth: Letters to Writers.* New York, Farrar, Straus and Giroux, 1993, pp. 30-31. April 8, 1960.

66. *Courage*, p. 31. May 20, 1960

67. *Courage*, p. 53. June 30, 1960.

68. *Courage*, p. 51. January 30, 1967.

corresponded about literary matters, some of which predated his move to the United States.

In one of these long letters Merton noted, "I am interested in Protestantism now." He mentioned having meetings with Protestant theologians whom he described as "pleasant, honest, and earnest men." He questioned how serious they were but indicated there was the same problem with Catholic theologians.[69]

Milosz had been critical of some of Merton's writings on peace. His experience in Poland during World War II and after made him skeptical. Merton was aware of problems. He was concerned about belligerent Christians, "on the one hand fundamentalist Protestants and on the other certain Catholics" who favored a nuclear attack as destruction in the name of Christ. As far as his writings on peace are concerned, Merton wrote, "I have just about said what I have to say."[70]

Merton maintained correspondence with Ernesto Cardenal, a former novice at Gethsemani who later became a priest and, eventually, the Minister of Culture in the Sandinista government in Nicaragua. In one of his letters Merton told Cardenal about his hermitage, "built primarily as a quiet place in which to receive Protestant ministers who come in small groups for retreats."[71]

In a letter of November 20, 1961, Merton said that he did not know what could become of his contacts with Protestant ministers and scholars, and noted that someone in Rome had said such activity was not appropriate for a contemplative. However, he added, "The only result has been to leave me with a profound respect for these (Protestant) men and an increased understanding of their spirit." Even so, he did not think that an ecumenical movement was important. On the matter of nuclear war, Merton was pleased that there was "at least a minority that is waking up and beginning to react, mostly among non-Catholics, but also among a few chosen Catholics."[72]

Merton enjoyed a correspondence with Pablo Antonio Cuadra, a Nicaraguan poet, journalist, and editor. Merton believed that his poetry was "the most authentically 'American' poetry of Latin

69. *Courage,* p. 68. May 6, 1960.
70. *Courage,* p. 80. March, 1962.
71. *Courage*, p. 123. March 11, 1961.
72. *Courage*, p. 129. November 20, 1961.

America."[73] In a 1960 letter, Merton told Cuadra that Jews had been coming to Gethsemani for retreats and that he had been spending time with Protestant theologians and ministers. He wrote that those relationships "promise to bring about a better understanding" and that the Pope had "personally blessed and encouraged them."[74]

Julien Green, of American parents, was a Paris writer known for his novels, plays, and essays. He liked Merton's *Thoughts in Solitude* which he said made him feel closer to God, as well as *The Seven Storey Mountain,* but was critical of Merton's essay "To Each His Darkness" in *Raids on the Unspeakable* on one of his novels. Merton replied that he had read the novel in haste and might have missed an important point. However, he did say that for him the Augustinian idea of sin is "impressive." Merton did not have the "taste" for Calvin that Green had, but added, "there are moments when I like to have him stand my hair on end for a change." He also indicated that he was having a copy of *Conjectures of a Guilty Bystander* sent to Green in which he states his own "Protestant likings," especially Karl Barth."[75]

Merton's continuing opposition to ecumenical organizations was expressed in a letter to the novelist Walker Percy. "I agree with you about the ecumenical sparks that did not spark. All movements fill me with suspicion or lassitude. I think the best thing is to belong to a universal anti-movement underground."[76]

WITNESS TO FREEDOM: THE LETTERS OF THOMAS MERTON IN TIMES OF CRISIS

Merton's poem about Nazi extermination camps was published in *The Mennonite* in 1961. He thanked the editor, Maynard Shelly, and indicated that he was very proud to appear in that publication. He also said that he had "respect and reverence" for the Mennonite tradition of peace and non-violence.[77]

The Shakers continued to be a strong interest for Merton. In

73. See the introduction to the Cuadra correspondence in *Courage*, pp. 178-179.

74. *Courage*, p. 187. January 4, 1960.

75. *Courage,* pp. 273-274. September 22, 1966

76. *Courage*, p. 283. July 20, 1967.

77. *Witness to Freedom.* Ed. by William H. Shannon. New York: Farrar, Straus and Giroux, 1994, pp.22-23. December, 1961.

1962 Merton had to express his regrets that he would be unable to see a collection of Shaker drawings in Williamsburg. He could not receive permission for travel for "social occasions." However, in his letter to Mary Childs Black in Williamsburg, he expressed his belief in the "deep significance" of the Shakers. He thought that they were an expression of the American paradise myth, a return to simplicity, unity, and the innocence of Adam. However, the Shakers saw that the secular vision of the earthly paradise was deceptive. It involved the slaughter of the Indians, the enslavement of the Negro, and the treatment of immigrants as inferior beings.

The Shakers knew their involvement with the secular world required a special conversion which captured the unique substance of the myth, which was something original, but which remained hidden to others. Merton was impressed that their vision was also eschatological and the fact that they basically ended.[78]

There continue to be references in Merton's writings to the Quakers. His mother had had a relationship with the Quakers. One of his letters was addressed to G. M. whom editor William Shannon suggested was probably Gwen Myers. The issue was Myers' concern that she, who obviously wanted to be a contemplative, was embarrassed that she and Merton were affiliated with two different church traditions. Merton's response was that this did not matter and noted that she had read authors that expressed the kind of contemplative life that was lived at Gethsemani. Everyone, he said, needs a community in which the Spirit of Christ can speak and guide people. Community life in religious groups is a "transparent medium" for the work of the Holy Spirit.

It seems that she belonged to a prayer group that did not seem to understand her contemplative aspirations. Merton advised her to trust God who will guide her "safely" if she will keep her heart pure and quiet. God will even provide books that will tell her things that her friends cannot tell her.[79]

Merton did have reservations about the tactics of some peace groups. He was opposed to people burning themselves to death as a way of protesting a war, and he was doubtful of the value of burning draft cards.

Merton attempted to set things straight with Allan Forbes, Jr. He said he had no intention of questioning the value of the Mennonites

78. *Witness,* pp. 30-31. January 24, 1962.
79. *Witness*, pp. 56-57. June, 1964.

and Quakers, and did not want to include them "indiscriminately" with all pacifists. He called the Quaker peace witness one of the most "reliable and stabilizing forces" and is of great spiritual importance. The spiritual witness of the Friends is a "most important" witness of conscience. However, Merton did not think it had significant political consequences.[80]

In an August, 1965 letter to his agent, Naomi Burton Stone, Merton indicated that he had sent something to *Motive* magazine which he described as "mostly Protestant" and published in Nashville. He thought they might be interested in "stuff" in the "Behavior of Titans."[81] In fact, *Motive* was a Methodist publication intended primarily for college students. The magazine was controversial among the Methodists, primarily for its liberal stand on civil rights and other issues. It was finally suppressed.

In 1961 Merton received the University Medal for Excellence from Columbia University. Of course he was not allowed to attend the ceremony in New York, but he did write to President Grayson Kirk a letter of thanks and appreciation for the award. Merton suspected that Professors Mark Van Doren and Jacques Barzun had something to do with it.

Merton mentioned to Kirk his interest in Oriental philosophy and spirituality and suggested that Oriental and African students at Colombia might benefit by visits to Gethemani. He added that several faculty members from Union Theological Seminary had visited and he hoped more would come.[82] In the 1950s and early 60s Union was considered by many to be the premier Protestant seminary in the United States. It had on its faculty Reinhold Niebuhr, Paul Tillich, and many other well-known scholars and theologians.

In the *Witness to Freedom* letter collection there is a long correspondence with Professor Herbert Mason of Boston University. In the first of these letters we see that part of Merton's spiritual evolution was growing disenchantment with institutional religion, which he described as "enormous and almost overwhelming." "Whatever fire there is in religion is not found in the external forms which so many want to preserve."[83]

---

80. *Witness*, pp. 61-62. August, 1962.
81. *Witness*, p. 147. August 31, 1965.
82. *Witness*, pp. 157-158. June 16, 1961.
83. *Witness*, p. 261. June 8, 1959.

In another letter to Mason, Merton described his continuing interest in the Shakers. Merton occasionally visited Shakertown, a community that closed in 1910. He referred to it as "an intense and rather wacky spiritual center," but called it "very significant." He saw in their simple handiwork a witness to something "tremendously genuine in their spirit." [84]

Three years later Merton expressed appreciation for the efforts to restore the Shaker village. He expressed his regrets to a Mr. McAllister who had invited him to a conference that he would not be able to attend, but did say that he looked forward to a forthcoming visit with McAllister and the Andrews when they could discuss their project. Shaker communities represented what Merton called "an authentic American form of the Monastic Life" with its "utopian and eschatological cast." He believed that there was much study to be done on the Shaker tradition in light of the various mystical traditions and Jungian depth psychology. The group represented vital religious forces that were at work in America in the nineteenth century.[85]

From time to time Merton wrote letters of spiritual counsel. In one to a Mrs. Nunn, whom he identified as a Methodist, he said that a deep experience of God should be a common experience for all Christians. It should be "familiar," he wrote, in the Methodist tradition. However, he counseled that too much emphasis on spiritual experience is not a good thing. Not everyone should think that they should have great experiences. Rather, they should abandon themselves in faith to God and focus only on what God shows them. He suggested that Mrs. Nunn read St. Theresa, Julian of Norwich, and Evelyn Underhill. He told her that many good books on the subject of mysticism were available.[86]

Merton did not write often on the subject of marriage, never having experienced it himself. However, the issue of interfaith marriages seemed to interest him. He received a letter from "Mrs. D," the wife of a Baptist seminary professor. She was ready to convert to Catholicism, but had not talked to her husband about it. In some Baptist circles this could be a very serious problem. That church generally did not have a good opinion of Catholicism[87].

---

84. *Witness,* p. 266. December 24, 1959.
85. *Witness*, pp. 303-304. October 29, 1961.
86. *Witness*, p. 310. January 10, 1964.
87. *Witness*, pp. 311-312. February 26, 1965.

Merton did not think such a conversion was impossible, but might require a certain amount of daring. She should go slow and not push it to the point that it would threaten their marriage. True Christian love was more important than identification with any institution. The Sacraments would be of great help to her, but, he wrote, "God gives grace without them," and is not bound by any system. She must, of course, talk this out with her husband, even if this means patient waiting. Merton told her that he had counseled with the wife of an Episcopalian priest. She converted, the family is together, and everything is fine.

One of the Protestant groups for which Merton always had a great interest was the Anglican Church. In April, 1965, he received a letter from Mrs. Mycock who suggested that if he had written *The Seven Storey Mountain* now (1965) he would have expressed a different opinion of Anglicanism. Merton agreed, saying that his writing had "hardly matured" at that time. He now regretted the injustice he may have done to that church and that he had been trying gradually to repair it.

Mrs. Mycock expressed a concern that the book might have a negative impact on the hope of the reunion of Christianity. Merton affirmed that there had been a "huge accumulation of injustice, faux pas, errors, cruelties, iniquities, on every hand," and that there was no hope of any reunion until they are "admitted, accepted, understood, painfully atoned for, (and) replaced by opposites." As for his early comments on Anglicanism, Merton said to her that he hoped for her forgiveness and assured her of his contrition.[88]

Gabrielle Mueller wrote to Merton in 1965 about negative comments he had heard from Protestants. Merton said that he was not surprised, but reported that he had had many meetings with Southern Baptists from their seminary in Louisville. They got along well together, and Merton thought that Protestant-Catholic animosity had died down. He told Mueller that he often explained Catholic practices and what the Church thinks about "relics, etc." The Baptists may not accept the ideas, "but they see that we are not totally nuts."

His advice to Mueller was to seek God in faith and focus on essentials, such as God's redemptive love for all people, her baptism, her reception of the Holy Spirit, and seeking first the Kingdom of God. Trying to get people to move from one church to another is a

88. *Witness*, pp. 319-310. May 10, 1965.

sign of a lack of being in touch with what the Holy Spirit is trying to tell the faithful. Merton said, "I personally have never encouraged Protestants to become Catholics even when they wanted to. I have never, never tried to persuade any Protestant that his religion is in error. It seems to me to be simply a matter of common decency and respect for another person's conscience. There I stand."[89]

THOMAS MERTON AND JAMES LAUGHLIN: SELECTED LETTERS

The volume *Thomas Merton and James Laughlin* differs from the five volume set of Merton's letters in that this collection has letters from both sides of the correspondence. Letters from both Merton and Laughlin are included. Both sides of the correspondence are seen in the collections of letters between Merton and Czeslaw Milosz, Rosemary Radford Ruether, Robert Lax, Robert Giroux, Edward Deming and Faith Andrewes, Jean Leclercq, D. T. Suzuki, and Victor and Carolyn Hammer[90]

James Laughlin had wanted to be a poet but was discouraged from that vocation by Ezra Pound with whom he had been studying in Italy. Pound suggested that he become a publisher. With help from his family, Laughlin founded New Directions Publication Corporation. He published Merton's poetry and a number of his

89. *Witness*, p. 321. November 10, 1966.

90. *A Catch of Anti-Letters: Thomas Merton and Robert Lax.* Kansas City: Sheed and Ward, 1994.

A Meeting of Angels: The Correspondence of Thomas Merton with Edward Deming and Faith Andrews. Frankfort, KY: Broadstone Books, 2008.

At Home in the World: The Letters of Thomas Merton and Rosemary Radford Ruether. Maryknoll, NY: Orbis Books, 1995.

Encounter: Merton and D. T. Suzuki. Ed. by Robert E. Daggy. Monterrey, KY: Larkspur Press, 1988.

Letters of Robert Giroux and Thomas Merton. Ed. by Patrick Samway, SJ. Notre Dame, IN: University of Notre Dame Press, 2015.

Letters of Thomas Merton and Victor and Carolyn Hammer. Ed. by F. Douglas Scuthfield and Paul Evans Holbrook, Jr. Lexington: University of Kentucky Press, 2014.

Striving Toward Being: The Letters of Thomas Merton and Czeslaw Milosz. New York: Farrar, Straus and Giroux, 1997.

Survival or Prophecy: The Letters of Thomas Merton and Jean Leclercq. Ed. by Brother Patrick Hart, 2002.

When Prophecy Still Had a Voice. Ed. by Arthur W. Biddle. Lexington: University of Kentucky Press, 2001.

books. Among other things he published the huge *Collected Poems of Thomas Merton, The Literary Essays of Thomas Merton,* and Merton's *Asian Journal,* as well as other works.

Much of this correspondence dealt with publishing issues, but there were occasional references to Protestantism. Laughlin had a Presbyterian background and, in this correspondence, Merton sometimes functioned as Laughlin's spiritual director.

In a July, 1947 letter, which predates *The Seven Storey Mountain,* Laughlin asked Merton to suggest some books that might help him "to increase the spiritual component in my life." He called himself "an essentially religious person," but he wanted some guidance from Merton. He explained that he grew up in a Presbyterian family amid much Bible reading and catechism learning, but with no interior religious feeling. Attending church with his mother seemed more social than religious. After a visit with Merton at Gethsemani he sensed a new kind of simple communication with God. There were times when his mind emptied of whatever he was thinking and "a sort of glow" entered which he identified with "the Idea of God." Laughlin confessed that he did not know what to say to God except "to enjoy the feeling and recognize its nature and be grateful for it."[91]

Merton replied five days later. He encouraged simplicity and integrity, and told Laughlin that God would guide him through people and events. He should be himself with God and realize "by faith" that God is with him and concerned about him. The most important thing was to cultivate a sense of the presence of God. However, Merton told him not to focus exclusively on contemplative union with God. He also needed a liturgical life, such as vocal prayer at set times. Merton also suggested certain Catholic practices such as praying the Our Father, the Hail Mary, and stopping in to Churches and hearing Mass. These would help bind his sense of God into his everyday life.[92]

A related letter of September 10, 1947 from Merton to Laughlin contains more spiritual guidance. He told Laughlin that when he was very busy the way to pray was to remember that the will of God is woven into everything he does. If he is working in union with God, a vital contact with God flows through Laughlin's own

91. *Thomas Merton and James Laughlin: Selected Letters.* New York: W. W. Norton, 1997, p. 22-23. July 12, 1947.

92. *Laughlin Letters,* p. 26. July 17, 1947.

work. If he is working against God, he will suffer a loss of energy, waste his strength, and leave him with his hands empty. He needs to develop a sensitivity to his union or non-union with God's will. If he asks, God will sharpen that sensitivity for him. But there is a caveat: he will have to be prepared to give up some things.[93]

The following year (1948) Merton advised Laughlin to cultivate tranquility, "the purity of heart that does things simply to please God." He should think of himself as swimming with the stream of God's will and not fighting the current of his own ambitions. If his own interests coincide with God's aims, "then things will move with a tremendous ease and swiftness." It is a matter of cultivating an awareness of God's presence by faith.[94]

Merton also shared with Laughlin his desire to have some small group sessions in his hermitage. He mentioned that he had two groups of Protestant seminary professors coming, but did not want that to be his specialty. He was also interested in "writers, beats, Protestants, Buddhists, intellectuals, who knows, even politicians."[95]

In 1961 Merton was saying that "The country is getting sicker all the time." As an example he cited criticism he had received because he supported the Dean of the Vanderbilt Divinity School who resigned after the University expelled an African-American student.[96]

I was a student there at that time. The expelled student was James Lawson, a Methodist minister, and the Dean was J. Robert Nelson. Lawson, who helped organize the sit-in movement in Nashville, told the mayor that his group would disobey segregation laws until they were changed. The Nashville Banner newspaper came out with a front page headline saying that a divinity student advocated breaking the law. The Chancellor of the University, Harvie Branscomb, author of a book on the ethics of Jesus, expelled Lawson. I well remember an all-day student body meeting in the Divinity School where we discussed how we should respond. Merton had an interest in the Divinity School because the first year church history students spent a day at Gethsemani every year. Those visits were rich experiences.

At the end of the collection of letters, Laughlin wrote a little

---

93. *Laughlin Letters,* p. 28. September 10, 1947.

94. *Laughlin Letters,* p. 38. July 8, 1948.

95. *Laughlin Letters,* p. 153. April 20, 1960.

96. *Laughlin Letters,* p. 169. April 5, 1961.

appendix which he called "A Portrait" of Merton. He appreciated Merton's ability to explain Catholic faith so that he, who described himself as "a heretic, benighted Calvinist" could get some feeling of what it is about. He described his own visit at Gethsemani as "a very novel experience," which his Presbyterian mothers would have regarded as an "invention of the devil." Laughlin, however, said it was "a place full of happiness and high spirits."[97]

AT HOME IN THE WORLD: THE LETTERS OF THOMAS MERTON AND ROSEMARY RADFORD RUETHER

One of Merton's liveliest exchanges of correspondence was an eighteen month series with Rosemary Radford Ruether, a Catholic feminist theologian. She and Merton both had many concerns about the Catholic Church, but Ruether exhibited a hostility toward monasticism and thought Merton was wasting his life. Merton's side of this correspondence appeared in the first volume of his letters, *The Hidden Ground of Love*, but the Orbis Books volume includes Ruether's side.

The correspondence began with a request by Reuther that Merton look at a manuscript she had written, *The Church Against Herself,* which included a chapter on Gabriel Vahanian. He was a theologian who wrote about the Death of God Theology, although he was not a death of God theologian himself. Merton replied that Vahanian was someone he must read. He had read Thomas J. J. Altizer, the father of the Death of God movement whom he respected, and William Hamilton about whom he had mixed feelings. He asked Reuther if she would send him anything she might think would be good for him to read.[98]

Ruether responded by recommending that Merton read Bonhoeffer, saying that her thought is increasingly being formed by him.[99] Merton replied that he had read Bonhoeffer's *Ethics* and his prison letters. "Certainly," he wrote, "you will find me liking Bonhoeffer."[100]

Being upset with the Catholic Church was a recurring theme

97. *Laughlin Letters,* p. 375. Appendix.

98. *At Home in the World: The Letters of Thomas Merton and Rosemary Radford Ruether,* Maryknoll, NY: Orbis Books, 1996, pp. 3-4. August 18, 1966.

99. *Ruether*, p. 5. Late August, Early September, 1966.

100. *Ruether,* p. 8. September 21, 1966.

in Ruether. She said that "it makes me shudder" and told Merton that she "hangs onto the fringes" and regularly celebrated with Protestants.[101] Merton shared her concerns, but in a mimeographed letter to friends he expressed gratitude for "the love that unites us," and that "union with Christ" meant much to him "though some of you are not enrolled in my church."[102]

One of Merton's theological concerns was Christology. He said that his entrance into the Catholic Church involved a "pretty strong and dazzled belief in the Christ of the Nicene Creed." He accepted this because he found new Christologies in Protestantism to be foggy, subjective, and messed up. However, Merton said that when one explores church history one finds a "bigger and bigger hole of unconscious bad faith." That caused him to question whether Catholicism was "the one authentic outfit that has all the real goods."[103]

Some of the correspondence had to do with the authenticity of the monastic life or, in Ruether's case, the lack thereof. She wrote that the logic of asceticism leads to salvation from the world and the dissolution of creation. Monasticism, she believed, had lost its soul and is no longer regarded as "the highest Christian state."[104]

Merton wrote a lengthy reply which included many references to the church fathers. He regarded her view of monasticism as both abstract and arbitrary. Merton saw himself in many ways as an anti-ascetic humanist. What had meant the most to him about the life was the contact with creation which leads to a "simpler, saner, and more human life than in the supposedly comfortable, pleasurable world." He now lived in the woods where it is naturally easier "to walk in God's light." He felt some guilt about having it easier than most, but he had not repudiated God's creation. He saw monks as the remnant of "desperate conservationists," and reported that he and the novices had planted hundreds of pine saplings only to see them bulldozed "by some ass" a year later. Responding to Ruether's criticisms he mentioned a thirteenth century lay-hermit movement where the solitaries preached to the poor and outcasts. These groups, Merton said, were forerunners of Protestantism and

101. *Ruether*, p. 11. October 10, 1966.
102. *Ruether*, pp. 14-15. January 22, 1967.
103. *Ruether*, p. 22. February 14, 1967.
104. *Ruether*, pp. 31-33. March 4, 1967.

pre-Protestant groups like the Waldensians.[105]

In March, 1967, Merton reported that Gabriel Vahanian had visited Gethsemani. He and Merton spent several hours early in the morning talking mostly about Faulkner, on whom Merton was working at that time. Vahanian suggested that monks needed to be "effectively iconoclastic in the modern world."[106]

For Easter, 1967, Merton sent out a form letter to many people, including Rosemary Ruether. It offered a recommendation for a new English journal, *Theoria to Theory,* edited by Anglicans. It was an effort to develop dialogue between theologians and contemplatives on one hand, and secular scientists, philosophers, and humanists on the other. Merton regarded it as the most promising venture he had seen, better than the new Catholic publications which he saw as "too formal and still a bit triumphalist."[107] Along with that letter Merton sent Ruether a copy of his vow not to be an abbot.

Ruether replied that Merton's letter revealed a dark but full faith "which is the only kind I can really take." Understanding the darkness of faith, she said, "was Luther's great genius." What matters is not achievement, but *fides sola*, faith alone. She complained that Catholics "crudely and stupidly" misunderstood Luther, because this was not a theology for beginners but for people who have tried many approaches to faith and discovered that such efforts were insufficient. Luther's theology, she wrote, "remains basically the result of his maturing monastic experience."[108] Merton replied that he told Protestants who visited Gethsemani that a monk does not really become a monk until he has gone through the kind of experience Luther had and discovered the futility of works.[109] In that same letter Merton told Ruether that he had just read a book by P. Parpet in German on Evangelical monasticism. Parpet suggested that the most contemplative-monastic people in the world then (1967) were nuclear physicists. Merton agreed and said that for him that meant Bohr and the Copenhagen group which he described as his "cultural heroes." Merton's universe of interest was ever expanding.

105. *Ruether,* pp. 36-37. March 6, 1967.
106. *Ruether*, p. 44. March 19, 1967.
107. *Ruether*, p. 68. Easter, 1967.
108. *Ruether*, p. 86. July 20, 1967.
109. *Ruether*, p. 87. August, 4, 1967.

THE LETTERS OF THOMAS MERTON AND VICTOR AND CAROLYN HAMMER

Two of Merton's best friends were Victor and Carolyn Hammer. Victor was an artist and printer who taught at Transylvania University in Lexington. Merton's letters are filled with requests for books from the University of Kentucky library where Carolyn Hammer was on the staff. They reveal Merton's interest in Protestants. For example, he asked for a copy of *The Christian Century*, a weekly periodical that represented the liberal perspective of what used to be called Mainline Protestantism. Merton was interested in an article in the *Century* on Religious Liberty in Russia.[110] He also asked for Herbert Butterfield's, *Christianity and History*, and said if the UK library did not have it he might be able to get it from the College of the Bible, a Disciples of Christ seminary later known as Lexington Theological Seminary.[111]

He was also interested in some of the leading Protestant theologians of his day. He asked Carolyn Hammer for Paul Tillich's *The Protestant Era,*[112] and Reinhold Niebuhr's *The Irony of American History.*[113] A later list of requested books included Eric Erickson's *Young Man Luther.*[114]

His major interest related to our topic in these letters was Shakertown. He mentioned a visit to Asbury Theological Seminary, a Methodist oriented seminary eleven miles south of Lexington. He wrote to the Hammers that he did not have time to visit them in Lexington, but on his way back to Gethsemani he stopped at Shakertown and took some pictures. He was thinking about putting together a small simple book with pictures of Shakertown and a prose poem about the place.[115] Instead, he wrote an article about Shakertown and sent it to *Jubilee*, a magazine published by one of his classmates at Columbia, Edward Rice.[116] Rice later wrote a book about Merton, *The Man in the Sycamore Tree.*

He sent the article to the Hammers who passed it on to three

---

110. *The Letters of Thomas Merton and Victor and Carolyn Hammer.* Lexington: University Kentucky Press, 2014, p. 48. June 6, 1958.

111. *Hammer Letters*, p. 74.

112. *Hammer Letters*, pp. 144-145. October 16, 1961.

113. *Hammer Letters*, p. 151. No date but after January 18, 1962.

114. *Hammer Letters*, p. 167. March 3, 1963.

115. *Hammer Letters*, p. 150. January 18, 1962.

116. *Hammer Letters*, p. 182. 1963.

members of the Shakertown committee. They wanted to know if they could have copies of it for the rest of the board members, or if *Jubilee* published it could they have off-prints. Carolyn Hammer said that they were moved by it and that "nothing yet has been written to bring out the ideal and spiritual qualities of the Shakers." [117] In a December, 1963 letter, to Carolyn Hammer, Merton urged the committee to write to Rice about off-prints. The article was to be published the following month.[118]

In 1963, Merton was to be awarded an honorary LLD degree by the University of Kentucky. As he was unable to attend, he asked if Victor Hammer would stand in for him at the occasion. In a letter to the Hammers, Merton said, "Victor is my first choice. After that, I could probably embarrass a professor at the College of the Bible into doing it." [119] After the event, Merton said that "he was especially grateful for Victor's Trappistic exploit as my secret agent." [120]

These letters, the five volumes first published, and those to James Laughlin, Rosemary Radford Ruether, and the Hammers, reveal Merton's growing appreciation for, and comfort with, varieties of Protestantism. It may not have been expected of a 1938 convert, but as Merton's understanding of the world, life, and religion broadened and deepened he was able to find truth in unexpected places.

---

117. *Hammer Letters*, p. 182-183. November 9, 1963.
118. *Hammer Letters*, p. 184. December 4, 1963.
119. *Hammer Letters*, p. 169. April 7, 1963.
120. *Hammer Letters*, p. 170. June 7, 1963.

MERTON AND THE THEOLOGIANS

In his books, journals, letters, and articles Merton referred to some 26 Protestant theologians. Some he mentioned briefly in passing; others were given much more attention. His reading of them was broad and, sometimes, deep, and he found many that resonated with his own theology.

KARL BARTH (1886-1968)

One in which he showed continuing interest was the Swiss theologian, Karl Barth, usually pronounced Bart. After his studies he served as a pastor in Geneva for two years and for 10 years in Safenwil, after which he became a university professor of theology. World War I led him to question the prevailing liberal theology which prompted his writing a ground breaking commentary on Paul's letter to the Romans, which a journalist once called a telegram to the twentieth century. It was first published in 1933 and had enormous influence in the first half of the twentieth century and the post World War II period. Its theme was God had sent Jesus Christ to deliver people from sin. That does not sound unusual now, but in the wake of late 19th and early 20th century liberalism it was a new approach in theology. Barth is known for his multi-volume *Church Dogmatics* which ran for many volumes and was never completed. Merton had access to a smaller volume, *Dogmatics in Outline,* a series of lectures given at the University of Bonn in 1946 which provided an outline of Barth's ideas in the *Dogmatics.* The lectures were delivered at 7:00 A.M., an hour necessitated because at 8:00 A.M. workers resumed the rebuilding of the area damaged during World War II. Before the war Barth had been dismissed from the university by the Nazi regime for his refusal to take an oath of allegiance to Hitler. In 1935 he became Professor of Theology at Basel, a post he held until retirement in 1962.

Barth reintroduced the western world to the Protestant Reformation, especially Luther and Calvin, although he disagreed with Calvin on predestination. The emphasis in Barth's theology was a sovereign God who takes the initiative in his revelation and was in Christ. Barth brought sin back into theology and emphasized the great distance between God and man.

Merton began *Conjectures of a Guilty Bystander* with an account of "Barth's Dream." Barth had a strong interest in the music of Mozart, and was known to play Mozart in the morning before beginning work.

Mozart was critical of Protestantism for being "all in the head" and thought that Protestants did not know the meaning of "*Agnus Dei qui tollis peccata mundi,* Lamb of God who takes away the sins of the world." In Merton's account, Barth was to examine Mozart on theology, but Mozart refused to answer any questions. Merton said, "I was deeply moved by Barth's account of this dream and wanted to write him a letter about it." He believed that the dream was about Barth's salvation. Merton suggested that perhaps Barth thought he would "be saved by the Mozart in himself than by his theology."[1]

In a Christmas sermon in 1931 Barth said that an unconditional belief in principles is the German version of unbelief. Merton agreed, but said the statement should not be restricted to Germany. He added that the coming of Christ into the world was "certainly *the most unprincipled reality* one can imagine." The Incarnation, Merton believed, could not be part of a system. Barth made many conclusions that Merton could not accept, yet he was more interested in Barth than Teilhard de Chardin who was very popular in Merton's time. He quoted a statement from Barth to the effect that Divine revelation cannot be discovered like beauty in art or genius in man. "It is the opening of a door that can only be unlocked from the inside."[2] Barth said that when Christians separated themselves from Judaism they denied that revelation came to both, and that a Christianity without Judaism was invented. Merton observed, "In consequence of this, Barth saw clearly that Nazi anti-Semitism was also an attack *on Christ*."[3]

Merton quoted a statement by Barth in his *Dogmatics in Outline* that unbelief should not be taken too seriously. "Only faith is to be taken seriously; and if we have faith as a grain of mustard seed, that suffices, for the devil has lost his game." Merton called this "one of

1. *Conjectures*, p. 3. See also *Turning*, p. 49.
2. *Conjectures*, p. 3.
3. *Conjectures*, p. 9. See also *Turning*, p. 49.

the great intuitions of Protestantism." As he put it, "Only faith is to be taken seriously because only the mercy of God is serious."[4] Is unbelief really serious? Merton said no. When we take faith seriously, we take God seriously, not ourselves. It is God who gives and renews faith, in spite of our unbelief. Barth also said that to regard God as pure power is not to see God as "the infinite, arbitrary will that flies into action unchecked by its own whim," but the power of truth and love. In addition, Barth saw evil as that which has been "denied existence by God, and which we affirm by our own choice, thus attempting to give it existence in spite of God."[5]

In *Dancing in the Water of Life,* Volume 5 of Merton's published journals, he made a number of references to Barth. He was obviously reading Barth in the fall of 1963. In a September entry he mentioned that while recovering in a Louisville hospital from back pain he read what Barth had to say about St. Anselm. Merton thought that Barth's explanation of Anselm's sense of God in his ontological argument was "very penetrating."[6] A few weeks later he wrote about Barth's "insistence" that "God is completely unattainable by any human tradition." He saw an "austere beauty" in Barth's absolutism, but also appreciated what he called another side to Barth: his love of Mozart and St. Anselm.[7] Five days after that he mentioned Barth's understanding of evil again. God has denied its existence, but we affirm its existence by making a choice.[8]

From October 24 to October 30, 1963, there are virtually daily entries on Barth, indicating his steady reading of the theologian. He mentioned Barth's idea that if we are in God's presence as Jesus was, we are "bearers of the wrath of God." Merton said that we need "the shock of this sentence." Then Barth said that, "while Jesus bears that wrath, the wrath is on us." In the same entry, October 24, 1963, he praised Barth's "terrific" chapter on the meeting of Pilate and Jesus. Pilate's duty as a state official was to decide between right and wrong. He admitted Jesus was innocent, but rather than free him he decided to maintain order in Jerusalem and preserve his own position of power. The king of the world met the kingdom

4. *Conjectures*, p. 304.
5. *Conjectures,* pp. 304-305.
6. *Dancing,* p. 1. September 20, 1963.
7. *Dancing,* p. 22. October 4, 1963.
8. *Dancing*, p. 24. October 9, 1963.

of God, and the world prevailed. This, said Barth, was the nature of politics. Merton's response was, "I think I will have to become a Christian."[9]

Two days later, Merton provided a long quotation on Barth making the point that the only thing that is really serious is that "Jesus is victor." Looking back is not "Christian seriousness." In the present we are called to take this victory of Christ seriously "and to be joyful in him." Merton added that Christ's victory makes joy possible even in the presence of evil.[10] The next day he wrote about Barth's comments on the Last Judgment in art. The Jesus who comes is the one who offered himself to God's judgment, and that is not clear in the Last Judgment of Michaelangelo.[11]

Merton's October 28, 1963 entry contains a long account of Barth's take on St. Anselm's ideas on the atonement seen in his *Cur Deus Homo.* Then Merton added a section on Barth's understanding of the Holy Spirit through which we participate in the work of God. He quoted Barth's belief that the work of the Holy Spirit is the work of God on earth, the outgoing of the Spirit from the Father and the Son. For Merton, the idea of Church makes no sense without a trust that humans are capable of grace and cooperation. Our hope is in true community. The Christian way, according to Barth, "is to hope for myself and all others." Merton wondered why Barth was often thought of as a Protestant individualist.[12]

The breadth of Merton's contacts with theologians as revealed in his letters and journals is amazing. In a March 6, 1964 entry, he tells of meeting a Czech Protestant theologian, Jan Milic Lockman. They had a late night conversation in which Barth was mentioned. Lochman said that Barth's book on Anselm was one of Barth's own favorites. He also revealed that Barth was "profoundly impressed" with Pope John XXIII and wanted Protestants to take another look at the papacy. Lochman also told Merton that in Prague there are important discussions going on between Catholic and Protestant laymen, an openness that is a beginning. Merton said he felt like they were sitting in Emmaus.[13]

A final comment on Barth in *Dancing in the Water of Life* was

9. *Dancing*, pp. 26-27. October 24, 1963.
10. *Dancing*, p. 27. October 26, 1963.
11. *Dancing*, p. 27. October 27, 1963.
12. *Dancing,* pp. 28-29. October 28, 1963.
13. *Dancing*, pp. 86-87, 1963.

a disagreement. The issue was natural theology which Merton believed Barth had neglected. Merton saw creation as the beginning of revelation. God was revealed to us when God made us in God's own image, which makes union with God our vocation, and our life cannot help but speak of the Divine.[14]

In a *Road to Joy* letter Merton recommended to his friend Seymour Freedgood a new journal published by the Carmelites in France called *Dieu Vivant*. Among other things, they published Jesuits and Karl Barth side by side. He found that very encouraging.[15] The 1950 date of this letter indicates that Merton had found Barth early in his monastic career.

In *The School of Charity* letter collection he has an interesting letter to Killian McDonnell, the Benedictine ecumenist. Merton had been reading "a little Barth" whom he described as "almost the one among theologians alive today that I like best."[16] To Hans Urs von Balthasar, whose writings were read at Gethsemani, Merton said, "I am very fond of your neighbor Karl Barth and have written on his book on Anselm."[17] Almost two years later Merton wrote to von Balthasar expressing the hope that his new book on Barth will be translated into English.[18]

DIETRICH BONHOEFFER (1906-1945)

In the Merton body of literature there are many references to Bonhoeffer, at least as many as to Barth. Some are scattered throughout *Conjectures of a Guilty Bystander*. In the Preface to *Conjectures*, Merton noted that although he wrote in appreciation about Barth and Bonhoeffer, he did not see it as a book of professional ecumenism. He saw this interest as "a Catholic sharing the Protestant experience—and other religious experiences as well."[19] He did not agree with everything they said, and some of their statements would not be accepted by Catholics. Nevertheless, Merton found their books "relevant and stimulating."

Part Two of *Conjectures* is on truth and violence and contains an opening statement by Bonhoeffer, "One is distressed by the

14. *Dancing*, p. 279. August 12, 1965.
15. *Road to Joy*, p. 124. February 25, 1950.
16. *School of Charity*, p. 189. December 20, 1963.
17. *School of Charity*, p. 219. July 3, 1964.
18. *School of Charity*, p. 312. September 12, 1966.
19. *Conjectures*, p. vi.

failure of reasonable people to perceive either the depths of evil or the depth of the holy."[20] Merton tells us that shortly before his execution by the Nazis, Bonhoeffer wrote that in a time of crisis moral theorizing was outdated. We should look for evil, not in the sins of good people, but in the virtues of the evil. There are murderers who love their families, gangsters who are loyal to each other. Such virtues mask evil so that it is not threatened by goodness. Bonhoeffer called the moral theorist a fool by seeing such good and ignoring "the abyss of evil underneath it." Only by focusing on the truth of God can one really see "the ethical reality."[21]

Merton expressed in many of his writings his concern about the breakdown of western culture. He referenced Bonhoeffer's belief that "our forefathers were the witnesses of the entry of God into history," and added that other forefathers have been unfaithful to this revelation. For him, a society that has received the mercy of Christ and has been unfaithful to Him will destroy itself.[22]

There is in *Conjectures* a quote by Bonhoeffer which states that the church has been ashamed of the name Jesus Christ "before the world," and has not opposed enough the misuse of the name. Violence and other evils have been committed "under the cover of this name." The Church, Merton said, has felt guilty because it has lost its hold on people, especially the young. There was too much concern for modernity, fashionableness, and respectability. Bonhoeffer, he said, saw the Church as thinking that her future belonged to the youth. For Merton, the last thing the Church should be concerned about is its survival. That is to deny "the Victory of Christ and the Resurrection."[23]

Both Merton and Bonhoeffer revealed continuing concern about how the Church related to the world. While reading Bonhoeffer's *Ethics,* Merton was interested in his comments on the Nazi persecution of Christianity and its attack on civilized values. Reason, culture, humanity, tolerance and self-determination had all been used as arguments against the Church. These concepts, said Bonhoeffer, had become homeless, and now they sought refuge in the Church. For Merton, the efforts of the Church to accommodate itself to the world in order to make itself respectable and popular

20. Quoted in *Conjectures*, p. 51.
21. *Conjectures*, pp. 53-54.
22. *Conjectures*, p. 59.
23. *Conjectures*, pp. 109-110.

in a world of science is "shameful to the Church and to Christ."[24]

Another element in Bonhoeffer's *Ethics* that appealed to Merton was an emphasis on the joy of living. Life is not just a matter of subordinating everything to the fulfillment of some purpose. A home, Bonhoeffer believed, was not just a shelter, but a place where people may relish the joys of family life. Eating and drinking are not just a matter of good health, but "they afford natural joy in bodily living." Play takes us away from all subordination to purpose. Sex is not just a means of reproduction, but brings joy in the love of two people for each other. "The life of the body assumes its full significance only with the fulfillment of its inherent claim to joy." Merton called this "genuine Christian humanism," and "a 'Christian worldliness' with which I thoroughly agree." He also said that it is "the voice of all that is best in the cultural tradition of Western Christendom." He also noted that Bonhoeffer based these ideas on quotes from Ecclesiastes.[25]

However, Merton did not believe that Bonhoeffer's purpose was to absolve the world of guilt. On the contrary, Bonhoeffer said that when livelihoods are destroyed in the interest of business or when violence is accepted as "a normal rational standard," the world is headed for chaos. Bonhoeffer had a clear understanding that the world is guilty and fallen, but has the greatest claim on Christian mercy. Merton said that optimism about the "torn and anguished world of the twentieth century" shows "the most pitiable lack of imagination and understanding."[26]

He quoted frequently from Bonhoeffer's prison letters: "It almost looks today as though the Church alone offers any prospect for the recovery of the sphere of freedom (art, education, friendship and play, aesthetic existence)." This prompted Merton to say that Bonhoeffer was closer to Catholicism than Barth was. Bonhoeffer believed that God is honored more when we accept the life God gives us, living it to the fullest and grieving when we have thrown away "the precious things of life . . . than we do if we are insensitive toward life." Merton saw this as the right kind of worldliness, "which sees the world redeemed in Christ."[27]

One of Merton's major criticisms of Protestantism was its

24. *Conjectures*, pp. 176-177.
25. *Conjectures,* pp. 182-183.
26. *Conjectures*, p. 231.
27. *Conjectures*, pp. 288-289.

lack of interest in nature. He believed that the Church could speak to the world on the basis of "nature and natural-law knowledge" which it has in common with the world. As a Lutheran, Bonhoeffer refused to believe this. He inherited the Lutheran tradition that a Christian has a duty to obey the state and go to war, and in so doing is obeying God. Merton did not agree and, of course, Bonhoeffer is known for his opposition to the Nazi state, an opposition that cost him his life.[28]

In July, 1964, Merton revealed that he was still reading Bonhoeffer's *Letters and Papers from Prison.* He called them "very monastic," and wanted to make a collection of what he considered to be "monastic texts" from Bonhoeffer.[29]

In the final volume of the journals, *The Other Side of the Mountain*, Merton copied out three quotations from Bonhoeffer. One of them, January 10, 1968, said that when one sees enemies living under the wrath of God, one knows what it means to forgive and love them. The next day he copied one in which Bonhoeffer said that the person who stands one's ground is one who sacrifices principles, conscience, freedom, and virtue, when called to be obedient and responsible to exclusive allegiance to God. Then Bonhoeffer asked where are such people?[30] A day later he quoted that the Christian world stands more under wrath than grace. This was to be the day for the election of a new abbot, and Merton hoped that the election may be a grace and "not the wrath we stand under," an oblique reference to the former abbot with whom he had so many conflicts.[31]

In his book, *Faith and Violence*, Merton made many references to Bonhoeffer, some less than appreciative. In a section subtitled 'Letter to a Southern Churchman' Merton announced that he was no longer going to comment on current events. He mentioned a comment by Bonhoeffer that it was an "Anglo-Saxon failing" to believe that the Church should have an immediate answer for every social problem. Merton said that none of us are free from evil, and a program of action "does not lift the curse."[32]

28. *Conjectures,* pp. 289-290.
29. *Dancing,* p. 129. July 21, 1964.
30. *The Other Side of Silence,* p. 39, January 11, 1968.
31. *The Other Side of Silence*, p. 40, January 13, 1968.
32. *Faith and Violence,* Notre Dame, IN: University of Notre Dame Press, 1968, p. 145.

He was bothered by Bonhoeffer's idea of religionless Christianity, although he did distinguish between Bonhoeffer himself and his disciples. It was a false attempt to speak to the world. For himself, Merton said that he needed to back away from commenting on current events because he was frustrated by manufactured news, making non-events important, the deceptions of advertising, and the myth-making of modern societies so that in quiet and solitude he could get a clearer perception of reality. "Someone," he wrote, "has to try to keep his head clear of static and preserve the interior solitude and silence that are essential for independent thought."[33] He quoted Bonhoeffer, "To be simple is to fix one's eye solely on the simple truth of God at a time when all concepts are being confused, distorted and turned upside down."[34]

Bonhoeffer, known for seeking God in the world, protested against Nazi worldliness and was hanged by the Nazis for his trouble. He protested knowing that the majority of Christians in Germany supported Hitler even though they knew Hitler would destroy their churches.[35]

Bonhoeffer believed that traditional dogmatic Christianity did not speak to modern people. But Merton knew that Bonhoeffer was well enough aware of evil in the world that must be resisted. Ideas about religionless religion were written while he was in a Gestapo prison. He wondered who Christ was for people in that kind of hopeless situation. He said, "The God who is with us is the God who forsakes us. The God who makes us live in the world without using Him as a working hypothesis is the God before whom we are ever standing."[36] Merton saw this statement as revealing how far from atheism Bonhoeffer was. He saw him using the language of the Bible. His theology implied a purity of faith. Bonhoeffer, said Merton, recognized modern peoples' discontent with a religiosity that "stifles and constrains," but no religion at all is not the answer.

Merton recognized that Bonhoeffers's statements should be read in the context of his whole work. His most popular book, *The* Cost *of Discipleship* was, in fact, a theologically conservative book. It is known for his attack on "cheap grace." The prison letters, Merton believed, revealed that this theology was not yet fully

33. *Faith and Violence,* p. 150.
34. *Faith and Violence,* p. 161.
35. *Faith and Violence,* p. 238.
36. *Faith and Violence,* p. 266.

formed. He died as a relatively young man executed by the Nazis a few days before American troops liberated the area. He was only 39.

REINHOLD NIEBUHR (1892-1971)

Reinhold Niebuhr was one of the foremost American theologians of the twentieth century. Born in Wright City, Missouri, he studied at Elmhurst College and Yale Divinity School. In 1915 he became the pastor of Bethel Evangelical Church in Detroit, made up primarily of men who worked in the automobile factories in Detroit and their families. *Leaves from the Notebooks of a Tamed Cynic* is a journal he kept during that experience. He became much in demand as an outstanding speaker, and his reputation began to grow. In 1929 he was appointed Professor of Applied Christianity at Union Theological Seminary in New York, a position he held until retirement. During Niebuhr's tenure, many saw Union as the premier Protestant seminary in America. He published many books. One of his best known was his Gifford Lectures, *The Nature and Destiny of Man.* He was also known for *Moral Man and Immoral Society, The Irony of American History, Faith and History,* and *Children of Light and Children of Darkness*, and others. He was sometimes called on by politicians, government officials and labor unions for advice. His thought was highly influential in Protestant seminaries in the 1950s and 60s.

Merton made only a few references to Niebuhr. In September, 1960, he reported reading a book on Niebuhr and called him "a great and lucid mind and profoundly Christian." He saw Niebuhr as a hopeful sign.[37] A few months later he said that he respected Niebuhr's intelligence and integrity and called him one of the few "authentically Christian voices" that have something relevant to say. Merton had been reading Niebuhr's *Christian Realism and Political Problems.*[38]

In *Conjectures of a Guilty Bystander*, Merton wrote about the killing of Jews in Nazi concentration camps. In that context he quoted Niebuhr on the point that if the Gospel really was a two-edged sword in the Church, white people might see their attacks on the Negro as "the evidence of an uneasy conscience.[39]

---

37. *Turning*, p. 53. September 29, 1960.
38. *Turning*, p. 91. January 1961.
39. *Conjectures*, pp. 221-223.

A. M. ALLCHIN

Merton had a strong interest in Anglicanism, and corresponded with a number of people in that tradition. One for whom he had considerable respect was A. M. Allchin, a priest who had broad interests. As mentioned earlier he had studied Eastern Orthodoxy, served as a librarian, been a chaplain to students, was a canon at Canterbury, and taught as a professor in Wales. He had three visits with Merton at Gethsemani, one of which included a visit to Merton's beloved Shakertown.

Merton's first letter to Allchin was about the Anglican's forthcoming visit in 1963 on August 6, 7, and 8.[40] The visit began an important friendship. Three months later Merton wrote to thank Allchin for sending him books. He mentioned that he had been reading George Herbert, Dame Gertrude More, and asked about the Cambridge Platonists.[41] Later, he thanked Allchin for sending him a book by Thomas Traherne, and said it would be valuable if he decided to write about Anglican mystics. He also said that everyone was "a bit numb" about the death of President Kennedy.[42]

In April of 1964 Merton thanked Allchin for a book, *The Blessed Virgin Mary: Essays by Anglicans.* He liked Allchin's essay on the seventeenth century Anglican divines, and reported that he was now reading Thornton's book, *English Spirituality.* He was also reading *Anglican Devotion* by Stranks and McAdoo's *Moral Theologians.* Allchin was providing Merton a good education in Anglicanism which prompted him to say, "It seems to me that the best of Anglicanism is unexcelled, but there are few who have the refinement of spirit to see and embrace the best." Merton feared a dreary rationalism. He concluded that he would try to be the best English Catholic he could be, given his position.[43] A year later he told Allchin that he was now using the Anglican Lancelot Andrewes's *Private Devotions* at night in the hermitage.[44]

From time to time Merton made comments about Allchin in letters to other people. In a letter to Etta Gullick, one of his frequent correspondents, he was concerned about Allchin's "overworking."

40. *Hidden Ground*, pp. 24-25. July 4, 1963.
41. *Hidden Ground*, p. 25. October 21, 1963.
42. *Hidden Ground*, pp. 25-26. December 1, 1963.
43. *Hidden Ground*, p. 26. April 25, 1964.
44. *Hidden Ground*, p. 27. May 22, 1965.

Merton said it is easy for that to happen if one is not able to say no to people's requests.[45]

In early 1967 Merton commented about religious turmoil in England and the United States. He feared that Roman Catholics were as confused as Protestants "with anyone and everyone rushing about in all directions." Monolithic religion was too rigid, but he did think that some agreement on basic truths would be desirable.[46]

Allchin made a second visit to Gethsemani in April, 1967. Merton commented that the weather was good and he enjoyed their walking and talking in the woods. He thanked Allchin for a book by R. S. Thomas, a poet, as well as one by Muir, another poet.[47] Merton wrote about that visit in his journal. Allchin had arrived a day early, and Merton saw him briefly in the evening. The next day it rained, so they had to talk in the gatehouse. The following day was beautiful and they walked to the top of the Lake Knob. Referring to a popular book, *The Secular City,* by Harvard theologian Harvey Cox, Allchin could not take it seriously, although he admitted that superficiality of this type was serious in America. Allchin thought that America was still in the nineteenth century religiously. Merton, in Louisville for an appointment with a doctor, took him to Southern Baptist Theological Seminary in Louisville on the final day of his visit.[48]

A few months after that visit, he encouraged Allchin to spend a few months in a monastery at Crawley Downs. He told Allchin that he had mentioned on other occasions that monasteries should be places where people could live for limited periods of time. There would be a group of permanent members, but others would be there for a year or two. He noted that Zen monasteries were like that.[49]

In a letter to Sister Penelope Lawson, an Anglican nun, Merton inquired about Allchin. He mentioned that they had had a "lovely" visit, but had lost touch and did not know where he was, although he thought maybe Oxford.[50]

Allchin's third visit began on April 3, 1968. The next day Merton took him to Shakertown. On their way back to the monastery

45. *Hidden Ground,* p. 377. September 30, 1966.
46. *Hidden Ground,* p. 28. January 14, 1967.
47. *Hidden Ground,* p. 28. June 16, 1967.
48. *Learning to Love*, pp. 209-210. March 31, 1967.
49. *Hidden Ground,* p. 29. September 15. 1967.
50. *Hidden Ground,* p. 31, p. 481. May 23, 1967.

they heard on the car radio about the death of Martin Luther King,

What was probably the last letter to Allchin was written from Delhi, India, on November 10, 1968. He said that the Indian journey was good and he had fine talks with the Dalai Lama and others. He said that he was trying to get permission to return to Gethsemani through England and asked, "Can we do Wales then?"[51]

Merton also mentioned his appreciation for Allchin in his journals. He praised Allchin's *Silent Rebellion* about Anglican monasticism which seemed to Merton as a "witness against the torpor of the Anglican establishment." He found the book both moving and disturbing, and said that he was very glad to be a Roman.

PAUL TILLICH (1886-1965)

Paul Tillich, the son of a Lutheran pastor, was one of the most dominant Protestant theologians of the twentieth century. His theology was influenced by his service as a chaplain in the German army during World War I. Forced out of Germany by the Nazi takeover in 1933, he came to the United States and taught at Union Theological Seminary in New York, Harvard University, and the University of Chicago. Tillich defined religion as "the dimension of depth in all of man's life functions." Religion, he said, is grounded in our ultimate concern. Some of his important works were his three volume *Systematic Theology, The New Being, The Dynamics of Faith, The Protestant Era*, and *The Shaking of the Foundations.*

Merton became interested in him, but contacts were only through Tillich's secretary, Mrs. Leonard. He had sent Tillich his *Prometheus* and *The Silent Life.* Mrs. Leonard replied that Tillich had enjoyed both. He announced that he was sending *Thoughts in Solitude* and *Monastic Peace.* He was busy working on a book on religious art and would like to see anything Tillich had written on that subject. He also hoped that Tillich would send him a signed copy of one of his books.

In this same letter Merton expressed his opinions about the ecumenical movement. He believed that what we have in common is much more important than our differences. Institutional differences are there, but they are not as strong as charity. He said that Christian unity has something to do with the Gospel.[52]

51. *Hidden Ground*, p. 31. August 27, 1968.
52. *Witness*, pp. 300-301, June 20, 1959.

Tillich sent Merton two more books along with an autobiography of Albert Schweitzer. Merton wrote Tillich that he was reading The *Dynamics of Faith* and found it "very congenial and practical." He also read and enjoyed *The New Being*. For Merton it was refreshing to hear Tillich talk about "deep matters that are spiritual and not just abstruse or intellectual."

Tillich had sent a speech he had given at a conference on art. Merton agreed with what he had to say about religious styles. "Our tastes are the same." In the book Merton wrote on *Art and Worship* which was never published, he advocated an expressionism like that of the Byzantines, the spiritual realism of icons. He liked Tillich's comment that there is more ultimate reality in a single apple by Cézanne than in a Jesus by Hofmann. Merton concluded the letter with a discussion of the solitary life in response to Tillich's mention of a friend who was considering it.[53]

In 1959 Merton wrote to Tillich, thanking him for books. He was reading *The Theology of Culture* which he liked very much. "All my Augustinian and Franciscan instincts (were) vindicated," Merton wrote. He was particularly attracted to the "Franciscan instinct for immediacy" which Merton saw as "the supremely important thing" in religious thought.

He found *Love, Power, and Justice* difficult until he read "the power of being is its possibility to affirm itself against non-being." From that point the book became illuminating. Merton called Tillich's interpretation of the power of being leading to love "the most existential and most Christian reality."

Merton had some doubts about Tillich's idea of ultimate concern. It did not seem to him adequately to embrace the Christian idea of faith. However, Merton said that from the point of view of Tillich's idea of the power of being, his idea of faith becomes "very noble as well as attractive." Merton closed the letter by thanking Tillich for his "enlightening thoughts" and assured him of "my complete sympathy and communion in Christ."

In one of his journals Merton wrote that he learned of Tillich's death on October 22, 1965. He did not comment further. After that he and his agent, Naomi Burton, went over the *Conjecture* manuscript and then took a long drive through the area.[54]

---

53. *Witness,* pp. 567-577. September 4, 1959.
54. *Dancing*, p. 317, November 20, 1965.

MARTIN E. MARTY

Martin Marty, the Fairfax M. Cone Distinguished Service Professor Emeritus of the History of Modern Christianity at the University of Chicago Divinity School, has often been called the Dean of American church historians. A Lutheran, his literary output has been enormous. Now, in retirement, he leads the Martin Marty Center for the Advanced Study of Religion at the Divinity School. Through its seminars, research projects, conferences and publications it fosters interdisciplinary research on religion.

Merton's first connection with Marty resulted from a negative review of *Seeds of Destruction* Marty wrote for the New York *Herald Tribune.* Specifically, Marty attacked the first part of the book "Letters to a White Liberal," saying that Merton was attempting to be a white James Baldwin. Merton's point had been that when a real racial crisis came, the white person's self-interest would take over. Two and a half years later Marty apologized to Merton in an open letter in the *National Catholic Reporter.* Marty reread the book and said, "You were correct." He wrote, "What bothers me now is the degree of accuracy in your predictions and prophesies in general."

Merton responded with a letter in 1967. "I long ago learned to live with the idea that I was half crazy." He thanked Marty for his generosity and told him that he had said what he thought needed to be said perhaps in a provocative way. Merton believed that the crisis had done considerable winnowing among liberals. He hoped that the summer's events might generate a collaboration between white and black on the left that could work for peace and constructive change. It might involve a "shaking of the foundation," a third way between anarchy and a police state.

Merton reported that he had been in Louisville soon after the Detroit riots. He found the "Negroes" very friendly, not hostile. There was no sense of racial war in the offing. It was a moment not to assume all Negroes are prone to riot. What the Black Power people want, he believed, was to get white liberals and radicals off the backs of Negro activists, so they can function freely by themselves. If they will stop trying to dominate and make up the minds of the Negroes and stay out of their way, such people will be accepted, not with thanks, but simply because that is what white people should do.

Injustice and cruelty will have to be overcome the hard way. The un-Christianity of American Christianity will be exposed and judged. Christians will kill in self-defense because of their fear that their affluent society will be menaced. What is called for is Christian non-violence in the face of Negro violence. The so-called order which defends the wealth of the slumlord and white businessman against the people they exploit is really disorder. White Christians should practice non-violence for the purpose of truth and the common good. Merton identified himself with the Christian non-violent left occupied by people such as Dorothy Day, the Catholic Peace Fellowship, and Joan Baez.

Merton concluded this long letter with "I am glad we understand each other after these four years."[55]

On the more positive side, Merton was impressed with one of Marty's early books, *Varieties of Unbelief* published in 1964. Marty was concerned with the unbelief of apparent believers. He saw a religious vacuum in which superstitions and neuroses combined with technology and nationalism produced a "curious and half-formulated creed" that is supported by "churchly institution" with references to Christ, the Gospel, and Christian ethics. Marty, said Merton, does not denounce these things; he meditates on them. The unbelief of moderns, Merton wrote, is a refusal to listen to God; it is a lack of interest in the idea of a God who speaks. It is a refusal of the spiritual security of any system of religion.

Merton heard the voices of the existentialists, such as Sartre, who were atheists and proclaimed it. These were not the unbelievers that Marty saw in American churches. These invoked a God who gave them security, but not a God who spoke or made demands. Their basic belief was in "success, prosperity, know-how, effort, and having fun." It centered around "individualism, nationalism, progress, and a hope that claimed to be Christian." Marty sensed in all of this a "nearness of unbelief" which is different from a "weak faith." This kind of faith, for Marty, was less intellectual and spiritually respectable than the atheism which implied "the courageous assumption of loneliness, dread and risk." A Christianity claiming to obey God when it was actually obeying "the imperatives of a marketing and affluent society" was certainly bad faith. Marty suggested that the "more vociferous ecstasies" of some Catholics and Protestants were based more on nationalism than faith. "Na-

55. *Hidden Ground*, pp. 455-458. September 6, 1967.

tionalism," he said "can produce an ecstasy which few others can."

Merton praised Marty for his refusal to condemn these situations, but to hope for possibilities of rational and civilized dialogue on the issues. Marty's perspectives were wider, and Merton, if anything, was a person of even wider perspectives."[56]

THE DEATH OF GOD THEOLOGIANS

There were two popular movements in the 1960s in which Merton had an interest and which he criticized. One was the Death of God Theology and the other was expressed in a popular book by an Anglican bishop, John A. T. Robinson, *Honest to God.* Merton believed that both should be heard, but he was highly critical of them. He regarded the Death of God Theology as part of a theological ferment that appeared after World War II. This ferment had been stimulated, he said, by Protestants such as Karl Barth, Paul Tillich, and Rudolph Bultmann, and Catholics such as Karl Rahner and Jacques Maritain.[57] Merton had doubts that the theologians in these new movements measured up to those in this ferment who inspired them.

Merton was fascinated by the Death of God movement in the 1960s. He strongly disagreed with it but thought that it was something that should be heard. In *Faith and Violence* Merton had three essays about it. The leaders of the group were Thomas J. J. Altizer and William Hamilton, whom Merton called "the apostle of Playboy," a lesser light whom Merton did not respect. Gabriel Vahanian was not part of the movement but wrote extensively about it. Merton described him as an iconoclast with whom he tended to agree. Most of what Merton had to say about it was found in *Faith and Violence.*

In Merton's essay, *Violence and the Death of God: or God as Unknown Soldier,* he said that the Death of God theologians believed if a modern person of good faith had any religious experience it was that of God's absence. Traditional theologians wanted people to experience God's presence, but this movement said that this effort had utterly failed. Not only does traditional theology prove nothing, it alienates modern people and makes it more difficult for them to find meaning in the idea of God. Experiencing

56. *Faith and Violence,* pp. 199-204.
57. *Faith and Violence,* p. 191.

God's absence has always been part of Catholic theology, and Merton added that Protestantism has said that a sophisticated and intellectual approach to theology tended to neutralize a personal encounter with the God of revelation. Traditional theology, Merton wrote, tended to objectify God and make God the servant of man's purposes, especially as the "guiding spirit of European-American civilization." This has led to slavery, war, and to submission to a church authority which ordered submission to civil authority. The identification of God with western civilization led to a crisis in which the remaining elements of Christianity in western culture "have all been bled away." God died in World War II.

Merton quoted Vahanian that it was easier to move from pre-Christian to Christian than it was from post-Christian to Christian. One positive element in Death of God Theology for Merton was that trying to make God relevant to man makes God irrelevant. The only thing to do is to declare God dead. "Then the true God, the God who is 'absent' comes to life again." Vahanian said that Biblical religion taught that our basic obligation was iconoclasm. Merton wrote, "That sounds wild, but it is only a reformulation of the first two commandments." His basic problem with Death of God thinking was that it was mere anti-religion and anti-clericalism, and subjected humanity to a post-Christian secularism. "We seem to end up rendering everything to Caesar." We must, said Merton, "renounce the mighty spirit that has let itself be set up in the place of God: the Angel of the West."[58]

In his second essay, *The Death of God and the End of History,* which Merton described as "reflective rather than polemical," he asked whether this theology was as "radical and as revolutionary as it claims to be?" It was concerned about relevance for the world, which cannot discover its potentialities, implicit and unrecognized. We act more freely when we recognize that God is not there, yet God is there in our freedom. Merton called that idea "ambiguous, elusive, deceptive." It does not mean that God does not exist or never existed; it simply means that the problem of God does not require any more attention. God is not needed to explain our existence. Merton saw this as a "justifiable" response to "a shallow and rationalistic apologetic" for Christianity which has no meaning for today. He remarked that this had nothing to do with an authentic understanding of God or of Christian mysticism. The Death of God

58. *Faith and Violence*, pp. 191-198.

Theology repudiates all discussion of God. Any claim to know God is dismissed as "infected with mythology." It not only repudiates traditional theology, but also repudiates metaphysics. It is post-Biblical and discards the Biblical revelation of God. Any claim to an experience of God is bound to be fraudulent.

So, the Death of God Theology chose the world rather than God. A new and more real "union with Christ" is to be found outside and beyond religious institutions. For Merton, this is the most valid critique. Churches tried to create a separate sacred world while at the same time gaining for themselves "every possible worldly advantage and privilege." They vilified all that was "real, valid, alive, creative, and forward looking." Merton had that same critique of modern monasticism.

The validity of the God is Dead theology's iconoclasm is determined not just by its readiness to confess that certain Christian myths are shallow, but whether it "can see through secular myths as well." Does it liberate one from traditional Christianity only to subject itself to a ready-made political ideology?[59]

For Merton, the problem with the Death of God Theology is not that it is "heretical, unorthodox, too iconoclastic, too radical, or "too modern." It is that it is a "tame and belated attempt" to be contemporary in a way that is already "behind the times." Merton wondered if it just reflected "a complacent acceptance of our affluence and highly organized society."[60]

HONEST TO GOD

Another example of an attempt at worldly religion was a best selling book, *Honest to God*, by John A. T. Robinson, the Anglican bishop of Woolwich, published in 1963. It was one of many efforts to make Christianity "more relevant" to modern times. Merton had an article about it in *Faith and Violence*. Robinson dismissed the mythical image of God "out there" seated on a heavenly throne ruling the earth. Merton said, "I should have thought it was about time."[61] He agreed with Robinson that mythical and poetic descriptions of God are inadequate, but when the Bishop tried to find new concepts, Merton thought that he did not see the depth of the problem. Robinson quoted

59. *Faith and Violence*, p. 252.
60. *Faith and Violence*, p. 293.
61. *Faith and Violence*, p. 225.

Tillich and Bonhoeffer, but Merton wondered if the bishop "measures up to them." The purpose of the book, Merton believed, was to present an image of the modern, secular Christian, freed from religious myth who can practice existentialism and the "new morality" without feeling guilty about it. Robinson seemed frustrated with a ministry that could not preach its message. The book, in Merton's eyes, seemed to be a more sophisticated Christian salesman like Robinson saying that he belonged to the bishop's world, but Merton believed that the book did not say enough or the right things for the situation. It appeared an effort at a theological revolution in Anglicanism, but for Merton, getting rid of theology does not make Christianity more comprehensible to moderns.

Nevertheless, Merton wrote that his own experience was close to that of Robinson. "the direct and existential discovery of God beyond concepts and beyond myths, in His inexpressible reality."[62] God is not just a Being beyond beings. The important thing is "a spiritual awareness of the supreme reality of God." Robinson's ideas, Merton wrote, were not new, they were traditional. He even suggested that Robinson should read Pseudo-Dionysius. God dwells in a light inaccessible who is manifest in the church through the spirit of Christ.

Merton still had a problem with a secular theology. For him, an acceptance of whatever there is in the world is no way to find God. *Honest to God*, as Merton understood it, was not a book that would convince an unbeliever. Thirty years ago he would not have read it. Now, however, in the 1960s, he has read it with "very real interest." The problems Robinson writes about are of no concern to an unbeliever, but are very real to the believer. The world, in Merton's opinion, is unchristian, and the faithful Christian lives in a diaspora. The faith of the Council of Trent and the Anglicanism of Cranmer are not coming back. Being "honest to God' for Merton is being faithful to the grace which has made him aware of the unknowable and unspeakable God who is present to him. He will do it on his own terms. He did see *Honest to God* as sincere and something which could not be ignored. He had seen some privately circulated letters of Bishop Robinson and found them deeper and more important than the book.

62. *Faith and Violence*, p. 229.

SØREN KIERKEGAARD (1813-1855)

Kierkegaard is generally known as the Father of Existentialism. He was the son of a wealthy Danish Lutheran and spent most of his life in Copenhagen. He had a classical education and university studies that included the liberal arts, aesthetic studies, and history. He was a prolific writer, and many of his books were written under a pseudonym. His major concern was what it meant to become and to be a Christian. Kierkegaard believed that the Christianity of the New Testament was unknown in his time. Being a Dane and a Christian were equated.

For existentialists, existence was more important than essence. Being a Christian, for him, required a leap of faith involving the whole self. Existentialists were not interested in philosophical theories or rational solutions. Rational arguments could not prove the validity of faith. Faith involves risk. It is not the acceptance of some theological formula or a belief that ancient events may have actually occurred.

Merton's primary interest in existentialism seemed to be in the writings of Jean Paul Sartre and Albert Camus. However, he did make a number of references in his writings to Kierkegaard. He wrote an article, "The Other Side of Despair: Notes on Christian Existentialism," in *Mystics and Zen Masters.*[63]

In this article Merton took upon himself the difficult task of trying to define existentialism. He saw it as an attitude and an experience, not a system of thought. Whereas other philosophies sought out the what and the how, existentialism is concerned with the who. He refers to Kierkegaard's concern about "leveling," where the individual is lost in the mass, "the vast emptiness of the public mind." It involves the abdication of identity and the acceptance of the "general myth." An existentialist does not allow oneself to be defined or determined by the public. One values "the inviolate sanctuary of the personal conscience." The existentialist theologians to whom Merton was drawn included Karl Jaspers, Martin Buber, Nicolas Berdyaev, the Protestants Rudolph Bultmann and Paul Tillich, and the Catholic Jacques Maritain and Etienne Gilson.

Other than the one article in *Mystics and Zen Masters,* most of Merton's references to Kierkegaard are found in his journals. We first see it in a Pre-Gethsemani November 26, 1940 entry. He

---

63. *Mystics and Zen Masters*, pp. 255-280.

bought a copy of Kierkegaard's *Fear and Trembling*, and said "have since talked about it so much I feel as if I had been reading Kierkegaard all my life."[64] A new discovery.

Later in that entry he wrote about a visit to Boston and Cambridge. In Harvard's Widener Library and the Boston Public Library he copied out long quotations from Kierkegaard's books. In *Christian Discourses* Merton was interested in the idea that unusually talented people are usually *superfluous* because they do not fit in where the business world would assign them. In *Philosophical Fragments* he found a passage that is best summed up by its last sentence, "All becoming takes place in freedom, not by necessity."[65]

The next day he wrote that he liked Kierkegaard's idea in *Fear and Trembling* that the great saints probably looked like "the stupidest bourgeois."[66] Later, he was driven to the Boston Public Library where he read more Kierkegaard. Although he had not yet become a Trappist, Merton was intrigued by Kierkegaard's comments of a vow of silence which he said was "necessarily imposed" on Abraham when he attempted to sacrifice his son Isaac. Abraham's faith was incomprehensible. Merton said it was "beyond ethics, beyond the universal, and beyond the intelligible." In light of Abraham's relationship with God it was incomprehensible. Abraham could not explain that kind of faith. "Hence the vow of silence." Likewise Mary's virgin birth was incomprehensible, "hence the vow of silence." Kierkegaard said that the angel came only to Mary. The mystery was not announced to the whole world that the world might easily have believed. Those who have the most faith appear the least heroic.[67]

At this point in his life Merton did not know how important silence would be for him. Kierkegaard's vow of silence idea, Merton said, kept coming up. There was so much noise in the world, and Merton said that to preserve their sanity people will become Trappist, not by joining an order but by being one in secret and private. No one will know they have taken a vow of silence. Merton said about himself, "I am impressed and awed by the fact that I cannot join an order," probably referring to the Franciscan's rejection of him in New York. He admitted that a vow of silence is not for

---

64. *Run to the Mountain*, p. 259. November 26, 1940.
65. *Run to the Mountain*, p. 261. November 26, 1940.
66. *Run to the Mountain*, pp. 265-266. November 27, 1940.
67. *Run to the Mountain*, pp. 265-266. November 29, 1940.

most people; it should not be sought after. Losing oneself in good works of faith and love must come first. "It is by this silence that we preach: by that we cannot preach."[68]

These thoughts led Merton to notice something else in Kierkegaard. He spoke of those who carry the secret of having seen God directly and cannot put the experience into words. Such folks will appear commonplace to the rest of us. Abraham was a "common, worldly, dull fellow, outwardly," and St. Francis, after Alvernia, was "like a little sick man."[69] This theme was picked up again in an October 8, 1941 entry. The life of Teresa of Lisieux, Merton said, illustrated Kierkegaard's point that the greatest saints' saintliness can only be contained under a mediocre and normal exterior "because it is an incommunicable secret."[70]

Years later, in July, 1965, Merton was still reading Kierkegaard, this time selections from *The Present Age*. He described them as "very fine and completely prophetic." He was impressed with Kierkegaard's understanding of the individual in mass-society. The communication of the "cosmic" in the individual without mediation to "pure humanity" can lead to liberation in "naked exposure to word (sic) of God."[71] Just a few months before his death, Merton was reading *The Attack upon Christendom.* He found the book "incontrovertibly true." It caused him to see his own life "so utterly false and trivial" in light of the New Testament. Trying to prove one is a Christian is really begging for attention from the world. He added, "What does one do when he realizes he is part of an organization whose members systematically try to 'make a fool of God?'" Then he admitted that he has done it too.[72]

REFORMATION THEOLOGIANS

Both journals and letters reveal that Merton had at least a passing familiarity with Martin Luther and John Calvin, leaders of the sixteenth century Protestant reformation.

Merton occasionally wrote a positive word about Luther: at other times just a passing reference. We have already seen his correspondence with Sister Penelope Lawson in England about

68. *Run to the Mountain*, p. 267. December 2, 1940.
69. *Run to the Mountain*, p. 287. January 11, 1941.
70. *Run to the Mountain,* p. 433. October 8, 1941.
71. *Dancing*, p. 275. July 25, 1965.
72. *Dancing,* pp. 138-139. July 5, 1968.

her new translation of a Cistercian father, Issac of Stella, where Merton critiqued her use of vivid images as "more a Luther's kind of thing."[73]

Merton had lengthy correspondence with Leslie Dewart, a professor at St. Michael's College in the University of Toronto. In an August 11, 1963 letter, Merton said that Luther's theology is pretty strong as long as he stays with scripture. However, his concern was that Luther had accepted the body-spirit split. He suggested that one of the strengths of Zen Buddhism is that it has no such division. He mentioned that he was thinking of writing an article on spiritual freedom from the perspectives of Zen, Lutheranism, and primitive Christian monastic documents. The problem with Luther was that sola fide was a matter of interior and spiritual graces alone. What happens in the interior justifies; what happens with the body is in the area of sin.[74]

He did like Luther's views on vows. In his journal he commented on Luther's "telling" critique of religious vows. Luther was right, Merton said, in believing that vows must be lived "fully and freely." Simply to enclose oneself does not give glory to God.[75]

Merton commented on Luther's distinction between God's "alien work," in which God reveals to us who we are through suffering and humiliation, and God's "own work," in which God's love lifts up and heals us. He wrote this in the context of his own suffering in his relationship with a young student nurse with whom he fell in love. He was torn between his love for her, simply referred to as M in his journals, and his commitment to his monastic vows. Part of his suffering was realizing that he would have to live without her after her graduation.[76]

Luther's theology continued to be of interest to Merton. He understood Luther's doctrine of justification as a matter of being forgiven and having a new future open for him. Merton wrote that if one added the Catholic idea of grace and does not make justification only this, then "it is a very acceptable and deep statement."[77]

The other sixteenth century reformer in whom Merton had some, not always favorable, interest was John Calvin, the reformer

73. *Hidden Ground*, p. 479. October 17, 1965.
74. *Witness,* pp. 295-296. April 24, 1964
75. *Dancing*, p. 74. February 10, 1964.
76. *Learning to Love,* p. 96. July 15, 1966.
77. *Learning to Love,* p. 142. September 23, 1966.

of Geneva. In *Conjectures* he compares the writings of Tertullian with Calvin in his having "a bitterness, a pessimism that are nevertheless salutary."[78] Later, quoting Barth, he said that one of the "great intuitions" of Protestantism is that unbelief should not be taken seriously; only faith should be. Calvin, he wrote, said that "the world is the theatre of God's glory." Humanity witnesses the acts of God and must express what it has seen. Merton's comment was, "It is a great conception, but it is inadequate." He is more attracted to the idea of Irenaeus who said that humanity itself is the glory of God.[79]

Writing about Anselm, Merton noted that for Anselm the death of Christ was not just a blind subjection to an absolute decree that he must die. Merton was interested in Calvin's intuition that Christ had to bear the wrath of God at all times. Merton saw that as true and had a more somber aspect of the same thing. A few pages later Merton saw agreement of Barth with this concept. Merton quoted from the Calvinist catechism, "That He all the time of His life, but especially at the end thereof had born in body and soul the wrath of God against the whole human race." Just describing the details of Christ's suffering on the cross missed the point. Merton feared that we have lost any sense of the wrath of God. The true wrath of God reaches into the very depths of our humanity. Merton concluded again, "I think I will have to become a Christian."[80]

MARTIN LUTHER KING, JR. (1929-1968)

King was born the son of a Baptist minister in Atlanta. He was educated at Morehouse College, Crozer Theological Seminary, and Boston University where he received a Ph.D. His dissertation was *A Comparison of the Conceptions of God in the Thinking of Paul Tillich and Henry Nelson Weiman.* In 1954 he became pastor of the Dexter Avenue Baptist Church in Montgomery, Alabama, where he expected to spend his time preaching and providing pastoral care to his congregation. However, the Montgomery bus boycott drew him into the civil rights movement where he attempted to make use of a non-violence philosophy for bringing about change. He wrote five books and, in 1964, received the Nobel Peace Prize.

---

78. *Conjectures*, p. 207.
79. *Conjectures*, pp. 264-265.
80. *Conjectures*, pp. 317-318.

One of Merton's major social concerns was racism and the civil rights movement. He made several references to Martin Luther King, Jr. in his journals. In 1961 he noted that he had been reading King and was impressed by the "moving" story of the Montgomery bus boycott. He added that in addition to King's actions he was interested in his spiritual development.[81] In 1963 he described King as "perhaps one of the few really great Christians in America." He was moved by King's "Letter from a Birmingham Jail," calling it a "terrific thing."[82] In the same year he commented on the March on Washington and praised the consolidation of civil rights leadership with King.[83]

In an article "Religion and Race in the United States" found in *Faith and Violence*, Merton called Martin Luther King, Jr.'s nonviolent approach to the problem as "one of the most positive and successful expressions of Christian social action that has been seen anywhere in the twentieth century."[84] However, by the time *Faith and Violence* was published in 1968, Merton believed that the days of its effectiveness were over. Racism was deep and more complex than many realized. The integration of African-Americans into white society had not been as successful as many had hoped.

Merton was more pessimistic in "The Hot Summer of Sixty-Seven," also in *Faith and Violence.*[85] The hopes for a non-violent solution were dashed by the violence that appeared in Detroit and other cities. The murder of three civil rights workers in Mississippi in 1964 and violence in Watts in California were the beginnings of more violence. For Merton, one of the causes was the war in Viet Nam. The official policy of the United States was to solve a political problem by violence, and African-Americans picked up on that. Black Power had replaced non-violence, and King was no longer the moral authority or the greatest leader of the movement. Those who had accused King of being a communist were regretting that power had now moved to the violent.

In a moving journal entry of April 6, 1968, Merton wrote about a visit with his Anglican friend Donald Allchin. After stopping by Shakertown, they visited with Merton's friends Gene Meatyard and

---

81. *Turning*, p. 119. May 16, 1961.
82. *Turning*, p. 325. June 1, 1963.
83. *Dancing,* p. 15. September 3, 1963.
84. *Faith and Violence*, pp. 130-131.
85. *Faith and Violence*, pp. 165-181.

Carolyn Hammer in Lexington. While having supper in a Lexington restaurant they saw the news of King's death in Memphis on TV. There was a replay of his speech in Memphis the previous night. Merton was impressed with King's "tenseness and strength. A sort of vague visual, auditory impression." Merton pondered 1968 which he called "a beast of year," and wondered why such things happened. Did people in desperation want them to happen, or did they have to happen? "Is the human race self-destructive?" Is the Christian gospel of love a "pitiful delusion?"[86] The previous day he had written a letter to Mrs. King and sent it by his friend June Yungblut who had been urging King to make a retreat at Gethsemani.[87]

On April 9, 1968, Merton noted the funeral of Martin Luther King, Jr. He received another letter from June Yungblut commenting about the "the calm and heroism" of Mrs. King. He also had a note from John Howard Griffin, who taught Merton photography, who asked, "When will they also shoot the rest of us?"[88] Griffin was known for his book *Black Like Me* in which he described how he used a chemical to change the color of his skin to black and then traveled around the South to experience what American African-Americans experienced. He was also to write the official biography of Merton but died before it was completed.

QUAKERS

The Quakers, or the Society of Friends, as they were officially known, were founded in England in the mid-17th century by George Fox. They believed in the Inner Light in every person and their worship was non-liturgical, consisting of sitting in silence until the Holy Spirit moved someone to speak. In the early years they were often persecuted. The state of Pennsylvania was founded by Quakers as a Holy Experiment. The Quakers were of some importance to Merton. His mother had occasionally attended Quaker meetings, and he had attended a few himself although he was not too impressed. Three meetings are mentioned in the journals and letters.

In a 1966 journal entry, he mentioned walking in the woods and reading in a collection of Protestant mystics which included the Quaker, Rufus Jones.[89] Jones spent his entire adult life as a

86. *The Other Side of Silence*, pp. 77-78. April 6, 1968.
87. *The Other Side of Silence,* p. 79. April 6, 1968.
88. *The Other Side of Silence,* p. 80. April 9, 1968.
89. *Learning to Love,* p. 114. August 15, 1966.

philosophy professor at Haverford College, a Quaker institution in Philadelphia. He devoted his career to a study of the history of Christian mysticism and, like Merton, published over 50 books on the subject including a multivolume history of the Quakers. He was greatly loved by Quakers in the first half of the 20th century.

Douglas Steere was also a well-known and published Quaker professor. He attended the Second Vatican Council and wrote briefly about it to Merton.[90] During his life he made visits to Gethsemani and gave talks to the monks. A journal entry in early 1962 revealed that Steere and his wife had visited. Merton liked them both, and said that Mrs. Steere impressed him as "a very spiritual person and a very typical Quaker." He described her as "Very simple, direct, earnest, completely good." Their conversation covered many topics, and Merton found they had much in common. Steere knew Dom Bede Griffiths, and admired him. He told Merton about Bede Griffiths's Ashram on a remote mountain side in India. While they were talking about nuclear war, Steere said that there were people in the Pentagon who had a more sober view of it than some theologians. For Merton, one of the most important points in the conversation was Albert Schweitzer's belief that the women of the world might be the most effective people in resisting war.[91] In a letter to his friend Daniel Berrigan, Merton mentioned that "Douglas Steere was here and we had a good talk.[92]

June Yungblut was a Quaker friend and frequent correspondent with Merton. She and her husband had worked in South Africa for the Friends World Committee. When they first contacted Merton they were the directors of Quaker House in Atlanta. June was close to Coretta King in the days that followed the assassination. She held a doctorate from Emory University in Atlanta. Her interests were literature and theology.

In January of 1968, Merton wrote to June about a proposed retreat with Martin Luther King, Jr. A new abbot, Flavian Burns, had just been elected, and a retreat with any publicity might be difficult for him. Merton suggested just a private affair rather than a special event. King and others could come later in the summer and "we could all do some developing here." A retreat before a

90. *Hidden Ground*, p. 413. May 20, 1963

91. *Turning*, pp. 199-200. February 5, 1962.

92. *Hidden Ground*, p. 73. March 10, 1962.

march would have "some symbolic public meaning," but this was not the time for that. The new abbot had just learned about the civil rights movement and knew there was a struggle going on, but that is about all.[93]

Two days later Merton wrote he was available anytime King might want to make a retreat. Having a new abbot complicated the situation a bit. In Merton's first "official" conversation with him, he said that he wanted Merton "to stick with my bloody mysticism" and not get involved with "outward works." Merton suggested going slow with any activity "that might signify a tie-in with some onslaught on the bastions of squaredom." The abbot, he said is open but inexperienced. Given time he can learn. Having King, Vincent Harding, and other notables for a "quiet, informal, deeply reflective session" would help the abbot see where Merton really belonged which was "halfway between in and out of the action."[94]

King was killed on April 4, 1968, and the retreat never happened. On the day of King's funeral Merton offered a Mass for him, joined by two Anglicans, his friend Donald Allchin and an Anglican seminarian. Merton wrote, "These have been terrible days for everyone. I feel that we have really crossed a definite line into a more apocalyptic kind of time."[95]

In March, 1968, June Yungblut wrote to Merton that she had plans for a post-doctoral study of four men of faith: Merton, Alan Patton, Elie Wiesel, and Thich Nhat Hanh. She told Merton that she had always seen herself as a Quaker-Catholic, but was now a Quaker-Catholic-Buddhist. Merton replied that he had been a Catholic Buddhist and also a Quaker. "I naturally feel happy about the new Church," he wrote. As he pondered her project he also pondered his own writing and evaluated some of it for her.

The books he was most happy about included *Conjectures of a Guilty Bystander, New Seeds of Contemplation, The Sign of Jonas, Raids on the Unspeakable,* and introductions he wrote on Chuang Tzu, Gandhi, and the Desert Fathers. He suggested that his essay collections, *Disputed Questions, Seeds of Destruction,* and *Mystics and Zen Masters* were uneven: some good and others way off from what he really wanted to say. He suggested that much of his writing

93. *Hidden Ground*, pp. 639-649. January 16, 1968.
94. *Hidden Ground*, p. 640. January 20, 1968.
95. *Hidden Ground*, p. 645. April 9, 1968.

was "beside the point" because it "was not in a creative manner that really suited me."[96]

BIBLICAL SCHOLARS

Merton made some effort to keep up with Protestant Biblical scholarship. The one to whom he seemed to give the most attention was the controversial Rudolph Bultmann. Bultmann spent most of his career at the University of Marburg where he gained an international reputation as a scholar. In his study of the Synoptic Gospels, Matthew, Mark, and Luke, he used form criticism as his method. Materials in the Synoptics were cast in literary forms by the early Christian community to meet its needs in communicating the Gospel. This meant that the Synoptics told us more about early Christianity that they did about Jesus. They are theological rather than biographical books. He believed that in order to understand the Gospels they must be "demythologized." It is impossible in his mind to know anything about the historical Jesus since he was presented to us in a mythological manner. It is also impossible to get behind the myth to the real historical person. The essence of Christianity can be found in the Gospel proclamation of the early church. He believed strongly in the basic message of the New Testament.

In a 1964 letter to his friend Etta Guillick, Merton replied to her request for spiritual books. He found a book of Bultmann's essays to be challenging and "terribly interesting." He thought Bultmann's anti-mysticism had a point. It was good, he believed, "to tussle" with things like this to get down to the most important point, which was faith.[97] To his Columbia classmate Seymour Freedgood, Merton wrote saying that he was sending some "curiosities that emerge from the hutch here." As Freedgood might know, Merton wrote, he has ended up getting interested in thinkers like Jaspers, Sartre, Merleau Ponty, and Rudolph Bultmann.[98]

In his essay, "Violence and the Death of God: or God as the Unknown Soldier," in *Faith and Violence*, Merton included Bultmann in a list of theologians who are important in a time of great theological ferment. In his critique of Bishop Robinson's book *Honest to God* found in *Faith and Violence*, he said, "With

96. *Hidden Ground,* pp. 641-642. January 16, 1968.
97. *Hidden Ground*, p. 364. January 7, 1964.
98. *Road to Joy*, p. 124, January 2, 1964.

Bultmann he will demythologize, and for this I am not so sure that he deserves to be 'trampled to death by geese.'" Later in that essay he mentions Tillich, Bonhoeffer, and Bultmann, whom he calls "profound thinkers." Even, he wrote, if one disagrees with them, one can accept their sense of urgency about the problems that concern them.[99]

There are several references to Bultmann in Volume Five of Merton's Journals.

In December, 1963, he quoted Bultmann to the effect that Paul's anthropology referred to new life and not anthropology in general. He rejected Paul's speech at the Areopagus and Peter's idea of our "partakers of divine nature" as "Hellenistic and strange."[100] On New Year's Day, 1964, Merton had a rather lengthy entry on Bultmann and his idea of God. While our care meets God at the end of its capacity, God is the one whose power limits us. Bultmann said, "It is God who makes man finite," and "who sets a terminus to his knowing." Merton said that this was a Biblical idea. Bultmann added, "Real belief in God always grows out of the realization that being is an unknown quantity . . . of which one is always becoming conscious in the 'moment' of 'loving.'" Belief in God, for Bultmann as Merton understood it, was not a "general truth." This is why the only valid knowledge of God is found in Christian revelation. "Belief in God," Bultmann said, "is never something we can have as a possession." If we encounter God as "thou" which demands love, we are in a constant struggle of hate against love because of our selfish disregard in maintaining our own interests.[101]

A few days later Merton wrote, "Bultmann's *Essays* have been a revelation to me, so powerful, so urgent, so important that every sentence stops me." He appreciated Bultmann's knowledge of Greek thought and the influence of Heidegger which he develops in a "New Testament and Kerygmatic way." Bultmann, Merton said, revealed the limitations in his own work, so that he can abandon or revise his own old ideas. A quotation he particularly liked in Bultmann was, "Grace can never be possessed but can only be received afresh again and again." Merton believed that institutionalized religion was always tempted to keep people constrained by its

99. *Faith and Violence*, pp. 225, 233.

100. *Dancing*, p. 45. December 15, 1963.

101. *Dancing*, pp. 52-53. January 1, 1964. Bultmann quotes are from his *Form Criticism: Two Essays on New Testament Research*, pp. 5, 7, 15.

own and society's past, but this constraint interferes with a person's freedom to respond to grace. He thought that Bultmann had a weak concept of the Church. However, for him, "Real loyalty does not involve repetition but carrying things a step further." [102]

Merton disagreed with some of Bultmann's statements about non-Christian religions, but strongly supported his idea that grace supports our whole existence. We can conceive of it as grace only when we surrender our whole existence and let ourselves fall "into the unfathomable dizzy depths without seeking something to hold on to." Merton's hope for the church is not that it will dominate as a world power, but that "the Spirit will shake the world when Christians have lost what they held on to and entered the eschatological kingdom—where in fact they already are." [103]

A year and a half later Merton was still reading Bultmann. Contact with God, he realized, was "word and event." It is not just sitting and recollecting which leads to no decision. What is important is the renunciation of one's own wisdom "in exchange for the foolishness of the cross, in which is pure light." [104]

There were several other Biblical scholars that interested him, but he made only fleeting references to them. He wrote into his journal a brief quote from the British scholar, C. H. Dodd, who said "We shall get at the truth of our present situation only by exposing ourselves to the judgment of God in it." Our own behavior, Dodd said, contributes actions that have brought us to the current situation.[105] In *Conjectures of a Guilty Bystander*, he mentioned Walter Eichrodt as one of the fine Protestant scholars writing Old Testament theologies who are making the greatness of the Old Testament evident. In the same sentence he referred to Gerhard von Rad, who said "Living praise is the fullness of man's being with God and 'the mystery' of the spirit." Faith in God's mercy and promises makes history for the Psalmist a theological fact.[106] In a March, 1964 journal entry, he wrote about another Protestant scholar, Amos Wilder, who made a statement that resonated with Merton. "The solitude of the Christian to the world and its institutions will be based on the word of the Cross," the Good News of the

102. *Dancing*, pp. 55-56. January 6, 1964.
103. *Dancing*, p. 59. January 11, 1964.
104. *Dancing,* p. 267. July 9, 1965.
105. *Turning*, p. 65. November 14, 1960.
106. *Conjectures,* p. 121.

Gospel, the righteousness of God, and the post-resurrection faith, not upon the social ethic of the Sermon on the Mount or natural law or the inner light of the Holy Spirit.[107]

WINSTON KING

Winston King taught comparative religions at the Vanderbilt Divinity School and shared Merton's interest in eastern religions. In 1967 contact between Merton and King began to develop. In April, 1967, Merton reported that King had spent a Saturday at Gethsemani and brought what Merton called "good information" about Zen people. He also brought a photograph of D. T. Suzuki which Merton placed on his table.[108]

In late November, 1967, Merton complained about being "intellectually overfed," and was giving up reading for a few days. He did go out in the afternoon and read some items on meditation in one of Winston King's books on Burmese Buddhism which he pronounced "good."[109] In March, 1968, King visited Merton. They had a good talk for several hours. He described King as "a good person to know," well informed on Buddhism and seriously interested in meditation. He loaned Merton copies of *Psycholofia* in which Merton found some good articles.[110]

The study of Merton's spiritual, intellectual, and theological evolution reveals a growing interest in Protestantism and its theologies. He always remained faithful to his Catholicism, but was not uncritical of it. The breadth of his reading in Protestant theology and his appreciation for some of its theologians reflects a growing openness to new ideas, at least ideas that were new to him. He sought out Protestant writers and always enjoyed conversations with students, ministers and professors. From time to time he would say that he had to give it all up, but in a few days new people would come and he would enjoy engaging them in conversation. He may not have wanted to be an ecumenist, but he just couldn't help himself.

Of course, Merton's ecumenism was not limited to Christians. He reached out to Buddhists, Hindus, Muslims, and even Cargo Cults. People who love Merton have often speculated about where

107. *Dancing*, p. 86. March 4 1964. Wilder quote is from his *Background of the New Testament and Its Eschatology*, pp. 5-7.

108. *Learning to Love,* p. 213. April 6, 1967.

109. *Learning to Love,* p. 216. April 8, 1967.

110. *The Other Side of Silence*, p. 18. November 18, 1967.

this would have gone had he not died so young. What new worlds would he have explored? Surely he would have continued to broaden his outlook and deepen his awareness of the religious and spiritual longings of the people of the world.

ECUMENICAL VISITS

Merton had visits from many people who came to see him at Gethsemani: writers, poets, artists, professors, theologians, publishers, social activists, and seminary students. Protestant students from Southern Baptist Theological Seminary, The Vanderbilt University Divinity School, Presbyterian Theological Seminary, Asbury Theological Seminary, Union Theological Seminary, Lexington Theological Seminary (originally known to Merton as The College of the Bible although it was a liberal graduate institution), and Episcopal seminaries made pilgrimages to the monastery. These visits had profound effects on many of the students, but also on Merton as he gradually came to know and appreciate these embryonic ministers. Mention of these visits is found in Volumes 3, 4, and 5 of Merton's journals.

The first such reference is found in Volume 3, dated March 29, 1960, where he said that he spent "an interesting afternoon" with Protestant students from the Vanderbilt Divinity School. He called the group "lively and intelligent" and said, "We got along well together, I think." He added that he might have gone more than halfway with the students in saying that every monk should have something like Luther's monastic experience when he discovered that faith and the reality of God's mercy were more important than formal observances and what Merton called "quasi-magical works." Merton spent an hour and a half with the students, and by the end of the day he believed a "deep and genuine understanding" had been established.

These visits had been started several years earlier by Professor Bard Thompson who brought his first year church history class to spend a day at Gethsemani each year. He always needed people to drive and, since I had a car, I managed to go on five of those trips while I was in seminary and graduate school. Two of those visits included visits with Merton. In the first one, Merton entered the room in the Guest House carrying a Revised Standard Version of the Bible under his arm. It was a new translation produced by the Protestant National Council of Churches, and it had not yet been approved for use by Roman Catholics. When we saw him with that Bible we thought this man must be something of a rebel and we were going to get along with him fine. Merton entertained our questions about the monastic life and spirituality in general, and we returned to Nashville that evening grateful for an inspirational and informative day. We had a new appreciation of the monastic life which we had studied in class, but until this day most of us had never had any experience of it. Beyond that, we had no experience of contemplative Christianity. We had been social action oriented in our faith, and this visit gave us something very important to ponder about our own ministries.

Merton also mentioned that Professor Langdon Gilkey, who taught us the history of doctrine, had been in a Japanese internment camp in China during World War II with a man who later became a Gethsemani monk, Father David Murphy. Both men were missionaries at that time. Gilkey was not present on this trip, but they did have a brief reunion the next year. Merton wrote him a letter about the coincidence.[1] Later, Gilkey became a professor at the University of Chicago Divinity School.

About a month later, Merton said he wrote to the College of the Bible and Asbury Seminary about their forthcoming retreats.[2] The ecumenical business was picking up. In one entry Merton said that he was becoming a Kentuckian "and a conscious one." This meant, he said, talking to people in Louisville and Lexington. He added, "I liked the Lexington Presbyterians who came over the other Sunday."[3] The College of the Bible group did come for a retreat. Merton gave them two conferences, and mentioned that Professor Richard Pope, who taught church history there, had trouble with the idea of annihilation of the "Self." Merton said it was no problem for him. His true self is the one "spoken by God." He concluded this entry with, "I know you are leading me, therefore there is *no conflict with anyone.*"[4]

Early in Volume 4 of the journals Merton described a visit with three men from Asbury Theological Seminary. The group included the President, Dr. Frank Stanger, who had a strong interest in spirituality matters, and two others. They walked to the woods behind the lake and discussed theology. Two other monks partici-

1. *Search*, pp. 381-382. March 29, 1960.
2. *Search*, p. 385. April 24, 1960.
3. *Search*, p. 391. May 18, 1960.
4. *Search*, p. 394. May 23, 1960.

pated. Merton indicated that "no one tried to dictate anything to anyone" and that they were "really seeking truth." This prompted Merton to reflect that "this retreat and the one from the College of the Bible have been very promising and rewarding." He believed that these encounters were valuable, and that there was mutual respect. He said that friendship with these people enabled him "to be friends with a hidden part of myself" which only happened if he gave friendship to them. He concluded, "all Christians should be making the same discovery."[5]

Two visitors, Earl Loomis and Jack Gruenwald, came from Union Theological Seminary in New York, regarded by many as the premier Protestant seminary in the United States. Merton said they had good conversations. He mused that such occasions tempted him to think that there was more point to his being at Gethsemani than there actually was.[6]

In October, 1960, Merton expressed concern that the Abbot, James Fox, had recently returned from a trip to Rome where he had a private audience with the pope. Merton was fearful that questions had been raised about his ecumenism. Dan Walsh, one of Merton's favorite professors at Columbia and now a resident, but not a monk, at Gethsemani told him that the abbot "is really keen on it" but said little about it to Merton. Merton was fearful that it was becoming a means to provide publicity for Gethsemani. His only interest in it, he wrote, was "the good that comes from simple and charitable conversation." There is no need for publicity or attention. If left alone, it will give glory to God.[7]

Negative thoughts about his ecumenical efforts began to enter Merton's mind in 1960. He suggested that it might be best to stop any efforts to bring Protestants to Gethsemani for dialogue. There were too many false motivations: the abbot's interest in the "façade," the fact that ecumenism was currently "fashionable," and Merton's own desire for friendship and conversation. Pope John XXIII had approved it and the abbot wanted it to continue. Merton was thinking that the abbot wanted any invitations to come from him. So, Merton decided not to plan any retreats for 1961 or to issue any invitations.[8] The next month, however, he noted in his

5. *Turning*, pp. 16-17. June 26, 1960,
6. *Turning*, p. 38. September 1, 1960.
7. *Turning*, p. 55. October 2, 1960.
8. *Turning*, p. 62. October 30, 1060.

journal that 75 seminarians from Southern Baptist were coming later in the day.[9]

In his first entry in his 1961 journal Merton mentioned one of the unique characters in his ecumenical relationships, Roscoe Pierson. Pierson was the librarian at the College of the Bible/Lexington Theological Seminary, a Christian Church (Disciples of Christ) institution. He was a politically conservative, gun loving, and outspoken character. Although they had very different personalities, Pearson and Merton developed a nice friendship.

The Gethsemani library did not have works by well-known Protestant theologians, so Merton would ask Pierson to send him books. He would often inquire about what he should read by Paul Tillich, Karl Barth, Reinhold Niebuhr, and others. In this particular entry he wrote that Pierson was going to send him a book by Nathan Söderblom, a Lutheran and a major leader in the ecumenical movement. In return for the loan of books Merton sent Pierson old Cistercian Latin liturgical books, mimeographs of some of his essays, and copies of his lectures to novices, among other things, for the seminary library. A lively correspondence took place for several years. Pierson had great appreciation and affection for Merton. Pierson was an excellent librarian, and the holdings in spirituality in the College of the Bible library were vast and of high quality. Merton said that he and Pierson would have a conversation about the faculty coming for a retreat. In the same paragraph he noted that Father Killian McDonnell from St. John's Monastery in Minnesota was coming to speak to the novices about the ecumenical movement.[10] Merton could not help himself; he was continually getting caught up in it.

In April, 1961, Merton reported that a group from Southern Baptist Seminary had come to Gethsemani the previous day. He said there was "good rapport. I liked them very much." While there was understanding and sincerity, differences were not minimized. The chief promoter of these visits was Professor Glenn Hinson who also taught church history. Merton described him as "a good and sincere person." He would come again with some faculty colleagues, and Merton hoped they would talk about the Church. But, Merton wondered if he had committed himself too much. He called this ecumenical activity "a strange, humorous game of God

9. *Turning*, p. 63. November 7, 1960.
10. *Turning*, p. 109. April 18 1961.

that I cannot quite take seriously." "I must not play it too madly," he concluded.[11]

In the late 1990s, Southern Baptist Seminary was taken over by a fundamentalist group in the Southern Baptist Convention. New trustees were appointed and non-fundamentalist faulty were terminated. Merton would have been sad at the loss of faculty friends and more open-minded students.

A May, 1961 entry, described an event at which I was present. It began with an ominous tone. "It started pouring rain. Protestants were coming." There was a large group, thirty or forty from Vanderbilt, he estimated, and a smaller group from a fundamentalist school. Merton called it a "good lively session" until they started to bicker among themselves.

The fact, from my personal observation, was that the fundamentalist students wanted to convert Merton. They quoted passages of scripture which they believed were anti-monastic, but Merton responded respectfully and lovingly, and by the end of the session he had converted them. They all rushed up to shake his hand and thank him. It was a fine lesson for all of us would-be ministers on how to handle a hostile situation. I have always been thankful to Merton for that. Merton commented, "The Vanderbilt group is always in general good and mature. I am sorry the more serious and profound of them did not come in a smaller party." Merton saw the event as a contest between "the sweet earnestness of Methodist, the polish and sophistication of the Anglicans (or rather Episcopalians) – the sometimes rather taut fervor of the Baptists—though I did not know exactly who was what." Merton said when it was all over he was exhausted because he imagined that he had something to say.[12]

In June of 1961, Merton reported a visit with three faculty members from Southern Baptist Seminary: Glenn Hinson, Dale Moody, and Les Garrett. They had an afternoon visit in the hermitage. Also present were two Methodists, but they had to leave early. Merton said the three Baptists were good friends of his now. He characterized them as having "great simplicity and goodness" and said, "We get along very well together and the hermitage is a fine place for free and uninhibited discussion."

There was conversation about the Church, but also about the problems of Southern Baptist ministers who wanted to support

11. *Turning,* p. 109. April 18, 1961.

12. *Turning*, pp. 129-130. May 1, 1961.

school integration. The Baptists told of meetings with Negroes in Louisville and what a wonderful Christian atmosphere they experienced. Merton saw this as an indication of "deep and genuine Christianity." "More and more," he wrote in his journal, "I see the validity of Protestantism and its spirit." But, he said Protestant weaknesses were greater than Catholicism's "in a way."

Still, he said that his unofficial dialogue "was a blessing." It was simply a matter of a Christian contact of people who are "in Christ" and people of good will. Merton had no interest in official ecumenical gatherings which he described as "a celebration of clichés." However, he said that in these conversations he was "fulfilling my function in the Church."[13]

Merton had two visitors from the University of the South at Sewanee, an Episcopal school. One of them was planning to attend Nashoda House, an Anglican seminary near Milwaukee. Merton liked both of these men, but the one going to Nashoda was preoccupied with demonstrating the "absolute identity" between the Anglo-Catholic liturgy and Gethsemani's. He showed Merton his Anglican Missal and Ordo and pointed out how they had adopted all of the latest changes in Catholic liturgy.

The other man was on his way to the Sorbonne to study political science. He had lived in Japan, the Near East, and Switzerland and showed an interest in monasteries. Merton gave him the names of monasteries he should see in France.[14]

Late in the summer of 1961, Merton visited the Southern Baptist Seminary campus to see some of the professors. He was particularly interested in Eric Rust who had ideas about Old Testament theology and history that Merton described as "very solid and alive." Rust had been an atomic scientist but became a minister and theologian after World War II.

He had lunch with some faculty in one of the campus cafeterias. It was in a women's dormitory, and Merton was surprised to see "some rather pretty girls studying to be Baptist ministers." He described the five or six faculty members with whom he had met as "very fine." He had met many of them before when they came to Gethsemani. He appreciated meeting Dr. Mueller who had studied with Barth and with Ray Petrie at Duke University who had published an anthology of medieval mysticism in the Library

13. *Turning*, pp. 129-130. July 21, 1961

14. *Turning*, p. 139. July 4, 1961.

of Christian Classics series.[15]

The next month Glenn Hinson brought his church history students from the Baptist seminary to Gethsemani. Merton spoke to them about peace. He thought that they had a good conversation and understood each other "completely." He mentioned in the journal that it had been about a year since the first Baptist seminary group had come.

Merton was surprised to see some of the students questioning the validity of popular assumptions about "the American way of life and whether there was anything particularly Christian about them." Merton thought that there was growing doubt in the United States which was producing "indecision and guilt."[16]

In January, 1962, Merton made another seminary visit, this one to Asbury Theological Seminary in Wilmore, about 11 miles south of Lexington. It had a Methodist orientation and is one of the larger Protestant seminaries. He had lunch with the faculty and talked to some of the students. He described those he met as "good, grass-roots American people," and saw the atmosphere of the school as one of "warmth and friendliness." He was somewhat frustrated with the chapel. He missed "any altar of sacrifice," and saw it as more of a synagogue than a temple. He described the hymn singing as powerful and joyous.[17]

Protestant visits seemed to be increasing at Gethsemani. In the winter of 1962 Merton wrote, "Big group of Protestants here yesterday—Episcopalians, Methodists, Disciples of Christ."[18]

On the 24th anniversary of his baptism, Merton had a journal entry in which he expressed some of his complaints about the Catholic Church. He said he had never had any doubts about his Christian faith or the Church as the visible Body of Christ. It was the institutional side of things that frustrated him. He did not like having to yield to officialdom and follow the regulations and decisions of bureaucrats when there was a conflict between the "dead regulation" and "living spontaneous moral action." What kept him at Gethsemani, he wrote, was the community and especially the novices in which he saw the Church.

It was in this context that he wondered how long he was going

15. *Turning*, p. 165. September 29, 1961.
16. *Turning*, p. 175. October 30, 1961
17. *Turning*, p. 194. January 12, 1962.
18. *Turning*, p. 204. February 20, 1962.

to be able to talk to the Baptist seminarians "with such uninhibited frankness," and suspected that they probably wondered too.[19]

The next group to visit was Anglican seminarians from Nashoda House on retreat. Merton gave a talk to them. The session was lively, and he liked the students. He wondered if too much was being made of these meetings. They were something new at Gethsemani. Perhaps, he said, they are events, but ordinary ones. "It is good that they are," he wrote.[20]

Another Anglican, A. M. Allchin, who is frequently mentioned by Merton, had published a book, *Silent Rebellion*, which Merton liked. There was, Merton said, "a special quality and excellence in the Anglican view of monasticism." It seemed to be a protest against the "torpor" of the Anglican establishment. He wondered if this was only a "precious indulgence" of a small minority. Merton said he was disturbed by the book and "certainly glad to be a Roman." [21]

In the latter part of September, 1963, Merton found himself in the hospital. He had a problem with a disc in his back as well as an injury to the vertebrae of his neck. He feared that these problems would slow him down. He would not be able to do as much writing and would have to reduce his project with the novices. He also wanted a deepening of his grasp on spiritual reality. Among other things, he believed that he should reduce "the more superficial type of ecumenical contacts" and many of the visits of people.[22] But the visits continued. A month after his entry he reported a visit from the Baptist Seminary in Louisville.[23] The following month some ministers from Louisville, people from the Baptist and Presbyterian Seminaries, and a group from Bellarmine College visited. They came for discussions but Merton said that he was dubious about it. What was more important to Merton was simply their being there. He liked Glenn Hinson "who knows and loves the fathers of the church" and Dale Moody who said that glossolalia, speaking in tongues, was sweeping through southern Protestantism. Moody favored it. Merton saw it as "a manifestation of spiritual insecurity and confusion." A group of Episcopal nuns from Versailles, Kentucky,

19. *Turning,* p. 265. November 16, 1962.
20. *Turning,* p. 268. November 24, 1962.
21. *Turning,* p. 347. July 29, 1963.
22. *Dancing,* p. 18. September 20, 1963.
23. *Dancing,* p. 29. October 29, 1963.

said the same thing was happening in Episcopal churches too.[24]

Early in 1964 Merton reported that faculty and students from the College of the Bible had visited. This item is followed by a comment on existentialism. In this context he mentioned Martin Luther's criticism of religious vows. Merton agreed that Luther was right "if the vows were not lived fully and freely." Just enclosing oneself does not give glory to God.[25] A week later there was a group of students from Asbury at Gethsemani. He visited with them briefly before the office of None.[26]

During the summer of 1964, Merton had a visit with a group of children from the Christian Church (Disciples of Christ) in Carrolton, Kentucky. He described them as "good, simple children, open, unspoiled." He said that he had compassion "for their simplicity which they will probably lose."[27] In the Fall he had another visit from the Baptist seminarians. He said that he enjoyed talking with them but he did not know if he could meet them next year. The meeting was "fruitful and meaningful," but he said, "you can't have everything."[28]

The final journal entry about his ecumenical contacts with Protestant students is dated January 10, 1965. It is a long passage in which he reflects on his life, his weaknesses, his growing maturity, the people he loved and who influenced him. It is a fascinating autobiographical statement. He affirmed that the happiest and most profound times in his life had been at Gethsemani. In this context he mentioned "good moments with Protestants coming here," especially the Hammers, Ping Ferry, and J. Laughlin.[29]

These visits of seminary students had profound effects. Most of us had never been inside a monastery, or for some, had any real idea what the monastic life was about. To see men who had given up the possibility of marriage and family life, successful careers in a variety of fields, and enjoying what American culture can offer, was a shock to the system. We did not know any who took their religion that seriously. Celibacy, obedience, stability, enclosure, and voluntary poverty just did not fit what we thought our ministries

---

24. *Dancing*, p. 40. November 30, 1963.
25. *Dancing*, p. 74. February 10, 1964.
26. *Dancing*, p. 77. February 17, 1964.
27. *Dancing*, p. 131. July 28, 1964.
28. *Dancing*, p. 164. November 10, 1964.
29. *Dancing*, p. 199. January 30, 1965.

would be. The impact of those visits for some of us would last a lifetime, and it contributed to a growing sense of the importance of spirituality in the Protestant ministry.

This impact worked both ways, because the visits turned out to be very important for Merton. In December, 1964, Merton informed Glenn Hinson at Southern Baptist Theological Seminary that meetings with seminary students would have to stop. For one thing, Merton was about to become a full-time hermit, and he wanted to explore its possibilities. Among other changes, Merton had to end his work as Novice Master and his teaching duties in the monastery. He told Hinson that these meetings with Baptist students had a profound impact on him too. He wrote, "I have learned very much from my contacts with my friends at the Seminary, and I don't think I will ever be capable of returning to a narrow and rigid view of the Church anymore." Definitions had to be made, but the reality was that God was greater than "anything we can explain, predict, or define." God's actions and mercy always "overflow" expectations and "we can never expect Him to fit into the limits we have assigned." Merton concluded, "I know that I have gained incalculably from knowing you all."[30]

Before leaving this section of the book there is one more ecumenical event that took place at Gethsemani in 1964 that had considerable impact on the United States. It was a gathering of peace activists who explored the spiritual roots of protest with Merton. They were Protestant and Catholic. One of the best known Protestant participants was A. J. Muste, a Quaker and former Dutch Reformed Church minister as well as former executive secretary of the Fellowship of Reconciliation and current chair of the Committee for Nonviolent Action. John Howard Yoder was a Mennonite who would later publish *The Politics of Jesus.* W. H. "Ping" Ferry was vice-president of the Center for the Study of Democratic Institutions in California, a Unitarian at the time of the retreat. Elbert Jean was a Methodist minister who had been active in the civil rights movement and paid dearly for it. Finally, John Oliver Nelson was a Presbyterian professor at Yale Divinity School, a leader in the Fellowship of Reconciliation, and founder of Kirkridge Retreat Center in Pennsylvania whose motto was "Picket and Pray." He was a co-organizer of the retreat along with John Heidbrink of the

---

30. William Apel, *Signs of Peace: the Interfaith Letters of Thomas Merton,* pp. 120-123.

FOR who, unfortunately, was unable to attend because of illness. Gordon Oyer was a Mennonite and an administrator in the University of Illinois system. He is also the author of a fine book on this retreat, *Pursuing the Spiritual Roots of Protest*.[31]

Catholic participants included Jim Forest who had joined Dorothy Day's Catholic Worker community in New York in 1961 and edited their newspaper *The Catholic Worker*. He had been discharged from the Navy as a conscientious objector. His editing of the *Catholic Worker* put him in touch with Merton whom he visited at Gethsemani in 1962. Tom Cornell, a Catholic Peace Fellowship organizer had joined the Catholic Worker at the age of 19. His work with the Committee for Nonviolent Action (CNVA) led to introductions to A. J. Muste and John Oliver Nelson. Cornell was involved in draft resistance and burned his nine consecutively issued draft cards. He developed a close friendship with Jim Forest.

Probably the best-known participant, other than Merton, was Daniel Berrigan, a Jesuit priest. He had been a professor of New Testament at LeMoyne College and a poet, but was known for his concerns about poverty and civil rights. During the Viet Nam war he and his brother Philip became two of the most prominent peace protestors. Philip also participated in the retreat. In 1962 Daniel and John Heidbrink, a Presbyterian minister, had led a series of retreats for Protestant ministers. In that same year Heidbrink began correspondence with Merton, visited Gethsemani, and lectured to the novices.

Other Catholic participants included a Canadian, Anthony Walsh, who eventually established Benedict Labré House following the Catholic Worker model. John Peter Grady became the editor of *Jubilee*, a journal founded by Merton's Columbia classmate Edward Rice. Robert Cunnane was a classmate of Philip Berrigan at Holy Cross College. He had worked with the Packard Manse Ecumenical Center in Massachusetts and tried to build relationships between Catholics, Protestants, and Jews. Charles Ring taught in the religious studies department at Catholic University in Washington. D.C. and later joined Cunnane at the Stigmatine retreat house.

Needless to say this was an eclectic and ecumenical group. They did not gather for that purpose. Their interest in civil rights, peace, and nuclear war brought them together, and a common con-

31. Gordon Oyer, *Pursuing the Spiritual Roots of Protest*. Eugene, Oregon: Cascade Books, 2014, p. xii.

cern for these issues overrode any theological and ecclesial differences. This was a much deeper unity than any official ecumenical organization could accomplish. Ecumenism was not the purpose of the retreat, but was a happy byproduct. Gordon Oyer wrote in his book on the retreat, "In ways both tangible and mystical many barriers holding at bay Protestant and Catholic fellowship melted that week through the power of relationships, cultivating a model for those who would follow."[32]

Gethsemani never saw itself as an ecumenical agency, but Merton's growing openness to the wider religious world, his correspondence with people of many religious traditions, the visits of Protestant ministerial students, not to mention Protestant theologians, professors, lay people, and the peace retreat, all had an ecumenical impact. The monks have had many conferences and lectures by Protestants. Today the retreat house has its share of Protestant retreatants, some ministerial and some lay. In that regard, Gethsemani is performing an ecumenical ministry that it never intended or expected.

The last word in this section belongs to Merton. During his fateful journey to Asia he gave a talk at Calcutta in October, 1968. Merton said:

> The deepest level of communication is not communication, but communion. It is wordless. It is beyond words, and it is beyond speech, and it is beyond concept. Not that we discover a new unity. We discover an older unity. My dear brothers, we are already one. But we imagine that we are not. And what we have to recover is our original unity. What we have to be is what we are.[33]

---

32. *Pursuing the Spiritual Roots of Protest*, p. 205.

33. *The Asian Journal of Thomas Merton.* Ed. by Naomi Burton, Brother Patrick Hart, and James Laughlin. New York: New Directions Books, 1973, p. 308.

PART II
PERSONAL REFLECTIONS BY PROTESTANTS

THOMAS MERTON'S LIVING INFLUENCE

Stephanie A. Paulsell

I don't remember when I first heard the name Thomas Merton. When I was growing up, though, it seemed like everyone around me was always talking about him. Merton was one of those presences that gave depth to life, a marker of radical human possibility. Whenever I saw my parents reading his books with a pen in their hands or heard his voice coming out of our portable cassette player or saw his frank, open face and laughing eyes in a photo, I knew he was pointing in a direction I wanted to go, even if I didn't know where it led.

While I don't remember when I first heard Merton's name, I do remember the first book I read by him—my father's copy of *The Sign of Jonas,* an Image paperback held together with a rubber band because its glue-stiffened spine had broken. I had tried reading the book I always heard my parents and my father's students talking about—*The Seven Storey Mountain*—but had gotten bogged down in the first chapter. I had tried *New Seeds of Contemplation*, another book they all loved, but found it too abstract. After reading the first few pages of *The Sign of Jonas,* however, I was hooked. With its short entries and vivid observations of the weather, the birds, and the silence of Gethsemani's church on late afternoons, Merton's diary was just right for me. I could dip in and out of it over days and weeks without losing the thread. It felt less like a book and more like a row of bread crumbs, perfect for a girl picking her way along towards something unknown.

The passage that has remained most strongly in my memory from that first reading was an entry in which Merton described going around the property with another monk, blessing the fields and the animals with holy water:

> Yesterday Father Macarius and I went out and blessed the fields, starting with the wheat and the oats and coming around in Saint Bernard's field and Aidan Nally's and

> across to the bottoms. Out in the calf pasture we blessed some calves who came running up and took a very active interest in everything. Then we blessed the pigs, who showed some interest at first. The sheep showed no concern and the chickens ran away as soon as we approached. The rabbits stayed quiet until we threw holy water at them and then they all jumped.[1]

Even now, whenever my eyes fall on *The Sign of Jonas* in my bookshelf, I see those rabbits sitting tense and still as the monks approach. And I feel them suddenly spring.

When I first read *The Sign of Jonas,* I was a Disciples of Christ kid growing up in eastern North Carolina. As in Merton's monastery, worship in my church centered around what Merton called the Eucharist and we called the Lord's Supper. We passed trays of bread and tiny cups of grape juice down the pews and served communion to each other. I knew there was a family resemblance between the Lord's Supper and what Merton called "the mystery of the Blessed Sacrament," but I also knew there were differences between them that I didn't understand. When Merton wrote things like "There, on the altar, in the midst of these various discrete sounds of homage, in the midst of the order ruled by love for Him, the Lord of all things said nothing, but filled the room with peace," I had no idea what he meant. But at the same time, the silent God, the God who said nothing and yet communicated something, felt familiar. Merton gave me language to think about what might be happening in the silence as I sat dreaming over his book but also as I received the tray of bread from the person sitting next to me in church.

There were a lot of images and phrases like these in *The Sign of Jonas* that marked out the territory between Merton's Catholicism and my low-church Protestantism. They included references to the face of God, the consecrated life, guardian angels, feasts and fasts, the making of retreats and thanksgivings, contemplative prayer, the Queen of heaven. These half-understood phrases and ideas entered my imagination, not as concepts to be defined or debated but as a kind of poetry that opened a space for thought and wonder. As with poetry, I didn't have to understand every word in order for

1. Thomas Merton, *The Sign of Jonas*. Harcourt Brace, 1953, 1981, p. 103 (Paperback Version).

those phrases to do their work on me, and they did. They enlarged my own religious desires.

Thomas Merton's influence did not reach me only through his books, however. It also came to me intertwined with the relationships that meant the most to me, and the idea of him accumulated meaning as I encountered people who loved him and shared his commitments.

In the second grade, I had spent a year in a Catholic school. When the courts insisted, more than ten years after Brown vs. the Board of Education, that the schools in my small southern town had to become fully integrated, the town closed the public schools and did not open them again until after Christmas. My parents sent me to the already-integrated St. Therese Catholic School, where I was taught by nuns who were serious about racial justice in the south and who taught us with a wry, intelligent humor. As they interacted with us in the classroom and on the playground, in the chapel, in the gym, and when we were fidgeting in line, Sister Mary Griffin and Sister Mary Ann communicated to us that the capacity for friendship and community was a religious capacity, a practice of faith. When the schools reopened, I went back to public school. But when I began reading Thomas Merton, his voice brought back to me the voices of my teachers at St. Therese and the things about which they cared most deeply.

When my father was a graduate student at Vanderbilt, one of his professors, Bard Thompson, used to take his students out to Gethsemani to speak with Thomas Merton. Merton would sit with the students in the afternoon, answering their questions about monastic life, talking with them about cultivating a life with God through prayer and study and serving others. All of this made a tremendous impact on my father and initiated his lifelong relationship with Gethsemani and its monks. When he became a professor at a college in North Carolina, he took his students to Gethsemani as well. By then, Thomas Merton had died in Bangkok. But other monks sat and talked with them and even taught them to chant the Divine Office. My father and his students formed a group that met twice a week to sing an office and discuss a book together. I would walk over to the college after my ballet lesson and listen to them talking about *The Rule of St. Benedict*, or Merton's *New Seeds of Contemplation*. I can't remember any longer the exact substance of those conversations, but I remember the melody of them, with their notes of love and longing and the ominous drone of the war in Viet Nam that ran beneath them. Everyone had been touched by the war, many feared being sent to it, many looked for ways to resist it. Merton's exploration of prayer and contemplation, war and fear, faith and despair seemed to have everything to do with our lives. Merton's insistence in *New Seeds* that all of life is holy, that our fears and doubts and loves and desires were in no way separate from our life with God felt as necessary as air to breathe. "The saint knows that the world and everything made by God is good," Merton wrote in *New Seeds*. Sitting in the back of the classroom, listening to them talk, those questing young people and their teacher became my saints, pointing beyond themselves to the God whose presence they sought together.

My father also took our family to Gethsemani whenever there was an opportunity. On long car trips from eastern North Carolina to my grandparents' house in the Rio Grande Valley of Texas, we always stopped off at Gethsemani, staying in the Holiday Inn in Bardstown. My sister and I would sit in the first pew of the balcony, peering over the railing at the monks as they stood, sat, knelt, sang. Compline was our favorite office, the last of the day. I remember how the last note of the monks' hymn to Mary would rise and rise into the high ceiling, spreading itself among the eaves until it turned back into silence. When I read in *The Sign of Jonas* about the frustration and confusion that Merton sometimes felt in choir, I wondered if Compline had the power to lift and dissolve that as well.

Merton had a strong interest in experimental monastic communities and often wished he could join one, perhaps in Latin America. When a young man wrote to him to ask how he ought to follow his own monastic vocation, Merton recommended that he check out some of those experimental communities, including Holy Mother of God Monastery in Oxford, North Carolina.[2] Gethsemani eventually took over the care of that small monastery, about 90 miles from our home in eastern North Carolina, and a Gethsemani monk who had known Merton well, Father Matthew Kelty, came out to run it.

Father Matthew had been born in South Boston and grown up in Milton, Massachusetts, where, he once explained to me, the Protestants lived at the top of the hill and the Catholics, who worked

2. Thomas Merton, *The Road to Joy: Letters to New and Old Friends.* New York: Farrar, Straus and Giroux, 1989, p. 362.

for them, lived at the bottom. A former missionary of the Society of the Divine Word, Matthew had entered Gethsemani in his mid-40s. His novice master was Thomas Merton. Merton was often hard on Matthew, keeping him inside to type his manuscripts on beautiful days and sending him out to work outside on cold, dark ones. Matthew remembered Merton once coming down on him "head-first, total-thrust, full-power."[3] Matthew was afraid he wouldn't be allowed to stay. But he was, and he eventually became Merton's confessor. Merton's greatest, and most unexpected, gift to him, Matthew has written, was a profound understanding of the role of solitude in human life. Matthew eventually spent nine years as a hermit in New Guinea, where he had once served as a missionary.[4]

Matthew embodied many of Merton's commitments, and he got to do some of the things that Merton had wanted to do. He got to live as a hermit far from Gethsemani for a time. He got to take part in a monastic experiment at the monastery in Oxford. Like Merton, Matthew was a contemplative and a writer of lyrical power. He was deeply committed to nonviolence, removing the phone from the Oxford monastery so as not to pay the war tax and making a pilgrimage of peace from Oxford to Washington, DC, with the monastery Dalmation to protest the war in Viet Nam. He was witty and kind and full of stories, in love with solitude, but also with people. He was a gay man who believed it was crucial for men and women to cultivate their whole selves, with all of their masculine and feminine dimensions.

Matthew was much more than a reflection of his novice master; he was himself a singular monk, with his own remarkable gifts and commitments. But he was part of Merton's influence on my life, bringing to life some of those words and phrases I had come across in *The Sign of Jonas*: vocation, consecration, contemplation. Matthew embodied the consecrated life for me, showed me what it looked like when contemplative prayer kept opening someone up to the world around them, taught me about the ways in which the psalms take us, as he used to say, "all the way in and all the way down."

---

3. Matthew Kelty, *Flute Solo: Reflections of a Trappist Hermit*. Kansas City: Andrews McMeel, Inc., 1979, p. 19.

4. For an account of Father Matthew Kelty's life, and a collection of letters he wrote from his hermitage in New Guinea, see William O. Paulsell, *Letters from a Hermit*. Springfield, Illinois: Templegate, 1978.

One of my father's students told me a few years ago about a talk on the monastic life Matthew once gave at the college. One particularly fierce professor stood to ask him, "How, in the twentieth century, can anyone justify living as a monk?" Matthew's answer: "Somebody's got to walk in the damn rain." Thomas Merton would have liked this answer, I think. He was himself a lover of rain—it is a "festival," he wrote in his essay "Rain and the Rhinoceros." "The time will come when they will sell you even your rain. At the moment it is still free, and I am in it."[5] That freedom was for Matthew, as I think for Merton, the whole point of the monastic life: the freedom to make oneself wholly available, without defense, to what is really real. Somebody's got to walk in the damn rain. Thank God.

Thomas Merton's influence followed me as I grew up. In college and graduate school, where I was taught to take apart every argument and lay out its parts like an old car engine, I sometimes wondered if it were possible to continue to believe in God. In the elevator of my graduate school, someone had scratched the words "God was a tidy little concept" near the ceiling. Some days I looked up at those words and wondered if that was what I believed—that God was a tidy little concept human beings had put to work, for good or ill, in every age. Somehow Thomas Merton always figured into my internal debates. Although he did not solve the problem of God for me, he did something even better: he bore witness to a God who was not tidy but rather excessive, paradoxical, and creative, a God in whose image we are made, a God who continually offers us freedom, a God who is with us.

Just as the God I encountered in Merton was more challenging than any glibly confident answer to the question of God might be, so was Merton's understanding of what God asked of us. Merton's moral commitments—to nonviolence, to civil rights, to peace—were uncompromising. Like many of his devoted readers, I had turned to Thomas Merton to learn something about the contemplative life. And, like all of us, I learned that, for Merton, contemplation implicates us completely in the life of the world and the suffering of others. If contemplation awakens us to reality, then it will lead us, as it did him, more and more deeply into the life of the world. Merton taught us to mistrust the separation of contemplation and

5. Thomas Merton, *Raids on the Unspeakable.* New York: New Directions, 1964, p. 9.

action. In this, as in many things, Merton insisted on a third way, an integrated way, a way that asked much more of us than occupying a neatly-defined space.

These days, as a teacher myself, Merton continues to speak to my most pressing questions. Teaching in a divinity school where students and teachers from many religious traditions and none study alongside one another, working out our vocations, I find myself once again turning to Thomas Merton, especially the Merton who sought and cultivated friendships with people from many different traditions, to help me be a better teacher. For Merton, it was not enough to compare doctrinal and liturgical information in dialogues with other religious people. He wanted us to be able to talk with each other about "religious intuitions and truths which may turn out to have something in common."

The point of intersection that interested him the most was the mystical. Sharing beliefs was important to him, but even more important, as he wrote to his friend, Abdul Aziz, a Muslim civil servant in Pakistan, was sharing "the experience of divine light." His profound interest in how others experience the presence of the divine was the engine of his intellectual life, the reason for his travels to Asia, the lifeblood of his friendships. "We live in dreadful times," Merton wrote to Aziz in 1961, "and we must be brothers in prayer and worship no matter what may be the doctrinal differences that separate our minds."[6]

It is worth noting, in a book about Merton's influence on Protestants, that he regarded resistance to interreligious conversation about the mystical dimensions of our religious lives as born of "the characteristic 'Protestant' reaction to mysticism," our emphasis on the "prophetic" at the expense of the "contemplative."[7] The emphasis on the prophetic, of course, has born a great deal of fruit in interreligious dialogue, helping us focus on the work we can do together for the life of the world. But Merton, as always, urges us to integrate the prophetic and the contemplative. When I reread Merton these days, I am often trying to figure out how better to open space in my classroom for conversations that engage, with attention and

---

6. Thomas Merton, *The Hidden Ground of Love: The Letters of Thomas Merton on Religious Experience and Social Concerns*. New York: Farrar, Straus and Giroux, 2011, p. 49. Letter from May 13, 1961.

7. Thomas Merton, *Mystics and Zen Masters*. New York: Farrar, Straus and Giroux, 1967, p. 205. From essay on "Contemplation and Dialogue."

reverence, both our shared commitments to justice and the hidden, mystical aspects of our diverse religious lives.

Thomas Merton's influence on me has been, and continues to be, profound. In truth, it is difficult for me to separate it from the influence of others—my parents, my sister, my father's students and my own, Sister Mary Griffin, Sister Mary Ann, Father Matthew Kelty. But perhaps that is not surprising. To encounter Merton is to encounter a universe of others—writers he loved, people with whom he corresponded, the monks by whose side he worked out his vocation in fear and trembling, frustration and joy. To feel the influence of Thomas Merton is to feel the influence of many. It is to be invited into a living conversation that springs into motion, like the rabbits Merton once blessed, with every new voice that enters.

THE BROKEN SILENCES OF THOMAS MERTON

Stephen V. Sprinkle

Turning a flesh-and-blood human being such as Thomas Merton into words takes a considerable effort for a Protestant academic like me. I am not sure I am up to it. After all, reducing flesh-and-blood to thought is the original sin of my tribe. Merton surely deserves better than that. It takes closer witnesses than I, eyewitnesses, to do justice to his complexity and earthiness, though these are among the very qualities that continue to draw me to him. You see, I never knew the man, not in actual life. I knew people who knew Thomas Merton. That is as close as I ever got to Fr. Mary Louis.

As if the original sin of Protestants were not enough to turn Merton into "The Big Idea," consider how ironic it is to break silence about a Trappist contemplative monk. For all his books and correspondence, Merton remains surrounded by silence. Rumi, the Sufi mystic, is rumored to have said that everything beyond silence, especially when dealing with godly things, amounts to no more than bad translation. Yet, since the Pope of Rome has flung open the public conversation on Merton before the United States Congress and the whole world, then perhaps His Holiness's wayward children might dare enter the dialogue about this controversial monk at a considerably more modest level.

My first visit to the Abbey of Gethsemani was in the second semester of my freshman year in college, nearly three years after Merton's death. So, you might say that my relationship with Thomas Merton originated as more of a residual or literary experience than a full encounter. There was always something of a barrier between the two of us: of time, of absence, and yes, of imagination, too. My world at the foot of the Baptist-dominated Blue Ridge Mountains was far too small to have room for many Roman Catholics at all, much less cloistered ones. When my religion professor broached the idea of visiting a monastery in Kentucky with himself and a group of students, the notion amused me. The only monk I ever knew of previously was Friar Tuck, portrayed as a corpulent, comic foil to Robin Loxley in the television series, "The Adventures of Robin Hood." To say I had no frame of reference for monks and monasteries in those days is an understatement.

Whatever I expected on that first trip to Gethsemani was up-ended the moment we entered the Guesthouse. My prejudices gave way to curiosity, and by the time I had experienced the three days of our retreat, something new had awakened in my spirit. Though I did not possess the vocabulary for it yet, the experience of devotion I encountered with the Guestmaster, Fr. David Murphy, was at once disorienting and reorienting. The beauty of the Divine Offices brought me to tears—tears of awe and not inconsiderable consternation. Especially the office of Compline at the end of the day hit me in a primal way, outflanking my youthful bias against reverence for the Blessed Mother. Each day I wrote in my journal about my experiences as best I could with inadequate words. I could not explain nor reason away the impact of the strains of "Hail Holy Queen" on my soul, sung so earnestly in the echoing dark by these monks who had prefixed her name, Mary, to their own monastic names. What I encountered on that initial trip to Gethsemani was my first conscious tryst with the Divine Feminine along a track I naïvely believed I had discovered myself there in the Kentucky knob country, a well-worn path trod by many generations along the way, and bears fruit.

Something else equally fundamental was set in motion by Gethsemani. My conversion experience as a child in a revival meeting was challenged and deepened. My Protestant spiritual practices of Bible reading and occasional prayer, as well as my offering of myself as a theological student and candidate for ministry, were being re-formed by what I had seen, heard, and tasted in this new species of evangelic context previously unknown to me, which by then had already flourished for nearly a thousand years: Cistercian spirituality. I suppose that is what first drew me to Thomas Merton. He offered me a credible, contemporary interpretation of the monastic life through his writings and, beyond that, to the claims of faith upon my thought and action in the world.

I have read that many Catholics after World War II were drawn to monastic life by Merton's books. My experience was the opposite of theirs. I was attracted to Merton by the impact of the monastery. His books were a portable medium by which I could take something of Gethsemani with me, back to my college campus, and later on, to seminary and the parishes I served as an ordained Protestant minister. If pontifex means bridge building, then I suppose Merton became my pontiff, helping me bridge the psychic and literal distances between the world where I lived, moved, and had my being, and the Trappist world that welcomed me on retreat—worlds that became increasingly integrated in my search for wholeness of life.

Chiseled into the stone lintel above the cloister gateway leading to the professed monk's quarters is the chilly epigram, "God Alone." That stark, beseeching demand confronted me every time I exited the main Guesthouse doors, one part grace-filled summons and another part indictment. Merton, who had struggled to express his life as a contemplative in a world of action, became a chief interpreter of those words for my faith. The Trappist of Gethsemani broke open the once unimaginable monastic life for me. Merton, my adopted honest broker of faith and action, helped me to reconcile the demands of an active Protestant ministerial life with its myriad pressures to do everything acceptably or be deposed by the parishioners I served and the contemplative values of Christian spirituality I had discovered at the Abbey—a process that has never at any point been without some degree of turbulence. Merton's is the only photograph of a Christian heavy hitter I have in my study, a black and white head shot I scavenged from a secondhand book and framed. Wherever I go to live and work, he goes with me, in testimony, I suppose, to the role I have invited this troublesome monk to play in my life.

Whatever tension existed in my mind that oscillated between a brief personal flirtation with Catholicism and the anti-popish propaganda that was still robust in the South of my youth, eased pretty quickly thanks to the matter-of-fact atmosphere of welcome and absence of proselytizing pressure at the Abbey. Guests were received as Christ. That was plainly truthful as the simple food served up to all of us in the Guesthouse Refectory three times a day, or the quiet, kind acknowledgement of our presence as retreatants by the monks who passed us by morning and afternoon going to and from their work assignments.

Any romanticism I harbored about the monastic life passed away rather soon, too, as I came to understand that the rawness of human nature resides in the heart no matter what sort of monastic habit drapes over it. As I got to know new Guestmasters and other monks through the years, their compelling humanity no matter what monastic garment they wore, kept me mindful of how much everybody shares the stuff of life in all its complexities. Like the incident on the stairs to the church balcony, for example when Gethsemani's other author, ancient and fierce Fr. Raymond Flanagan, belayed me for resisting conversion, the only time any monk ever suggested in my presence that Protestants were defective in faith. Or the manic delight of Dom James Fox, a hermit by that time, at the bare feet of a teenaged retreatant in the Guesthouse, expressed with an enormous Cheshire-cat grin and a booming exclamation loud enough to shake up the whole hall, "Bare feet in the monastery! Bare feet in the monastery! What a rebellion hah, hah, hah. I'm something of a rebel around here myself!" Then to the young barefoot man, "I've been to Harvard Business School, do you hear me? Eh? I was going to be a millionaire! God put me on an elastic string and snapped me right back here! Now look at me! I don't even own my own clothes! Hah, hah, hah!"

According to more than one commentator, Merton had strong meat on the bone like that. He lived in friction with Dom James for decades, as Abbot Fox kept Merton on a short tether denying him a hermitage. Merton responded by mocking Dom James' reliance on cheese and fruitcakes to line the monastery coffers with money and by protesting his flinty authoritarianism. But they worked it out between them, hard as it was. Fox is remembered complimenting Merton as an obedient monk. I am such a professional sinner myself that outbreaks of obstinate human nature do not disturb my attraction for characters like Fox, Fr. Raymond, and Fr. Louis, Thomas Merton. Takes one to know one. Christianity is an incarnate faith, after all.

Once, longtime Guesthouse chaplain Fr. Matthew Kelty, told me, "The day I watched Merton leave on his Asian journey, I felt we would never see him again, and I said so, out loud. I said, 'There goes the best of us. We'll not see his like again.' And we haven't." Many of his former novices felt that way about him, taking for granted that a person who had such dissonant commitments with his monastic vocation, as an anti-war and civil rights opinion maker and a correspondent with religious and secular figures worldwide, could still keep the Rule of St. Benedict and conduct an exemplary contemplative life. Some monks, though, only knew him as Fr. Louis in the monastery. Once on a long walk in the monastery woods, I happened upon a small shelter built for a rotation of monks to take "hermit days" away from the community. I inadvertently barged in on this monk's solitude and became his noonday devil, a distraction from what he had disappeared into the woods to do. I asked him, "Did you happen to know Thomas Merton, Brother? "Who," he asked in reply, "You know, Thomas Merton the writer," I said. "Oh, Louis, You mean Louie," the monk shot back offhandedly. "Yeah, I knew him. We all did. I'll tell you this about him; he did okay with the little solitude God gave him."

The welcome of the Gethsemani community has kept me returning on retreat for better than thirty-five years now, customarily on the days between Christmas and New Year's Day when the pressures of parish leadership and academic life ease up a bit. That same hospitality drew me to other Trappist houses in the States: St. Joseph's in Massachusetts, Our Lady of Mepkin in South Carolina, and Holy Cross in the Shenandoah Valley of Virginia—but the knobs of Kentucky always beckon me back.

Merton's stock and trade was words, but the secret of his writing remains the silences between his words: the silences before words and after them, forming the power of his prose and poetry. In the hubbub of everyday life outside the monastery we want to fill all the spaces for silence with heaps of speech, and as we clatter away, we build our lives upon sand—like stacks of bricks with no mortar between them, no seams of quiet strength to hold them together against the furies and the corrosive boredom of living.

Merton understood that the word and silence combine to break open ordinary human language, to crack apart our petty human meanings, and let the light in and out. Merton broke the words like he broke the bread and thus let the possibility of God shine through. He was cunning like that, our Thomas, writing in an age of doubters. He understood that for God to get a hearing in this day and time, only broken language would do. Wordsmiths who ply broken-open words most effectively are broken people. Broken on the wheel of life. Broken by the bombs of war. Broken from emptiness of heart. If you are able to find love at all, it will have to be in amidst the ruins. Our Thomas carried that broken wisdom in the ache of his bones. It's all there for those who can read between the lines.

I remember a sunny afternoon at Gethsemani. I took a copy of *New Seeds of Contemplation* with me across Odo's Road, and then up the gravel trackway that led to the bronze statues of the sleeping disciples and the desolate Christ called "The Garden of

Gethsemani." I didn't make it that far, but settled down instead beneath a big tree by the side of the path to read from my book. For hours I read the essays, tasting the lucidity and clarity of them, soaking in the honesty of Merton's search for God and humanity. Then, the force of these words broke upon me like a wave:

> The ultimate perfection of the contemplative life is not a heaven of separate individuals, each one viewing his own private intuition of God; it is a sea of Love which flows through the One Body of all the elect, all the angels and saints, and their contemplation would be incomplete if it were not shared, or if it were shared with fewer souls, or with spirits capable of less vision and less joy.
>
> I will have more joy in heaven and in the contemplation of God if you are there to share it with me; and the more of us there will be to share it the greater will be the joy of all. For contemplation is not perfect unless it is shared.[1]

As I sat and read, the meanings multiplied as the common significations he used fractured and refracted into new possibilities. His reach exceeded his grasp with one upward sweep, one sharp dart of longing love, stretching to touch the hem of the mystery:

> The more we are alone with God the more we are with one another, in darkness, yet a multitude. And the more we go out to one another in work and activity and communication, according to the will and charity of God, the more we are multiplied in Him and yet we are in solitude.
>
> The more we are alone, the more we are together; and the more we are in society, the true society of charity, not of cities and crowds, the more we are alone with Him. For in my soul and in your soul I find the same Christ Who is in our life, and He finds Himself in our love, and together we all find Paradise which is the sharing of His love for His Father in the Person of Their Spirit.[2]

Even despite the passage of the years and the change in customs and gender consciousness usage and capitalization, Merton's message comes through to me undimmed, with refreshing grace and power. The core of true spirituality is mutuality and accountability,

1. *New Seeds of Contemplation*, p. 65. Personal Reflections.
2. *New Seeds*, p. 66.

human and divine. These are not parochial values, either Catholic or Protestant. They are touchstones of the unity which we all seek. These are the threshold steps of a true, holy dialogue among the whole human family. Though I returned to the Abbey that evening by the same route I traveled, I knew I had to be different now. I could no longer be the same.

In his address to the Joint Session of Congress on September 24, 2015, Pope Francis reintroduced Thomas Merton to the world as a man of prayer, a bridge builder among peoples and religions. Merton's explorations into Buddhism, Taoism, and Islam, had aroused opposition among fellow Catholics. His very existence as a cloistered monk had stirred up questions about his political and social relevance among non-Catholic Christians and secular activists. A complicated past cast a shadow across his monastery. Yet the Holy Father was undeterred by any of that. I was inspired to hear Merton lifted up by his Pope as an exemplar of openness to God and of dialogue across chasms of difference.

Pope Francis broke silence about Merton to commence a conversation with believers and non-believers alike. His books are appearing on store shelves again. His birth centennial is inspiring new editions of his most famous works, and given a renewed impetus to the publication of letters and essays that had not seen the light of day. Merton's literary corpus has grown more after his death than during his lifetime—a distinctive achievement for any writer, if not an unprecedented one. But no matter how many works of his are finally published, the silences around the man remain: the contemplative silences that invite us to converse with him and about things he lived for and loved. Good jazz. Belly laughs. A sharp eyed camera. The vocation of monastic communities in the modern world. Prophetic witness for justice. Peace.

Insofar as Thomas James Merton, a.k.a. Fr. M. Louis, OCSO, fulfills the hopes of Pope Francis and engenders a renewal of contemplative and dialogical values for Roman Catholicism, he will inevitably do the same for the rest of Christianity. On the sea of faith and doubt, all boats, as they say, rise together. Let us pray that Merton the diaologian—equal parts conversation partner, practitioner of prayer, and theologian—will continue to find his audience among the great and humble.

As for me, Merton has helped make a better Protestant out of me, a better lover of humankind in the name of Christ. At least that is my hope. His example is not singular at all really. He learned never to take himself that seriously. Rather, in my mind's eye, he stands silhouetted in the candlelit darkness among his brothers, facing forward toward an icon of the Queen of Heaven, written in Greco-Russian style by Brother Lavrans Nielsen. He sings to Her, and for me, and for us all in the beloved silence.

THOMAS MERTON AND ME: SIGNPOSTS ON A CONTINUING JOURNEY

Libby Falk Jones

March 2016

Today I'm walking in the woods with Thomas Merton. What does that mean? I don't exactly envisage him tromping along by my side in his old work clothes and boots, camera swinging from a sturdy strap around his neck. But I see through his eyes. I see the beauty of the rotting stump cradling dusty-brown leaves, the single yellow blossom in the middle of the path, the lines of trees and hazy mountains beyond. "Stop looking . . . and begin seeing!" his voice rings in my head. "Because looking means that you have something in mind for your eye to find . . . But seeing is being open and receptive to what comes to the eye." [1]

I'm not carrying my camera on this walk, but I'm making images in my mind. I stopped to see. The tunnel of rhododendrons and the sloping path up to the light. The sound of my feet through the leaves. The shape of rhododendron leaves downward from a bud, like a ballerina slowly twirling, always balanced. The way the light makes shadows on those leaves, a dance of light as I move slowly past.

Back home I open a Merton book at random and read, "To go out to walk silently in this wood—this is a more important and significant means to understanding, at the moment, than a lot of analysis and reporting on this 'of the spirit'" [2] How can Merton have read my mind?

November, 2003

On the Bellarmine campus during my sabbatical. I first see Mer-

1. Thomas Merton, *The Paradox of Place: Thomas Merton's Photography*, p. 20. Louisville, KY: Thomas Merton Center, 2003.

2. Thomas Merton, *When the Trees Say Nothing: Writings on Nature*, p. 163. Ed. Kathleen Deignan. Notre Dame: Sorin, 2003.

ton's photographs. In "The Paradox of Place: Thomas Merton's Photography," Paul Pearson has arranged a stunning display of images and writings.

I spend a long time in front of Merton's photos of the Buddha, reclining and standing.

I carry these images in my head all month, through the drive from Kentucky to Boston to help my son pack up for seven months' travel in Asia then back home to Kentucky as he departs on his journey. Merton's photographs infuse the poem I draft.

Blessings For My Younger Son

Yesterday, your father raking Japanese maple leaves
in our Kentucky yard, an Indian gentleman,
a stranger stopped at our walk,
blessed our garden Buddha in his own tongue,
insisting that your father, the Buddha's guardian,
place the statue higher, near the pool.
In Merton's photograph, the Buddha
claims our eyes, he lies on his side,
large and still, hand pillowing his head,
eyes open to inner world.

Like Merton,
you've left Kentucky's woods,
in a few hours you'll bury your cell phone,
squeeze your travel pillow into your carry-on,
board the bus for JFK and twenty hours through the air
to walk with those who bless
the Buddha daily. Wrap these blessings
around your grandfather's cuff link in your pack;
may you find wonder even as you sleep,
may you not cross over the mother's edge
as you carry your grandmother's name forward
may you become again the *newperson*
she called you. Know that on the other side
of your new world your father, mothers, brother
watch over your spirit alongside the Buddha
now atop our rock, smiling into air.[3]

---

3. Libby Falk Jones, *Above the Eastern Treetops, Blue*, "Blessings, for My Second Son," p.20. Georgetown, KY: Finishing Line, 2010.

March 2016

This morning I awaken with Merton. I see the patter of light and shadow through the white sailcloth curtain on the window. I walk onto my porch where a straightbacked chair with a woven seat catches the edge of the sun, casting a curved shadow onto the logged wall. I go for my camera to investigate the lines and textures and patterns. In my mind's eye, I see Merton's photograph of the wagon wheel standing against the tall wooden cross outside his hermitage. Daily he saw that wheel, really saw it. Saw its sameness and uniqueness. His camera helped him see. His writing helped me see.

I have sat in Merton's hermitage, have seen that wheel through the screen door. I've also seen the screen itself, curved, graceful merging of protection and filter. I've known the happiness that Merton felt in that space, a nameless happiness born out of silence, solitude, and seeing. "Lay in bed realizing that what I was, was happy" he writes in his journal.[4]

October 1993

Parker Palmer has come as a visiting professor for a year at Berea College, where I teach writing and direct faculty development. To help faculty better explore the vocation of teaching, Parker leads discussions of some Chuang Tzu poems, including "TheWoodcarver." Thus I become acquainted with the work of Thomas Merton, translator and scholar. I love Chuang Tzu's poems.

Later I will read Merton's Asian Journals and his essays in *Zen and the Bird of Appetite*. I will read that he called his camera "a Zen camera." Who is this Trappist monk who studied Eastern religions—whose mind and spirit ranged comfortably among many ways of thinking?

January 2011

In the Winter 2010 issues of *The Merton Seasonal*, I come across a poem about Merton's teaching, written by Brother Paul Quenon, himself an accomplished poet and photographer. Brother Paul was one of Merton's novices. He wrote a poem, "My Novices: Late 1950s."

---

4. *Trees*, p. 100.

Young men came
Looking for
—don't know what—
Left the place
Looking for
—don't know what—
Of these I had no regrets.

Some came, seemed like
    looking—
heard some talk about
    —what—
stayed a while
and left
talking like—Well,—
    like somewhat.

Serious young men came looking,
took up talk about
    —don't know what,
stayed long and left
talking
about everything what-not.

Some came completely
clear and sure about
    what—
Those I sent away.

Silent young men, a few,
came looking for
—don't know what—
    Stayed
and kept looking
stayed and never got to
    what—
wore out
died,
and never stopped looking for
    what—
For these I have no regrets.

All of these I loved, but
Seems the part I loved about them best
Was—
  don't know what—[5]

I've taught now for almost 50 years, and I like to think that, like Merton, I've learned some things. I can still see myself standing in front of my first college composition class in 1968, wearing bell bottom cords with an oxford cloth shirt, in my hand an index card with key questions—and expected answers—about *Othello*. Today, I approach writing and literature classes with a more open, relational mind concerned with students' questions as well as my own, with listening and learning from both talk and silence as we puzzle through important, sometimes strange, ideas and words.

Like Merton, I have pondered why my students come and what I have to give them. I have known and loved, in some fashion, all the different kinds of students Merton catalogues: those who leave after looking for "—don't know what—" or who leave "talking about everything/what-not," or who come incapable of learning because they are "completely/clear and sure about /—what." Like Merton I've known and especially valued those who come looking and stay, still looking who never stop looking "for—don't know what—." Merton's approach affirms the centrality of questions and the power of silence and presence in learning. Like him, I stand humble before what's finally the mystery of teaching and learning, all we don't know.

And Merton speaks to me as a teacher when he writes that sometimes he finds himself in his students. "I am grateful to my students," he writes in *A Search for Solitude*, "simply because . . . they are what they are."

O let me be always, with my students, like Merton: a seeker.

MARCH 2016

Photography, like life, is about mystery. "If you can't see more than is visible," writes photographer Ruth Berhard "you won't see anything." Merton sees the visible and invisible. He writes about seeing constellations at night, in his hermitage, then becoming able to see

5. Paul Quenon, *The Merton Seasonal: A Quarterly Review* 35, 4 (Winter 2010) "My Novices," pp. 28-29.

them in the daylight in his mind's eye, precisely where they should be. "The sun is rising in Aquarius and so I know that in the blue sky overhead the beautiful swan, invisible, spreads its wide wings over me," he writes in his journal. "A lovely thought, for some reason." Yes. I can think of the closing image in Gerard Manley Hopkins' "God's Grandeur," the Holy Spirit spreading its wings over the "bent earth." Comfort, protection—and an invitation to fly?

January 2013

My contemplative writing students walk with Merton. We are reading *Echoing the Silence,* a collection of excerpts from Merton's writing about writing. One student responds to Merton's ideas about the purpose of writing, about the ways a writer must examine her motives in writing: "The selection of writings of Thomas Merton really encouraged my thinking and examination of myself . . . ."

For Merton, the sacrifice of self is essential to writing. This is because he is not writing for himself . . . but to purify his motive through God so that what he writes, through the mortification of himself, is the reality and evidence of God dwelling in him.

This means a lot to me in my own life now. I feel I am going through something similar to what Merton went through when he was young, as I believe most do. Using a good goal as a façade for not truly giving to God what should be given. Using effort, false humility, and struggle to "repay" God for what he has done in my life and mask the fact that I have not surrendered what I should surrender. I am fearful that I may end up walking so many years on the ground when I could have flown simply because I am afraid of what would be required of me by surrendering myself to something greater. Yet, though I am afraid of what I must surrender, I am more afraid of what I will lose if I never surrender to God. As Merton said, I am all "mixed up in illusions and attachments."

January 2008

On retreat at Desert House of Prayer in Cortaro, Arizona, on the edge of Saguaro National Park. I check out from the library the final volume of Merton's journals. I type pages of quotations that speak to me. One passage is from Merton's writing in late June, 1968, the last year of his life. He was 53 years old:

> Thinking deeply of . . . my own need of discipline. What a fool I have been, in the literal and biblical sense of the word: thoughtless impulsive, lazy, self-interested yet alien to myself, untrue to myself, following the most stupid fantasies, guided by the most idiotic emotions and needs. Yes, I know, it is partly unavoidable. But I know too that in spite of all contradictions there is a center and a strength to which I *always* have access if I really desire it. And the grace to desire it is surely there.
>
> It would do no good to anyone if I just went around talking—no matter how articulately—in this condition. There is still so much to learn, so much deepening to be done so much to surrender. My real business is something far different from simply giving out words and ideas and "doing things"—even to help others. The best thing I can give to others is to liberate myself from the common delusions and be, for myself and for them, free. Then grace can work in and through me.[6]

When Merton died in December, 1968, I was 24 years old. In 2008, when I encountered these words in my simple retreat room in the Arizona desert, I was 64. No wonder I copied down this passage. How well Merton's reflections speak to who I am now. I used to think that age would bring wisdom, certainty, a settled-ness. Not only do I no longer think this, I no longer want it (well, certainty, at least; I still hope for wisdom). I know I am still, like Merton, a fool, but I know my center and I know I can reach it. Yes, there is, still, for me "much deepening to be done . . . for grace [to] work in and through me . . . "

MAY 2011

If Merton's life speaks to me, so too does his death.

On a visit to Gethsemani with my contemplative writing class, Brother Paul Quenon shares with us his poetry and his memories of his novice master Merton, known in the monastery as Father Louis. Later Brother Paul leads us out to Merton's hermitage, where we circle on the concrete porch to reflect on solitude, nature's beauty, and community.

That evening, as the class's retreat continues, I read some of

6. *The Other Side of the Mountain*, Volume 7, p. 135. Ed. by Patrick Hart. HarperSanFrancisco, 1998.

Merton's poems[7] and think about his life and death. In particular, I ponder the paradox of dying too soon but dying well. Among the fragments of Merton's words in my mind, a poem finds its way. I work on my first draft into a sonnet, the quintessential love poem. I share it with my students and, near the anniversary of Merton's death publish it in *The Merton Seasonal*, Winter 2014.

Swift Passings

It's good to go like Father Louis, fast;
for him no slow disintegrating ooze
of oil crushed. No, let waxen candle
flare, and there he is Andromeda,
his mind now light years deep. Did he feel
the shower's heat air unmoving, fecund,
in his soul's new land, did he seek
a breeze to blow him fresh like golden ginko
leaves across his Abbey garden's grass?
His fingers on the switch, a single pulse
into the light that seems to sing? "I think
I'm dying," my mother told the nurse who gripped
her hands and tried to call her back. O let
all pilgrims swiftly pass through the air alight.

"We who are poets know that the reason for a poem is not discovered until the poem itself exists," Merton writes.[8] Until I had drafted my poem, I didn't know that at its center would be my unresolved feelings about my mother's sudden death that had occurred 30 years before. Thank you, Thomas Merton, for indirectly leading me to understanding and a kind of peace.

February 2013

For me, this section was a climax: Merton's own reflection on life, and the questions he has sought answers for. His questions are deep and drive at the core of existence, from his own existence, life's meaning, what is evil and what is good, and such. As writers we have to learn to ask the right questions in our lives and in our writing. Every piece of writing will have a core, something that

7. Thomas Merton, *Selected Poems*. Enlarged Edition. New York: New Directions, 1967.

8. Thomas Merton, *Echoing Silence*. Boston: New Seeds, 2007, p. 94.

brings it to life, a question that it seeks to answer, a theme that may repeat itself through most of your work; however, these questions will not help you produce your writing but through your writing you will find answers you did not know you knew. Asking about life and love and truth is part of the journey Merton took and part of the writers' journey we all must take.

MARCH 2016

In publishing Merton's photographs in 1979 in *A Hidden Wholeness*, John Howard Griffin, noted photographer and Merton's friend, says that he selected images Merton himself marked as "coming the closest to what he hoped to convey through the visual image."[9] Griffin goes on to note that these images tell us who Merton was: a person tough and sensitive, a love of nature, silence, solitude, an artist pursuing a contemplative vision. Griffin describes that vision: "Merton held that it was not so much what you did that counted, but what you allowed to be done to yourself. He worked for photographic images which, when viewed without haste or pressure, might accomplish the slow work of communicating 'a hidden wholeness.'"

I too believe that we are defined by the things we love, the art we make, the calling we respond to. Knowing Merton's photographs and writing, seeing through Merton's eyes and mind, helps me to understand what sounds deepest in my own soul.

I also love Griffin's photographs of Merton and his camera. Sometimes Merton has an impish grin, sometimes a thoughtful, listening slant to his head; once a triumphant smile. The camera is cradled carefully in his hand or swings easily along his body as he walks.

In many of Merton's photographs I see that he has captured emptiness, the spaces between the spokes of the wheel, snow broken by only a few feathery weeds. Like Hopkins, Merton loved what is counter, original, spare, strange. Where presence dominates, the subject is usually the ordinary often overlooked: texture of bark, carpet of fallen leaves, peeling paint, buckets and ladders.

APRIL 2013

A third contemplative writing student pursues Merton's journey

9. John Howard Griffin, *A Hidden Wholeness.* Boston: Houghton Mifflin Company, 1970, p. 5.

through photography and poetry. In Paul Pearson's catalogue, *A Hidden Wholeness: The Zen Photography of Thomas Merton* (November 2004), she encounters Merton's comments on the paradoxes of a mountain—in this case, Mount Kanchenjunga, in Darjeeling—as something seen and not seen. His insights provoke her imagination and understanding. She writes:

> I can understand what Merton was saying in his discussion of the mountain: it exists and it doesn't. From close up, a mountain is not a full mountain, one can't see its entirety. But from a distance, a mountain no longer exists, either, because it has become intangible. From far away, one can see the entirety of the mountain, but one is now so far away, it is impossible to consider experiencing the mountain any other way but by sight. The paradox is that the mountain is still there: it exists as a physical structure, but as a tangible reality it does not. I found myself while looking at the mountain imagining it as the ocean, its trees as a sea of hands waving at me, their branches masses of tangled hair on a lumpy head. It took a while for any imagination to settle around the concept of the mountain as a mountain, but when I did, I was able to see myself in relation to the mountain and felt surprisingly at peace.

March 2016

Drafting this essay, I re-read Merton's advice to young, aspiring writers:

> 1. Never write down to anyone.
> 2. Never write simply what you think they want.
> 3. Write rather what is deepest in your own heart and what you know . . . is also deep in theirs.[10]

I know that, as I work to deepen my ways of being in the world, my ways of seeing the world's beauty and mystery, my ways of working with word and image, I will continue to walk with Merton.

---

10. *Echoing Silence: Thomas Merton on the Vocation of Writing*. Ed. by Robert Inchausti. Boston: New Seeds, 2007, p. 202.

TWO GIFTS FROM THOMAS MERTON

Brian L. Cole

Thomas Merton died on December 10, 1968. I was born on December 7, 1967.

My father, Bruce, died on February 12, 1990. I made my first visit to Gethsemani during the summer of 1991 and purchased a copy of *The Thomas Merton Reader*, the green paperback version, shortly after that time there.

I grew up in Missouri in a very conservative Southern Baptist congregation. Almost everyone I knew was some kind of Baptist. The exceptions were either Methodist or Church of Christ. We were always worried about the condition of their souls.

Our worry for their souls, however, was nothing compared to the ongoing concern about our own. Was I really saved? We would have two revivals a year, one in the spring, one in the autumn. The evangelist in the spring would get us all saved and rededicated. Then the evangelist in the autumn would ask us to consider whether it had all been an act, not truly heartfelt and real. So, we would get saved again. It was an exhausting way to live.

Today I am an Episcopal priest, serving a parish in Lexington, Kentucky, roughly 70 miles from the Abbey of Gethsemani. When I try to make sense of how I ended up here, miles from home, both geographically and spiritually, I always come back to discovering Thomas Merton when I was a young Baptist seminarian in my early 20s.

I have now known of Merton and read him consistently for 25 years. No other Christian writer/theologian has shaped me more.

I am aware that Thomas Merton entered my life shortly after the death of my father who, like Merton, died while still in his 50s. In the aftermath of my grief, I can now see that I was a young man searching for the next father, the next mentor, a guide to make sense of a world where I was far from what I had known, but not certain as to what was ahead for me, or even all that clear about where I stood at that moment.

When I try to get at the essence of why Thomas Merton looms so large in my spiritual landscape, I come back to Silence and Conversation. Merton introduced me to the importance of silence, both as a human and as a Christian. From that center of grounded silence, I grew to appreciate that Merton then had the courage to converse with *everyone*.

Before that trip to Gethsemani on a blazing hot summer day, my complete understanding of the Christian life was filled with sound, with noise, with, at the very least, background music. The presence of silence, of no sound, had no place in my life.

Before visiting Gethsemani, I might have told you that silence showed a kind of emotional absence. In my youthful upbringing, we were instructed on how to be prepared to give our personal testimony in under three minutes, as if we were seated next to someone about to board an airplane. I had never boarded an airplane in my life. But, I was ready, I thought, to give a witness, to fill those three minutes with words about Jesus. I now realize the unwitting stranger probably would have welcomed the silence, and probably benefited from it more.

In a world given to filling spaces with sound, the presence of actual silence, intentional silence, was simply too loud for me when I first encountered the Trappist monks and Merton. Along with needing to be prepared at a moment's notice to give a witness, my life, at that point, had been completely outward-focused, seeking out the next friend, the next group to join, the next activity to fill up a schedule so I did not have to sit alone in my room, by myself. Merton said:

> We do not go into the desert to escape people but to learn how to find them; we do not leave them in order to have nothing more to do with them, but to find out a way to do them the most good. But this is only a secondary end. The one end that includes all others is the love of God.[1]

In other words, silence was not something simply for introverts. Seeking a time of silence and solitude was not an anti-social act. Rather, for Merton, and for those who would find wisdom from him, it was essential for being in right relationship with self, others, and God.

Before I read Thomas Merton, silence was not something I

1. *New Seeds of Contemplation*, p. 82.

understood as holy or something to seek. If pressed, I would have thought of silence as what happens toward the end of our twice a month visits to my grandparents in northeast Arkansas. After Sunday lunch and an initial burst of conversation and reveling in old family members, we would retire to the living room. There we would sit, all gazing out a picture window, until the words gave out, the awkward silence arrived, and we waited for my father finally to say we needed to get back, wishing, somehow, we could stay longer.

Before reading Thomas Merton, I believed the religious life required words and sound and song. Merton's writings on silence encouraged me to consider how other Christians consider silence. Only after Merton did I come to know the Quakers and their unprogrammed tradition of gathering for worship in silence, waiting for the Divine Spirit to lead a participant to speak. If speech came, it would come from silence. Like Merton, the Quakers treated silence as the ground, the beginning place for words, if necessary to emerge.

I continue to draw wisdom from Merton's writings on silence because the world we now inhabit is even louder, with more sound coming from more places. Years ago, I heard Father Berrigan speak of contemplation as a countercultural act in a world filled with noise. With each passing year, his words become even truer.

Merton's understanding is that we go to the desert in order to return from the desert to be in relationship with self and others, ultimately seeking to rest in God's love that keeps the practice of silence from turning selfish and sectarian. In discovering silence, I now recall feeling smug in comparison to all those noisy Protestants.

Smugness, however, was not the goal. The goal was to find a place of love, for me, for others, especially the noisy Protestants, and to trust that love was God's native land.

A recent documentary by Morgan Atkinson on Merton (*The Many Storeys and Last Days of Thomas Merton*) includes the quotation that "silence is God's language; all else is poor translation." The quote has been attributed to Rumi and to St. John of the Cross. The spirit behind the saying helps us locate silence as a core value in the story of God. Silence is not the minority report. Thomas Merton helped me see again the story of the Bible, of Jesus, of God's presence as properly understood only if I could live with silence sitting in my own room, at rest.

It seems from a reading of Thomas Merton's life that when he was not in prayer, sitting in silence, he was in some kind of conversation, either in person with pilgrims to the monastery, or more often with letter writers. From a rural setting in central Kentucky, located in the deeply Catholic place of a Trappist monastery, Merton conversed and read widely.

Prior to encountering Merton, I had known a religious life insulated with a carefully prescribed list of the right kinds of books to read, the right kinds of movies to watch, the right kinds of people to know. In attempting to check out a copy of *The Grapes of Wrath* from my high school library, I was encouraged to reconsider my choice by the librarian, a member of my local Southern Baptist congregation, since "there were *words* in that book."

Merton, however, appeared to have crossed the rigid boundaries of my pious youth. For every letter from Dorothy Day there was also one from Henry Miller. For every reflection on a canticle, Merton also wrote to young people about his preference for the Beatles and jazz. Whether intended or not, I had approached life before the trip to Gethsemani by believing when in doubt, be afraid. Merton turned that idea on its head in *New Seeds of Contemplation*:

> You cannot be a man of faith unless you know how to doubt. You cannot believe in God unless you are capable of questioning the authority of prejudice even though that prejudice may seem to be religious. Faith is not blind conformity to a prejudice—a "prejudgment." It is a decision, a judgment that is fully and deliberately taken in the light of truth that cannot be proven. It is not merely the acceptance of a decision that has been made by somebody else.[2]

For Merton, because he was in Christ, because he was seeking to rest in his true self, encountering the stranger did not have to be a frightening event, something to avoid. Rather, the stranger could be the source of new wisdom, or at the very least, a means to clarify the wisdom already in him. Merton famously spoke of going to Asia, in the final year of his life, as a pilgrim. If God is perfect love, then we do not have to be afraid. We know that from scripture because of the letters of St. John. I was now learning it from a contemporary pilgrim in Merton.

Just as Merton's words on contemplation gave me the ability to appreciate the Quakers and their deep commitment to silence, so I found several new conversation "partners" by reading Merton

2. *New Seeds*, p. 107.

and discovering how widely he read in his personal library. My own travels to India were partly inspired by Merton's interest in the East. Upon arriving there, I quickly realized how small my story of Jesus was and that the East could teach me much about the Christ I thought I knew. I am a more faithful follower of Jesus because I traveled to India, well outside my comfort zone. I would not have traveled to India if I had never gone to Gethsemani. Merton:

> If I can unite in myself the thought and devotion of Eastern and Western Christendom, the Greek and the Latin Fathers, the Russians with the Spanish mystics, I can prepare in myself the reunion of Christians. From that secret and unspoken unity in myself can eventually come a visible and manifest unity of all Christians. If we want to bring together what is divided, we cannot do so by imposing the one division upon the other or absorbing one division into the other. But if we do this, the union is not Christian. It is political, and doomed to further conflict. We must contain all divided worlds into ourselves and transcend them in Christ.[3]

Along with lessons on silence and conversation, I have come to admire the deeper wisdom from Merton that we need to seek wholeness, integration. If I learn to make room for silence in my life, it is no good if I then make caricatures of those Baptists back home, who, though imperfectly, did their best to love me.

Like Merton standing at the corner of Fourth and Walnut in downtown Louisville, we all need to wake up to an epiphany, to the dream, hopefully someday realized, that we love each other, that we need each other. Merton did not make me a monk, a converted Catholic in the Roman Catholic sense. He made me a better Protestant, a better pilgrim in seeking wholeness.

With Merton as a guide from the past, I go forward, realizing that our best attempts to name this wholeness fall short. On the other side of Merton's conversational life, silence returns to him, to us, to all. This is not the awkward silence of Arkansas Sunday afternoons. This is the Silence, the "sound" of Easter, the sacramental place where the hope we have in Christ holds all things spoken and unspoken.

Thomas Merton, as a young man heading to the Abbey in 1941,

3. *Conjectures of a Guilty Bystander*, p. 12.

was eager to trade New York City for Gethsemani. In his youthful vigor he was trading one story for another. Two decades later, the Merton of the mid-1960s knew that that call was not to seek one preferred story over another, as much as he was called to live in a wider story, in God's story.

My father, who died young at 59, has now been dead more years than I knew him. When I dream about him now, he is no longer stricken with cancer. He is healthy, younger, probably my age now in my dreamscape of him. If we were to speak, how could I possibly explain to him who I am, how I have changed, what has become of his son? I would not know what to say, how to begin with words.

Rather, I believe I would ask him to drive with me 70 miles from here, to a place where we would not need to speak in order to understand each other, and to love each other.

Thomas Merton taught me that.

THOMAS MERTON: THE STAMP OF GRACE

Bill J. Leonard

On March 20, 1947, Thomas Merton wrote from the Abbey of Gethsemani:

> So yesterday I made my solemn vows. I do not feel much like writing about it. This does not mean that I am not happy about profession [of monastic vows]. But I am happy in a way that does not want to talk. One thing I will say: that *the stamp of grace* is on the memory of yesterday. And by that I mean that I am left with a deep sense of deep union with all the other monks. I do not know what I expected to feel after my profession, But afterwards I was left with a profoundly clean conviction that I have done the right thing and that I have given myself as best I could to God.[1]

Merton set those words into his monastic journal on the day my Texas born and bred family celebrated my first birthday in this world. Almost seventy years later, Thomas Merton has placed a profound *stamp of grace* on my own memory, not because I knew him personally, but because his writings have contributed extensively to my own spiritual formation. It took a while.

Growing up in Baptist-infested Texas, I didn't know a lot of Catholics. In fact, Pauline Gidley, one of my mother's coworkers, was often referred to as "our Catholic friend," largely because she was the only one we had. In those years, when a Baptist married a Catholic it was like a death in both families. When John F. Kennedy ran for president in 1960, many Texas Baptists believed that Catholics were religiously unqualified to become the nation's chief executive. I've thought of that often with polls suggesting that a

1. Thomas Merton, *The Sign of Jonas* in *A Thomas Merton Reader*. Garden City, NY: Image Books, revised edition 1974, pp. 39-40. Portions of this essay appear in Bill J. Leonard "Thomas Merton: Spiritual Identity and Religious Dialogue: The Walls of New Freedom," in *Perspectives in Religious Studies*, Summer 2011, pp. 195-214.

current generation of Americans feel similarly about Muslim or Mormon candidates.

During my undergraduate studies at Texas Wesleyan College (now University), Merton (*The Seven Storey Mountain)* showed up on my academic radar along with Catholics Teilhard de Chardin (*The Divine Milieu)* and Michael Quoist (*Prayers*). But I discovered him really in Louisville, almost a decade after I joined the faculty of the Southern Baptist Theological Seminary. My senior colleagues, Glenn Hinson and Dale Moody, knew him reasonably well, having taken Baptist students to Gethsemani in the halcyon days after Vatican Council II when we were all so hopeful about Catholic-Protestant "dialogue." Early in my tenure in Louisville I also met Father Clyde Crews, a professor at Bellarmine University, scholar of Kentucky Catholics "Holy Land" and began a close friendship that endures to this day. It was Clyde who took me to Gethsemani in assorted Advent seasons, and got us hosted inside the monastery, rising at 2:00 A.M. to fight the forces of darkness, keeping vigil and shivering with the Trappists in the stone-cold Abbey church.

It was Clyde who got our friend Brian Cole and me to a Trappist funeral where, on a steamy summer afternoon, we watched them lower the body of an ancient monk, unembalmed and uncoffined ten feet below ground as the Abbot read the burial liturgy: "When we came into this world we brought nothing with us and when we leave this world we take nothing away," and I confronted mortality as never before. It was Clyde who gave me two copies of *A Merton Reader*, fostering a tradition of taking one of these volumes with me every time I leave the country reading pieces of Merton's collective works in settings from Viet Nam to Israel.

Those memories carry me as close to Thomas Merton as I guess I can get in this world, even as Merton's writings have carried me closer to the *stamp of grace* than I could ever have imagined. This Merton retrospective is offered not by a Merton scholar but by a faithful Merton student and "guilty bystander."

The *stamp of grace*—God's gracious favor—is, Merton insisted, the presence of Christ within individuals. He wrote, "For Christianity is not a doctrine or a system of beliefs, it is Christ living in us and uniting [us]to one another in His own Life and unity." The *stamp of grace* also reflects a strange paradox, for Merton as it turned out, and perhaps for us as well. In reflecting on our collective journey, I wondered if we might revisit Merton and grace at this moment in American history. Can the work of a Trappist monk, dead for almost half a century, continue to inform and form? Can his response to questions of peace and war, born of our Viet Nam incursion, help us address war as a constancy in American life? Does his approach to something now called "spirituality" have any implications for a society where one in five adults often refer to themselves as "spiritual but not religious?" Is Merton still a viable guide in the quest for the *stamp of grace*?

In the monastery, Merton discovered an environment—*a stamp of grace*—in which he could pray, read, reflect, and most of all, write. And could he write. Even today his books fill the trade stores and Amazon.com. Paradoxically, however, Merton's compulsion to write was at times a terrible warfare, within himself and with his monastic superiors. On one hand he was a contemplative writing, "God has put me in a place where I can spend hour after hour, each day, in occupations that are always on the borderline of prayer. There is always a chance to step over the line and enter into simple and contemplative union with God."[2] Yet he was quick to acknowledge, "This morning before the Blessed Sacrament it seemed to me that these vows will mean the renunciation of the pure contemplative life. If Jesus wants me to be here at Gethsemani, as my Superiors insist He does, then perhaps He does not want me to be a pure contemplative after all."[3]

Trappists were to lose themselves in community and contemplation, not distinguish themselves in the world. Merton struggled with the tension between writing, thinking, praying, and living in community. Was writing a calling or a distraction from his real monastic vocation? He suggests that tension incessantly, as in this comment, "As soon as I get into a cell by myself I am a different person! Prayer becomes what it ought to be. Everything is quiet . . . . Plenty of time. No manuscripts, no typewriters, no rushing back and forth to church, no Scriptorium, no breaking your neck to get things done before the next thing happens."[4]

His abbots, particularly Dom James Fox, pressed him hard about the relationship between his literary work, his growing obsession with solitude, and his commitment to his monastic community. It was a struggle that led him to move from Novice Master to hermit

2. *Merton Reader*, p. 31.
3. *Merton Reader*, p. 33
4. *Merton Reader*, pp. 187-188.

even as his fame seemed to explode with each new publication.

Almost fifty years after his death, Merton's works continue to mentor writers and other artists challenging them to claim and explore the grace of art and contemplation. He wrote that true artists did not need "an ideal of freedom," but "freedom from the internalized pressures by which society holds" the artist down. This, he said, was the "freedom of conscience."[5] Thus he concluded, "In the last analysis, the only valid witness to the artist's creative freedom is his or her work itself. Artists build their freedom and form their own artistic consciences by the work of their hands. Only when the work is finished can they tell whether or not it was done "freely."[6] The first *stamp of grace* for Merton's monastic experience seems to be the grace to nurture contemplation while also writing prose and poetry.

Another *stamp of grace* came from the community. Merton asks himself and those who read him, "Do we, can we, nurture community and let community nurture us?" Much of Thomas Merton's early writing involves his celebration of and struggle with the nature of community in a monastic environment. In fact, he calls it a "furnace of ambivalence which nobody in the monastery can fully account for and which is designed, I think, to serve as a sign and a portent to modern America."[7] "A furnace of ambivalence" is a great term for community whether found in a monastery, a church, a family (especially a family), or the world at large. Merton writes with honesty about the difficulties of his early experiences in relating to a monastic community:

> In the Scriptorium you find a book in the Common Box that begins to interest you intensely; and then someone else gets interested in it too, and every time you want it you find that he has got there first. Out at work you may be put to work to saw a log with someone who just puts his head down and closes his eyes in prayer and doesn't care how he pulls his end of the saw, so that it continually jams in the log and you have to do five times as much work as usual, with practically no result. All this becomes more interesting when it happens that the same person is the one

5. *Raids on the Unspeakable*, pp. 126-127.
6. *Raids on the Unspeakable,* p. 135.
7. *Merton Reader*, p. 138.

> who coughs down your neck in choir, and takes the book you want in the Scriptorium, and fails to get your portion [of potatoes] for you at the table . . . .[8]

Christian community, monastic or otherwise, is messy, cumbersome and sometimes ornery—its own theological and ecclesial "furnace of ambivalence." From the beginning of his monastic journey, Merton celebrated and refined his experience of communal life concerned less about the personality clashes and the quirkiness of a bunch of men living together in almost total silence, than in the way in which communal responsibilities—work and prayer—kept him from his burning desire for solitude and contemplation. In *The Sign of Jonas* he complains about all his communal responsibilities, duties and tasks, writing:

> To belong to God I have to belong to myself. I have to be alone—at least interiorly alone. This means the constant renewal of a decision. I cannot belong to people. None of me belongs to anybody but God. Absolute loneliness of the imagination, the memory, the will.[9]

It was that commitment to "absolute loneliness of the imagination" that ultimately sent him to the cinder block hermitage, not because of an excessive individualism but in search of solitude.

Yet even in the hermitage he was never geographically and spiritually far from the community. Indeed, he summed it up for them and for us, when he wrote, "In fact, so marked is the importance given to [communal] brotherly love in our monastic ideal that it occupies a crucial position in the structure of Cistercian mystical theology. The ascent of the individual soul to personal mystical union with God is made to depend, in our life, upon the ability to love one another."[10]

There is a third aspect of *the stamp of grace* involving spirituality and solitude. For Merton, and perhaps for us, the spirituality of personal and communal pilgrimage remains rather dangerous, because he was and we are forced to confront the meaning of the ideas we encounter in biblical texts (where will the text take you?); in

8. Thomas Merton, Unpublished from the original manuscript of *The Seven Storey Mountain* in *A Thomas Merton Reader*, p. 146.

9. *Merton Reader*, p. 202.

10. Unpublished from the original manuscript of *The Seven Storey Mountain* in *Merton Reader,* pp. 145-146.

history (what is the context of your faith?); theology (what concepts keep you awake at night?); and ethics (where will your conscience take you?). And, through it all, we may ask with Merton, where and what is the Presence of God? On spiritual pilgrimage then and now we confront *hierophany,* those moments when the Sacred appears in the ordinary. Merton writes, and writes, and writes about such hierophany in these words from *The Sign of Jonas*:

> God, my God, God whom I meet in darkness with You it is always the same thing! Always the same question that nobody knows how to answer! I have prayed to You in the daytime with thoughts and reasons, and in the nighttime You have confronted me, scattering thought and reason. I have come to you in the morning with light and desire, and You have descended upon me, with great gentleness, with most forbearing silence, in this inexplicable night, dispersing light, defeating all desire. I have explained to You a hundred times my motives for entering the monastery and you have listened and said nothing, and I have turned away and wept with shame. Is it true that all my motives have meant nothing? Is it true that all my desires were an illusion? While I am asking questions which you do not answer, You ask me a question which is so simple that I cannot answer. I do not even understand the question.[11]

Merton never really tells us what the great question is, but reading him pushes us from the rational to the non-rational, from left brain to right brain and back again, from objectivity to vulnerability. Indeed, the depth of his spiritual insights is probably the most important element in Merton's continuing influence and impact as we move further into the 21st century.

His extensive literary corpus offers guidance in meditation, contemplation, self-examination, and spiritual discipline for individuals inside and outside the Church, Catholic or Protestant. Ironically, he now represents certain monastic ideals at a time when almost no one (at least in the West) wants to become a monk.

To read Merton is to be captivated by his use of words, his spiritual insights, and his quest for the mysteries of life and death, grace and love. Sometimes his essays are so incredibly profound that you return to them again and again. Sometimes his ideas are

11. *Merton Reader*, p. 213

so obscure, convoluted or frightening that you revisit them at your peril. In certain works he seems far too Catholic for many moderns, in others he may not appear Catholic enough, even too secular for some readers. Sometimes I read him and have no idea what he is talking about—his poetry affects me that way in particular—but often I return months, or even years later, and something clicks. I've changed; he hasn't, it would seem. The *stamp of grace* carried Thomas Merton, and now his readers, into an ever broadening spirituality amid moments of unanticipated hierophany.

The fourth element of Merton's approach to grace is relatively easy to articulate but often costly, even dangerous, to fulfill. It is grounded in what I would call gospel worldliness, a willingness to take spirituality into the world and do something about it. Thomas Merton channeled the natural worldliness that sent him tumbling from New York night clubs to a Kentucky monastery into a worldliness that looked beyond the monastic walls to the struggles of human beings worldwide. We discover that gospel worldliness in his response to the civil rights and peace movements, the Vietnam War, and ecclesiastical renewal through Vatican II, as well as in the passion for interfaith dialogue that took him to Bangkok in pursuit of shared spirituality with the Buddhists. In *New Seeds of Contemplation,* Merton wrote of the worldliness of prayer:

> I do not mean to imply that prayer excludes the simultaneous use of ordinary human means to accomplish a naturally good and justifiable end . . . . In fact, a believer should normally do both. And there would seem to be a reasonable and right proportion between the use of these two means [praying and acting] to the same end.[12]

Then, in words that seem frighteningly contemporary, he noted:

> When I pray for peace I pray God to pacify not only the Russians and Chinese but above all my own nation and myself. When I pray for peace, I pray to be protected not only from the Reds but also from the folly and blindness of my own country. When I pray for peace, I pray not only that the enemies of my country may cease to want war, but above all that my own country will cease to do the things

12. *Merton Reader*, p. 280.

> that make war inevitable.[13]

Lest you think this is mere sentimentality, remember that so outspoken was Merton about our Viet Nam incursion, that when he died in Bangkok, it took a long time to put to rest the rumor that our own CIA or another intelligence agency might have had a hand in this death.

While Merton calls for radical social action against racism, war, and poverty, his worldliness is always centered in the gospel as the ultimate source of personal and social renewal. In an essay on "Mysticism in the Nuclear Age" he declared:

> If the salvation of our society depends, in the long run, on the moral and spiritual health of individuals, the subject of contemplation becomes a vastly important one, since contemplation is one of the indications of spiritual maturity. It is closely allied to sanctity. You cannot save the world merely with a system. You cannot have peace without charity. You cannot have social order without saints, mystics, and prophets.[14]

The world, Merton insisted, is "Christ-haunted," to use a Flannery O'Conner phrase, noting in words that sum up the heart of his gospel worldliness:

> Into this world, this demented inn, in which there is absolutely no room for Him at all. Christ has come uninvited. But because He cannot be at home in it, because he is out of place in it, and yet he must be in it, His place is with those who do not belong, who are rejected by power because they are regarded as weak, . . . tortured, exterminated. With those for whom there is no room, Christ is present in this world.[15]

From his early, best-selling autobiography, *The Seven Storey Mountain* to his final thoughts in *The Asian Journal*, Merton's life is in full review, ever a struggle with sin and salvation, doubt and celebration. What draws us back to Merton, years after his death, is his haunting ability to unite the spiritual and the worldly, the inner

13. *Merton Reader*, p. 281.
14. *Merton Reader*, p. 375.
15. *Raids on the Unspeakable*, pp. 51-52.

and outer life with wondrous prose and occasional poetry. Through it all, there is the Christ, haunting Merton to the end. Which brings us back to the "Fire Watch" and Merton's own response to the question, "Will it come like this, the moment of my death?" And his "answer" moves prophetically from Gethsemani to Bangkok and all our futures:

> There is greater comfort in the substance of silence than in the answer to a question. Eternity is in the present. Eternity is in the palm of the hand. Eternity is a seed of fire, whose sudden roots break barriers that keep my heart from being an abyss. The things of Time are in connivance with eternity.[16]

---

16. *Merton Reader*, p. 221.

HEART TO HEART

Gary Hall

A gathering of Catholic missioners had invited me to lead a study day with Merton at its heart. Pope Francis had not yet hailed Merton as a beacon for our turbulent times, but the fresh breeze of his peculiarly Franciscan Jesuitry carried the fragrance of a little springtime. The day together was laced with inspiring reminiscence and rich reflection, plenty of jesting and strong bonds of mutuality, all flowing together in an easy blend of lightness and seriousness. Fine fellowship, as we used to call it. With a room full of priests, the day naturally culminated in the Mass. As the only person in the room with no formal Catholic credentials, I discreetly stepped away as the bread and wine were about to be shared in order to avoid any awkwardness for worshippers, or celebrant in particular. He was having none of it. "You're one of us, aren't you?" Of course I was, and am. But thank God for those with the grace to risk saying as much, and acting accordingly.

The memory surfaced when I was invited to write this personal reflection on reading Merton, for a book on Thomas Merton and Protestants. Grateful to be asked, I was at the same time troubled by the "protestant" part of the equation. I don't tend to think of myself under that category until situations like the Mass remind me, and I had to stop and think about how it might influence my reading of Merton. I'm still thinking about it, as may be all too apparent. For sure, I am a Presbyter of the British Methodist Church, and gladly so, but by all accounts an accidental Methodist, due in no small part to circumstances and the strength of my Methodist mother over my Baptist father. The Methodist people were my people in a family way before I had a clue about what it meant to be Christian, let alone Methodist. Perhaps this is a typical way of things. A more nuanced sense of religious identity evolved over time, but any experience of being "this not that" or "one of us not them" was rarely defined in terms of simple Catholic/Protestant dualism. There were people with whom I shared perspectives, moods, commitments, tastes, passions, and so on, and the need to think systematically about denominational identity tended to be imposed by external pressures from those for whom exclusion and control seemed to matter more than, say, love and or service. That's how I remember it anyway. In due course I discovered the riches of the legacy of the Methodist revolution (and that term will still cause a stir), which was like finding a suitcase full of letters and diaries of the ancestors in the attic, where a younger self was not only glad to leave it, but hardly noticed it was there.

As for the day with the Catholic missioners, I didn't know whether to mention it. I don't want anyone to be in trouble or offended. Other episodes with Catholic friends and colleagues I keep under my hat, because we learn to edit or censor ourselves, treading cautiously, if ignorantly, around assumed ecclesial sensibilities. Too much delicacy or misplaced deference perhaps; until, now and then, clarity is restored and we know how it feels to be amongst people with whom we belong.

It's not a matter of sitting lightly to church order, or dishonouring the carriers and upholders of inherited traditions. It's more about experiencing enough moments when we recognize what living traditions actually *are* and what they do. Neither does our unapproved communion imply a careless disregard for the often-painful complexity of our tangled histories. To be intentionally committed to Church does not imply an acceptance of our belonging to that long and fractured story, acknowledging that we are from the same gene pool as any dysfunctional ancestors or cousins we happen upon during those pivotal episodes of our lives when identity or relations become especially interesting to us.

To talk of accepting this fractured reality does not mean either approving or justifying any of it, but simply means a willingness not to reject that we are related, interconnected, more profoundly than I can imagine. Whatever stories I happen to have heard about Church can hardly do justice to the vast array of human interactions which make us who we are. We seem to make sense of who we are (and who we are not) as followers of Christ by weaving patterns out of the most prominent stories, themes, and habits which have currency amongst the Christian people with whom we identify. Which is fine; there is always more, another perspective, an unheard voice. We are held within particular manifestations of church and, if pressed, we might describe these as more valid or authentic or faithful than contrasting versions. This is understandable enough. I am instantly aware when I come across, say, Joseph Kony's version of the Lord's Resistance army, that I carry criteria by which I judge what it means to carry the name of Christ. There are aspects of the bigger picture we prefer to sweep under the carpet or lock securely into a closet. In between are historical agreements, theological debate and talks in high places, and degrees of dispute about acceptable behavior or ways of believing. Then there are relationships between people who continually work at understanding and loving one another, perhaps because they recognize a family resemblance, or are simply responding to the relentless love of God.

All of the above is a kind of preamble, musings on the question about what might be a peculiarly Protestant experience of reading Merton. A willingness not to reject the bigger picture is something he awakens in readers, but in no straightforward way. Christian history is brimming with stories of separating from what is seen as destructive, sinful, and corrupting, false, and so on. And Merton, we may say, is an archetypical separator, paradoxically moving to center stage in 1948 with a testimony of secession from the world of his time, a casting off from the shores of a society held in thrall to forces and trends he repeatedly described as hellish. Granted, this was not a separation from other Christians specifically, but from the context of social influences, trends and structures which seemed to choke off his better self and undermine his desire to rest in the transformative presence of the Christ-like God who appeared to him in Rome and Cuba and New York.

Merton remained at a distance from what we call the mainstream until his final fateful journey to the East. He was geographically and socially distant, whilst his separating from the noise and the fog allowed him to see and to rejoice in his unshakable belonging to the human race he loved. Time and again he saw a bigger picture, not just of church in any formal sense, but of human interdependence and mutuality undergirding the details of social organization and traditions. He remained separated, way beyond the corner of Fourth and Walnut in Louisville, in order to remain connected by compassion and the clarity of contemplation. In order to remain in love.

Merton's monastic separation is perhaps the thing which seems most alien to fellow Methodists. It's not that we can't, just that we don't. Of course, the same is true of most Catholics; but amongst Catholics there might be assumed a general appreciation of the intentions behind religious celibacy, and of contemplative life.

Methodism in Britain is continually evolving, but elected silence and separation will probably still be interpreted as opting out of some kind of responsibility toward fellow citizens. It was Merton's separating which intrigued and inspired me. He reasoned his way towards a recognition of the causes of war and social breakdown, and his own part in that sorry mess, then he faithfully stepped away from the causes as well as the effects. There are good reasons for separating, as well as bad reasons. Sometimes separating is an act of love, affection, and solidarity, and arises from an overwhelming sense of connectedness. That's what Merton showed me.

In better moments, when we manage to hold on to a sense of our part in the bigger picture (of church, or nation, or let's face it, the human race), we are perhaps also being tender towards our own contradictions and inconsistencies. We manage to hold them together, as Merton held himself in the thoughts of east and west and much else besides. Trouble seems to occur when, in our longing to get free or to be 'closer to God,' to create intentional communities of faith or to choose the better life, we can no longer sustain the tension and project all that we consider dangerous or corrupt or harmful or limiting onto particular persons or crudely-defined groups from whom we must distance ourselves. A desire to keep those others (or previous versions of ourselves) at bay naturally follows on from the projections and exclusions which, in their lighter forms, may be just tactless rather than aggressive, but which nevertheless diminish us.

Before his definitive act of separation, as his personal crisis was amplified by the furies of war, Merton probed the causes and effects of the ways in which we imagine one another, and I still find no better expression than *My Argument With the Gestapo* of the author's determination to get beyond the lazy and harmful categorizations which tribal violence requires. Thank God I stumbled across that strange book, written out of Merton's impassioned search for a way to live with integrity during wartime. I think I met the Merton of *My Argument* and of *Raids on the Unspeakable* before I met the Merton of *The Seven Storey Mountain.* This was the early-late Merton, the Merton whose parting gift was a published version of a pre-monastic journal which takes us to the origin of his monastic vocation. The Merton of 1941 had left behind the easy bourgeois options laid out before him. He also left behind the too-easy option of joining the ranks and traipsing off to launch sanctioned violence upon the latest enemies of the state. Instead, he joined a different band of brothers in the strange world of a Trappist monastery and, rather than launch unresolved inner turmoil onto an external world, he chose the harder way of surrender to a world of psalmody and saints where he engaged the turmoil quite differently.

It was soon after writing (though long before publishing) the imaginative journal that Merton would be knocking at the door of Gethsemani Abbey, having discovered which threshold he next needed to cross. A few years later, Merton again took up a Dantean autobiographical project, this time with a higher dose of realism, for which he became a celebrity archetype of a particular Christian idealism, somewhat at odds with the earlier journal and with much of what would follow. *The Seven Storey Mountain* gives us a restructured world and a reconstructed Merton. Stripped of comfort and distinction, he had by the time of its writing passed through several more veils of infidelity which, in the midst of the habitual compromises of our common life, prevent us from living in truth. *The Seven Storey Mountain* was written from within the liberating constraints of structures which necessarily upheld his living and his writing during transitional years in the monastery. His relationship with the structures of the church, monastery, and theology, continued to evolve as he diligently pressed on under the warming gaze of restorative love.

What Merton highlighted, by his choices and his ways of describing them, was that our life together as Church does seem to entail accepting as authoritative the self-limiting structures and patterns of institutions, even if they sometimes seem to be woefully inadequate representations of the transforming irruption of the risen Christ.

After all, how else has testimony to Christ reached us, other than through this tangled vine into which we are grafted? From a place of acceptance and commitment we then learn the depths of trust. We learn to love one another in ways more closely aligned with the one who took towel and bowl as he took bread and wine. We learn to recognize one another first and foremost as sibling, even if our faces seem unfamiliar, our accents strangely alien and some of our behaviors are hard to fathom. By grace we can learn to do away with sibling rivalry, not least when we celebrate companionship in bread and wine, grateful even for crumbs from a table whose host is our brother Christ. We rest in an intuition that, beneath the surface, we are already one. But "if we love our own ideology and our own opinion instead of loving our brother, we will seek only to glorify our ideas and our institutions and by that fact we will make real communication impossible."[1]

When asked for a personal account of reading Merton, I began to think about how I first came across the writer-monk, and what it was that held my attention. I cannot rightly remember the earliest encounters way back during late adolescent and early adult years. Attempts to recover those memories are in the end perhaps less about recollection and more about creative composition of half-remembered fragments and moods, woven into patterns which corresponded closely enough to what now seems true. I make patterns, and as I get older, it is Merton's pattern-making which intrigues me, his persistent re-telling of life as he saw and remembered it. He was continually finding fresh narrative form in relation to whatever he was reading or hearing or feeling, whilst discerning deeper currents beneath (and personal resonance with) news from abroad. How might he respond, if at all, to news of high-profile sectarian violence in Brussels and Paris? What might he make of the mayhem in Syria, and intensified debating across Europe and American about ideologies and large scale movements of people? Where would he fix his gaze? Grieving with the victims and the bereaved, would he nevertheless turn away from what in the end may be pseudo-events, media moments held before us to serve political, economic, and military ends?

It is this kind of question which sends me back to Merton's early imagined autobiography. There was something compelling about the creative urgency of the *Gestapo* book, and the impassioned insights of a young writer yet to find his literary voice. In retrospect we can read between the lines of that idiosyncratic journal, all that would unfurl for Merton over subsequent decades: his determination to drill down into causes and meanings; his discontent with unprocessed beliefs; his satirical deconstructing of the kind of tribal language which paves the way to war, and the weaponized vocabulary which is propaganda. He portrayed with comical precision the annexing of media and the distorting effect of a uniform. These and so many other themes signal later developments in his writing on deep ecumenism, or war and the crisis of language. His prophetic shredding of the deceptions hiding beneath a licensed pursuit of

1. Thomas Merton, *Faith and Violence* p. 163.

happiness may have been expressed with greater art in later work, but all is foreshadowed in the macronic journal's riffing on Blake, Dante, Joyce, and wartime newsreel.

I was captivated by Merton's style of protestation, by his imaginative yet deeply serious response for a turbulent world and his part in it. The uncharacteristic mode of *My Argument with the Gestapo* did seem oddly contrived, but communicated effectively enough the workings of a young author discovering why he could not simply get on with the life he was living. With its mythologized trek through the purgatory of wartime Europe and America, the book testifies to an estrangement and a longing: estrangement from the hardened and inadequate ways of thinking which divided people against one another and from their truer selves; and longing for another country he could call home. By contrast, *The Seven Storey Mountain* left this reader with quite different impressions of the author's having arrived at a place where, prematurely, all made sense. Perhaps Protestant sensibilities were awakened by the undercurrents of that post-war best-seller, though I am more inclined to think it was just that I had previously met a Merton with whom heart spoke to heart much more directly.

I don't remember the extent to which Merton was involved in kindling deep-rooted longings for shared silence and simplicity, for a more intentional living and for a perspective from which to see more clearly and act more decisively. I remember that when I went to Taizé to live with the questions, Merton's *Thoughts in Solitude* came with me. To read him is like following a treasure trail toward a clearer perspective on the world and our place in it. Between *My Argument with the Gestapo* and *The Seven Storey Mountain*, via *New Seeds of Contemplation*, *Conjectures of a Guilty Bystander* and *Raids*, Merton seemed to be continually writing himself into a more vital participation in the world.

Nothing remained static in Merton, even after his opting for a life of monastic stability. The restless, generative tensions were part of what made him compelling. More than a peculiarly unsettled personality, he became in some way representative of a Benedictine way of riding the rapids between desires for solitude and for community, between love of ancient traditions and innovative communication with contemporary life, between the world as we know it and the world as we dream it.

There was nothing particularly strange about the turbulent navigation through tensions and passions, just more immediacy than I found in John Wesley, whose letters and journals had always struck me as more captivating than his sermons and biblical annotations. The journals, despite their editorial crafting, take readers closer than the sermons to the untidy wrangling of ideas, emotions, insights, and relationships which constitute a lived public faith. They offer glimpses into what might, in a monastic setting, be called 'education of the heart,' awakening to the heart of the world in the heart of God.

The purpose of this essay is not to compare aspects of Merton and Wesley, but I have found it helpful to think how my reading of Merton compares with reading a source within the Methodism which nurtured me. Perhaps a twentieth century Methodist writer, such as Neville Ward, might have been a fairer parallel; but there is something intriguing about the ways in which mythologies of both Wesley and Merton revolve around moments of the heart. For Wesley it was a heart strangely warmed, awakened by grace to new depths of trust in Christ. For Merton, it was an awakening to the secret beauty of the hearts of persons that each one is in God's eyes.

Wesley's account of the moment at Aldersgate Street (where his heart was strangely warmed) seems to lack the renewed sense of human connection and belonging which Merton celebrates. We need to look elsewhere for that, such as his sermon on the Catholic Spirit, where Wesley emphasized how a genuine desire to respond to the needs and wants of fellow believers is evidence that 'your heart is right, as my heart is with your heart.' That being the case, he went on, 'give me your hand.' We are connected, related, in solidarity. We learn to recognize the fruits of the Spirit in the other who comes to us as a gift, through their very 'otherness.' Heart to heart, connections are forged which put our grappling with words and meanings into proper perspective, as we struggle not over against one another, but against whatever falsely divides and distorts our essential unity in Christ.

Thus the Church is always coming into being, repeatedly experiencing itself as the church of Pentecost, overwhelmed by a Spirit which disrupts our structures and habit and ways of seeing the world. Riding that wave can render the believer vulnerable to the disapproval of fellow believers and a world which associates church with a more rigid kind of stability. As Wesley puts it in his sermon on the Catholic Spirit, we need not share the same opinions; neither will we all worship in the same manner nor agree on church order. We will have our affiliations and particular congregations; but we will go on loving "in the kingdom and patience of Jesus . . . rooted in the faith once delivered to the saints, and grounded in love, in true catholic love" until we are "swallowed up in love forever and ever!"

THOMAS MERTON: SON OF A QUAKER AND FRIEND TO FRIENDS

Alan Klop

> My Lord God, I have no idea where I am going. I do not see the road ahead of me. I cannot know for certain where it will end. Nor do I really know myself, and the fact that I think that I am following your will does not mean that I am actually doing so. But I believe that the desire to please you does in fact please you. And I hope I have that desire in all that I am doing. I hope that I will never do anything apart from that desire. And I know that if I do this you will lead me by the right road though I may know nothing about it. Therefore will I trust you always though I may seem to be lost and in the shadow of death. I will not fear for you are ever with me, and you will never leave me to face my perils alone.[1]

Reading these words from Thomas Merton was my first encounter with the famous monk from Gethsemani. At the time, I did not know who Merton was and I had no clue what or where the Abbey of Gethsemani was. Growing up a Quaker in rural Indiana in the mid-20th century meant one did not read Catholic monks. Being ecumenical meant talking to our Methodist neighbors!

Becoming an adult and spiritual in the 1960s was both challenging and thrilling. The Vietnam War, Civil Rights, Feminist Movement, Vatican II, and massive immigration created the caldron of my spiritual formation. Going to a Quaker college afforded me the opportunity to own and deepen my inherited faith tradition. I became a real Quaker. During my college and graduate school days, I watched the Catholic Church implement the reforms of Vatican II. I visited my first monastery; it was not Gethsemani.

Going to graduate school at an urban world-class university put

1. *Thoughts in Solitude*, p. 79.

me into an ecumenical and interfaith laboratory where my education came as much from the people I associated with as the classes I attended. For a couple of years my back yard adjoined Harvard's Center for the Study of World Religions. The house next to mine was the Hillel House. It was into this spiritual and intellectual crucible that Thomas Merton also became a friend.

A bridge is the metaphor I will use to describe my engagement with Merton. Like so much I was reading, Merton at first seemed to be "over there" from where I was. Although I was provincial, I did not know it. It is only by meeting others that we become aware of our narrowness. You can literally visit others by having coffee with them. Or, you can figuratively visit others by reading their writings. This was how Merton began to become my friend. His books became a bridge to cross over for a visit.

There were two sides of the bridge. Merton sat in his Trappist monastery, and I occupied a Quaker meetinghouse. I realized the monastery and the meetinghouse were not contradictory, but rather complimentary. Just as Merton took vows, I vowed to learn more about my own faith tradition. In the process Merton helped me learn about a larger Christian and burgeoning interfaith tradition. I learned that much of that resonated so well with my own particular Quaker tradition.

In that context I first read Merton's words from *Thoughts in Solitude*. They spoke to my soul in that crucible. "My Lord, I have no idea where I am going." For someone who expected to travel the road back to an Indiana farm, I was now on a very different path. Now I could no longer "see the road ahead of me." I certainly did not know "where it will end." But the truest thing Merton said was that I really did not "know myself."

More precisely, Merton helped me to see that the self I thought I knew was not my true self. For example, I found words from the early Merton in *The Seven Storey Mountain* to be spot on: "The monastery is a school—a school in which we learn from God how to be happy. . . . What has to be healed in us is our true nature, made in the likeness of God. What we have to learn is love. The healing and the learning are the same thing . . . ."[2] I wanted love and I needed healing. I would not join a monastery, but I could be monastic.

There are two key assertions in this quotation that linked two

2. *Seven Storey Mountain*, p. 172.

foundational aspects of Quaker spirituality. They are part of my Quaker credo—my belief. Merton's words assume that human beings have a "true nature." This true nature was made in the image and likeness of God. Secondly, this nature has become sick and needs to be healed. I want to use each of these assumptions to connect with foundational Quaker spirituality which I had learned and which Merton helped me understand and appreciate even more fully.

The earliest Quaker phrase I learned was the affirmation that "there is that of God in every person." No one ever told me I had to believe this to be a Quaker, but all Quakers I knew accepted the truth of that phrase and based their lives on it. Merton helped me understand this was the Quaker version of the Genesis creation story of human beings. In Genesis God says, "Let us make humankind in our image, according to our likeness . . . ." (Genesis 1:26)

I was created in the image and likeness of the Holy One. This was my true nature, according to Merton. I now understood why Quakers said I had "that of God" within me. I know this does not mean I am good. But I am a child of God. I have the *Imago Dei*, the image of God, and that makes me special. The corollary is every other person is made in the image of God and is also special. It began to dawn on me that this creative gift and blessing was the cue to why Quakers believe everyone counts.

Thankfully, I had the theological key to why Quakers were anti-slavery and why they were pacifists. If some other person also has "that of God in him or her," then it is never right to take a life. The ethical implications were clear for many other social issues, such as the Civil Rights issues of the 1960s, like race, gender, etc. To read Merton's later works on these issues of rights helped me form more fully my own spirituality.

If "there is that of God in every person," I also realized that was only the beginning of the story. Anyone who knows the early chapters of Genesis, knows the first two chapters of creation are followed by Genesis 3 which narrates the disobedience of Adam and Eve and, consequently, the loss of human likeness to God. Merton and early Catholic theologians helped me understand that the sin of Adam and Eve erased their likeness to God. But they did not lose the *imago Dei*—the image of God.

I liked Merton's image of humans in need of healing. Metaphorically, it makes some sense to talk about sin as a kind of sickness—not being well. Just like being sick, when we sin we are "not quite ourselves." Merton was especially insightful when he showed me that sin is an existential problem, as well as a moral one. His use of existential language, such as alienation or lostness to describe sin opened my eyes. This resonated with what I had learned from the early Quaker, George Fox.

George Fox was very aware of his alienation from the culture of mid-seventeenth century England. He was not bad, so much as lost. Although he grew up in a religious context, he did not feel whole. He needed healing. And so in his late teens, he entered a serious period of religious searching. He knew *about* God, but he longed to *know* God—to know God experientially. He sought this sense of divine immediacy from a variety of religious preachers and teachers, but to no avail. Hence, he was tempted to despair.

Then, interestingly, in solitude he was addressed. In his own words Fox said, ". . . when all my hopes . . . in all men were gone, so that I had nothing outwardly to help me, nor could tell what to do, then, Oh then, I heard a voice which said, 'there is one, even Christ Jesus, that can speak to thy condition,' and when I heard it my heart did leap for joy."[3]

The condition in which Fox was living was not unlike the condition of Merton before his own religious searching brought him to the Catholic Church in 1938. Briefly, Merton considered finding a home among the Quakers, whom he had known as a boy, but his reading of Catholics led him to make his home among Catholics and, then a little while later, specifically with the monks of Gethsemani. Christ Jesus had also addressed him and had spoken to his condition. The healing process had begun.

Quakers do not have creeds, but individually we have a credo—some key theological points to describe our spiritual journeys. My first two creedal aspects are already in place: "there is that of God in every person" and "there is one Christ Jesus that can speak to our condition." Having crossed the bridge into Merton's thought and language helped me articulate these two points in more contemporary and meaningful ways. For example, I could talk about my true nature and, unfortunately, the life I lead as a false self. The false self is not necessarily sinful in the old way people talk about sin, but the false self is always inauthentic. With the experience of immediately encountering God, the healing process of being made

3. . *The Journal of George Fox*. Ed. by John L. Nickalls. Cambridge: Harper and Row, 1983, p. 11.

whole begins.

I now trace that process through two more creed aspects of my Quaker spirituality—with Merton's help, of course. My third creedal affirmation says, "All things are sacramental." As a young Quaker I noticed that we did not "do" sacraments the way most Christians did. Therefore, the sad de facto position Quakers assume is that "we did not have sacraments." I had to be educated to understand that was provincial ignorance. Reading non-Quakers on the sacraments enabled me first to understand something of the history and significance of sacraments. Secondly, reading a few Quakers who actually knew how to talk about Quaker sacramental theology made a huge difference in my spiritual maturity.[4]

Augustine taught me the classical definition of a sacrament: a visible sign of an invisible reality. Since Quakers do not use the outward element of water, I could understand why we unfortunately concluded that we did not believe in baptism. The same was true with the Lord's Supper or Eucharist. Never seeing the wafer or wine in a Quaker meetinghouse led to erroneous sacramental assumptions.

With the help of British Quaker scholar Maurice Creasy, and with the knowledge of how other Christians developed sacramental theology, I realized how to understand and maximize this third creedal aspect about sacraments, namely, "All things are sacramental." I occasionally heard this as a young Quaker, but it made no sense because I had no understanding of sacramental theology. But, with knowledge and understanding, that phrase became very important in my own understanding of the Presence of God in our world. Merton and monasticism played a significant role in that process.

The most important step in my process was to expand the arena for sacraments. This is exactly what the Quaker phrase does when it claims all things are sacramental. If not true, at least that claim is potentially true and is the hope. Before grasping the expansive possibilities for sacraments, I needed to understand better the traditional sacraments, namely, baptism and the Eucharist.

The Augustinian definition allowed me to understand that the water, bread, and wine were the visible signs. As such, they signified the invisible reality, which I knew was the Spirit or Presence of

4. See Maurice A. Creasy, "Quakers and Sacraments," *Quaker Religious Thought*, Vol. 5, No 1 (Spring, 1963, pp. 2-25.

God. I believed that if God were real, that reality had to be signified and symbolized in such a way that I could know it and talk about it. But I also realized that the Spiritual Presence of God was not captured in sign or symbol. The sign signified, so in a way, Quakers were on to something. For Quakers, the outward signs of water, bread, and wine, were not necessary. By themselves they were not sacraments. The necessary element was the Spirit of God, and to this Quaker gives assent.

My Quaker theological move, then, became simple. With such an understanding I would no longer say Quakers did not have sacraments.[5] With this new understanding, I realized while "doing sacraments" was not necessary for me, I was free to do them. With freedom comes liberty. This was a welcomed bridge to other faith traditions. I was free to join, to participate, and to commune.

The sacramental bridge would take me to an unexpected place. In the early 1960s the Dutch Dominican, Edward Schillebeeckx, published a work that built a bridge from sacrament to the person of Jesus. The book *Christ the Sacrament of the Encounter With God*, described Jesus as the "primordial sacrament."[6] Following the Gospel of John, Schillebeeckx opened me to understand the incarnation as the primary sacrament, "the Word became flesh." Jesus is the visible sign of the invisible reality. God became sacramental in a personal way. My Quaker mind had discovered the key to why "all things are sacramental." If creation is the expression of God's Spirit, the incarnation was the personalization of the same Spirit. This personal sacramental Presence continues even in our day.

Another profound help is Christopher Pramuk's book *Sophia: The Hidden Christ of Thomas Merton.* Pramuk offers an insight that helped me put it all together. His third chapter is entitled, "In the Belly of a Paradox: The Archaeology of Merton's Sacramental Imagination." Readers are mesmerized by Merton's words, which is why he is still popular. But Pramuk uncovered something deeper for me when he noted:

> Merton is not a word magician but a sacrament maker structuring religious discourse in such a way that the symbols and doctrines of tradition may be experienced not as mere

5. Alan Kolp, "Friends, Sacraments, and Sacramental Living," *Quaker Religious Thoughts*, Vol. 20, No. 3 (Summer, 1984), pp. 36-52.

6. E. Schillebeeckx, *Christ the Sacrament of the Encounter with God.* New York: Sheed and Ward, 1963, p. xvi

> words, explanations or as a 'heap of notions,' . . . but truly as vessels of memory and real presence, enablers of hope in the concrete circumstances of our lives.[7]

Merton is a sacrament maker. That's it! His words become visible signs of an invisible reality—the Presence of God. The idea of the sacrament creates multiple bridges.

The idea of sacrament bridges and ties together creation, incarnation, salvation and finally, community (monastery and meetinghouse). Long before I had the words, I had the sense and experience that it was the "gathered community," as Quakers call the worshippers joined in union with the Presence of God, that was our authentic sacramental experience. Indeed, sacrament is communal. Just as Jesus was the primordial sacrament, the community is the ongoing sacramental Presence in our world, although not the only opportunity for Presence.

Once again, Merton was a bridge to help me understand and articulate this in a much bigger, broader way. In *The Monastic Journey*, Merton commented on the monastic vow of stability and intriguingly linked it to sacrament. Merton said, "It is clear that the monk's 'stability' is not made in an earthly place so much as in a spiritual family . . . since St. Benedict is always concrete, the monastery itself is a 'sacrament' of the future home to which the whole monastic family is tending with all its efforts . . . ."[8] I realized the same thing could be said for the Quaker community.

Truly, the Quaker focus is on the community, not the building or place. That is why Quakers called their places of worship "meetinghouses." The place bears no sanctity, but the people gathering on a personal journey of sacrament making become saints. I also resonated with Merton's sentiment that the community is always an eschatological adventure. In one sense, the gathered community is potentially the experience of realized eschatology—the Kingdom is here. But it is never fully realized eschatology. In another sense, the community is a sign of what will be.

What is always true, however, is if you are a member of the community, you are a minister. Quakers took the Protestant idea of the priesthood of all believers to its radical conclusion—we did

7. Christopher Pramuk, *Sophia: The Hidden Christ of Thomas Merton*. Collegeville, MN: Liturgical Press, 2009, p. 114.

8. Thomas Merton, *The Monastic Journey*. Garden City, NY: Image Books, 1977, p. 97.

away with the laity! All Quakers are ministers and are called to serve. To be clear, ministry is not who I am, but rather what I do. To minister is an active verb—an action of service.

This leads to the fourth aspect of my Quaker credo. We are all ministers and, as such, are to "walk cheerfully" in service to the world. George Fox's 1656 letter to Friends in the ministry highlights the character of Quaker ministers:

> . . . this is the word of the Lord God to you all, and a charge to you all in the presence of the living God, be patterns, be examples in all countries, places, islands, nations, wherever you come; that your carriage and life may preach among all sorts of people, and to them. Then you will come to walk cheerfully over the world, answering that of God in every one . . . .[9]

There is much to note here, but let me mention two points. First, we notice how comprehensive and global this call to ministry is. Clearly, this connects to the later Merton whose spiritual interests had become equally expansive. More even than Fox, Merton models for me how to be specifically a contemporary Christian Quaker in the large, global spiritual world.

The second point reveals how clearly the call to ministry uses the same language as the first theme of my credo, namely, "there is that of God in every person." To minister is to serve the desire of God that every living person come to know that they are a beloved child of God. This is the generalized call to ministry that disciples receive. Of course, it has to be particularized and concretized for each individual, and this usually requires some individualized discernment. In my own journey it brought me back repeatedly to the words of the epigraph of this article.

One sentence from that epigraph stands out for me as I try to follow the desire of God. "And I know that if I do this you will lead me by the right road though I may know nothing about it." The road that God crafted for me has crossed many bridges—taking me places I never dreamed I would go. One of the main bridges given to me was the writings of Thomas Merton. Continual crossing into those writings enable me to know how to experience and appreciate the many "others" I have encountered.

---

9. *Journal of George Fox*, p. 263. See also Alan Kolp, *Fresh Winds of the Spirit*, 2nd ed. Richmond, IN: Friends United Press, 2007, pp. 109-131.

Merton's visionary words in Louisville at the corner of Fourth and Walnut put it as conclusively as anything I know. And those words match Fox's initial vision atop Pendle Hill in northern England, which galvanized the Quaker vision to be God's leaven for "a great people to be gathered." With Merton I see we are all priceless—diamonds:

> Again, that expression, *le point vierge,* (I cannot translate it) comes in here. At the center of our being is a point of nothingness which is untouched by sin and by illusion, a point of pure truth, a point or spark which belongs entirely to God, which is never at our disposal, from which God disposes our lives, which is inaccessible to the fantasies of our own mind or the brutalities of our own will. This little point of nothingness and of *absolute poverty* is the pure glory of God in us. It is so to speak His name written in us, as our poverty, as our intelligence, as our dependence, as our sonship. It is like a pure diamond, blazing with the invisible light of heaven. It is in everybody, and if we could see it we would see these billions of points of light coming together in the face and blaze of a sun that would make all the darkness and cruelty of life vanish completely . . . . I have no program for this seeing. It is only given. But the pure gate of heaven is everywhere.[10]

---

10. *Conjectures*, Image Book Edition, p. 158.

THE ENDURING PRESENCE OF THOMAS MERTON

James Baker

Thomas Merton made his first appearance in my life on a dark winter's morning in December, 1962. Glenn Hinson, the professor of my medieval church history class at The Southern Baptist Theological Seminary, had made friends with officials at the Abbey of Gethsemani in Bardstown, Kentucky, and particularly with its most famous member, the renowned writer Thomas Merton, whose religious name was Father Louis. Glenn was a naturally curious person and was dedicated to making his insulated Baptist ministerial students aware of their cultural traditions. We were all descended from medieval Catholics, whether we liked to admit it or not, and we needed to find our roots. In order to give us a bit of the old world, the monastic part of it, he arranged for his class to spend a day at the abbey. Although I knew little about monasticism, less about Cistercians of the Strict Observance (Trappist), and nothing about Thomas Merton, I went along. After all, it was a day away from the restraints of learning the strictures of Baptist orthodoxy.

We ministerial chicks were up long before dawn and in a convoy of cars going down the narrow road from Louisville to Bardstown, where Glenn got us lost around the square, then finally off the two lane road onto one with barely room to pass oncoming cars until we turned left at a small sign that read "Trappist" and found parking outside a formidable, closed wooden gate beneath a sign that said "God Alone." I did not get a sense of impending doom the way the three fellows in my car did as we entered what was then still a nineteenth century structure, without heating. Gethsemani was not exactly welcoming, but I alone among the Baptists in my group reasoned that it might make sense for people tired of the excesses of the modern world to come there. The monks we saw looked not exactly happy, but not at all in mortal agony about inhabiting a place which was something of an anomaly in the middle of the twentieth century. Still, I found Gethsemani on that bleak December morning dark, cold, and more than a bit forbidding.

After we had watched and listened with curious interest from the church balcony as white robed monks filed in below us and said their morning prayers, we went in and sat in a corner of the refectory for coffee as the silent monks conversed with sign language across the way from outsiders. Then we took a tour of the buildings, both living quarters for the monks, cold and comfortless, and the just as cold and comfortless barns for the cows that provided raw material for the abbey's famous cheeses. I would later learn that Merton complained about the winter cold in his cell and at the altar and that he liked to joke about making cheeses for Jesus. He was not the stereotypical sanctimonious monastic booster.

Despite my unwillingness to pass harsh judgment as my colleagues were doing, I had to admit that the entire place gave off a faint odor of decay, a sense that this was a place not so much to live as to die. The brothers who moved quietly down the darkened hallways looked very old, even the ones who were obviously young. I thought a person would have to be very fed up with the world to come here to spend their lives in work and worship.

The abbot met with us in a study room and told us the story of how the abbey was founded by monks from France, a bit of its history, and how it now functioned. We were impressed, but not exactly excited or inspired. Then in bounced Father Louis, Thomas Merton, entering my life never to depart. In contrast to the abbot and the other monks we met, all of whom carried an air of sad resignation to the inevitability of surviving this vale of tears, he was a dashing figure, still very much a man of the world while being a man of the abbey. His robe was not quite white and looked unpressed, and his shoes were a size too large so that there was space at the heel, but his eyes were bright with keen interest in every subject we discussed.

He could hardly sit still as he asked us more questions than he answered. What led us to the ministry? What were we reading at our seminary? What did we think of Rudolph Bultmann, at that time a very controversial provocateur in New Testament studies? What did we think about the goings on at Vatican II in Rome? When someone suggested that the abbey should have sent him to represent the Trappists at the Council meeting, he clapped his hands together and said wistfully, "Oh do I wish!!!" When one of the students asked him about an old monk he had seen breaking up rocks in the garden, whether it was some kind of punishment for transgression, Merton broke us up by saying, "Oh no, it's just senility. He likes hammering away at rocks."

After the abbot gave him a warning cue that it was time for him to go back to his monastic duties, Merton bade us all a fond farewell and with a wave was gone. As my friends and I left the enclosure wall and headed back to the city, the other three were still shaking their heads and saying how good it felt to be out of "that place," back into the real world. But I heard myself defending it, saying it was not such a bad place after all. I was at that moment on my way to a much later admission that had I been born in the Middle Ages, had I been baptized a Catholic even in the modern age, I might well have found myself living in a monastery, a monk who taught church history and wore a dingy wrinkled robe and listened with keen interest to every visitor who came by, longing for information about a world whose values I had with relief abandoned and rejected but still found fascinating. I might have been a variation on the Merton theme.

I finished my seminary training and became a chaplain at Florida State University where, in my spare time, I completed a Ph.D. in the interdisciplinary humanities program. I had not thought much about Gethsemani and Thomas Merton for a time until I realized I had to choose a topic for my dissertation. Then he came to mind. He was still a young man, barely past 50, with a long writing career in front of him, but my committee felt a preliminary study of his 50 or so books would be worth doing. I sent him a letter asking him to approve my plan, asking to meet him when I had the materials to begin writing, but there was no reply. I was not on the list of people whose letters were permitted to go through to him. I appealed to Glenn Hinson, who wrote a letter that did get through. One day in my box I found a letter from Merton. He seemed pleased that a Ph.D. candidate, a Protestant, was writing the first doctoral dissertation on him. He offered to send me any material I wanted and to meet with me at some time in the future. From then on we corresponded regularly. Our first meeting occurred on another cold December day, five years after I first heard him speak. He had arranged with his abbot for us to have an afternoon talk. He was now living as a hermit out in the abbey woods, but he would come in that day for our meeting.

The abbey had gone through some renovation, and it was warmer and better lighted than I remembered it. I saw him coming down a long hallway toward me, a warm smile on his face. He was never a shy person, never timid or self-effacing, not the stereotypical monk at all. "You'll have to wait," he said, "I need a haircut." I guess I looked perturbed, thinking that this would take time away from our conversation, but he said, "Don't worry. The kind of haircuts we get don't take long." And sure enough, he sat down in the chair, Brother Barber went zip, zip, zip, and Merton got up, completely shorn. "Okay, let's talk," he said, leading me to a lounge. On the way he dropped off a wad of dirty clothes and picked up a new outfit of jeans, shirts, and robes. They had been worn by someone else before they came to him. Like the other monks, he had nothing of his own.

We spent an exciting afternoon discussing my dissertation, with him once more asking as many questions as he answered, filling in gaps in my research, then turning to the news of the day. Once more, I felt his exhilaration when involved in discussions of world and national events. He was greatly interested in the civil rights movement and the war in Viet Nam, having written controversial articles on both topics, angering many conservative Catholics. He found sad humor in the fact that, because of his articles on race and war, one Louisville Catholic had advised his friends to burn Merton's books. He had hosted anti-war protesters and had made a tentative date to host Dr. Martin Luther King, Jr. the next year. Dr. King, of course, was killed before he could come to Gethsemani.

He was only vaguely interested in the presidential election coming up the next year. He seemed to feel that one politician was very much like another. When I asked him whom he would like to see elected, he said, "Oh, maybe someone like Nelson Rockefeller." He mused at the way our leaders, both political and religious, were fumbling around in the darkness on all of the important issues. His literary fame had given him a voice to speak out on social issues, and he intended to go on doing so, even though what he said might be unpopular among conservative Catholics. I saw clearly the irony of a cloistered monk acting as a social critic. At the end, as the sun was beginning to wane, he led me outside, wished me well at the abbey's back gate and headed down a worn pathway toward the woods and the hill where his hermitage lay. After many years living in the abbey itself he was farther away from the world than ever, yet more involved in world events than ever. It was gently snowing. He turned once, waved, pulled his cowl over his shaved head, and walked off into the gathering darkness.

I finished the dissertation at long last, sent him a copy, and got it back with corrections. He called it a "benign" treatment, and it was a long time later that I learned what he meant. In part it was benign because I am an historian, not a literary critic, and therefore offered little commentary on his fiction and poetry, which was probably a relief to him. I had also taken his autobiography, *The Seven Storey Mountain,* as objective fact. Merton knew that it was not a complete or even an entirely honest book. He had himself called it inadequate, although he had not specified what made it so. Censors had snipped out large parts of it, especially his love affair in England and the child that resulted from it. His friends would resurrect many sordid details later on, but at that time he was probably pleased that I did not probe deeper than his own account of the life he had led. He thought my summaries and evaluations of his books and their themes were accurate and would help readers understand him better. He was glad that I emphasized his social thought. What I had written pleased him, and what he said about what I had written pleased me.

He invited me to visit him again. I expected to spend several years bringing the manuscript up to par, bouncing ideas off him to make it a thorough and accurate study of his life and work before it was published. My second visit, however, would prove to be my last. It was late summer of 1968, and he told me that day that he was planning a trip to Asia the next month, where he would meet with monastic leaders from all over the world and from many different religious faiths. He expected to be gone for several months. He said there were rumors that he was leaving the abbey for good, but he said he would "always be a monk of Gethsemani," a cryptic comment that did not promise that he would ever live again in Kentucky. Later, the speculation blossomed that he had planned to join an abbey in Alaska, in order to make trips to both to the east and back to the west. I guess we will never really know. Perhaps at that moment he did not know.

A lady came with me on this visit, and it was obvious that Merton liked women very much. I would learn more about this when some of his university friends began publishing books about his early romantic exploits. He spent more time talking with my guest than with me, delighting in her company, patiently sitting for her to do sketches for a portrait. He had suggested that I bring a picnic basket, and he took us out to sit under the trees and share it. I was unsure of his dietary restrictions so I brought a variety of sandwiches and drinks. When given the choice of sandwiches he picked beef over cheese, and when given a choice of drinks he chose beer over cola. Again, when we had talked a lot and laughed even more, he left us. We went through the abbey bookshop where a couple of "hippy" youngsters recognized him and asked for his blessing, which he gave them, and where he picked his latest book of poetry off a display case, signed it for me, and left without paying for it. Royalties from his writings had, of course, enriched the abbey's coffers. Once more I watched as he went up the path toward his hermitage. Once more he turned and waved, but this time it was on a sunny day and it was goodbye forever.

The next month he flew to the west coast, then on to Asia. It was later reported that some religious leaders he met pronounced him a reincarnation of the Buddha, and he became an object of admiration in the Buddhist East as he already was in the Catholic West. He met and had his photograph made with the Dalai Lama. One of his stops was in Bangkok, Thailand, where he attended a conference of world monastic leaders. On the morning of December 10, someone called me and told me to turn on the news, that the monk I had written about was dead. That was when I learned that Merton had been accidentally electrocuted. He had attended a morning session of the conference and gone to his room to rest. He had taken a bath and with wet feet walked across a terra cotta floor to pull an electric fan over to his bed. The fan had a faulty wire. It shocked him, then fell over him, and it was several hours before he was discovered, the current still flowing through his body. His last public comment was that he would now disappear.

I noted that he died on December 10, exactly 27 years after he had first entered Gethsemani. He was almost 27 years old in 1941; he was almost 54 in 1968. He was the third person I admired to die violently that year, M. L. King in April, Bobby Kennedy in June. Merton's body came home aboard a military transport plane, his coffin alongside those of American boys killed in Viet Nam, in a conflict he had strongly condemned. Suspicion of the federal government being so strong, there were rumors that his death was no accident; but nothing ever surfaced to substantiate the talk. I was not invited to his funeral, but I mourned with all those who had met him and/or had read his books and knew they would miss him terribly. I had no idea at that time how deeply he had influenced me and would give light and direction to the rest of my life.

My dissertation was still in rough post-doctoral form when he died, but soon I began to have inquiries from publishers. Merton was hot news, more because of his death than because of his life, and a Merton book would be a hot item. As a young scholar, still wet behind the professorial ears, I was shocked by all the attention. I was still writing lectures in my first teaching assignment, but I went to work, and the book I produced was the first of a gathering and then a roaring avalanche of Merton books and articles by people who knew him and many who did not. My editor recognized right away that mine should hone in on his comments about the society which he observed from his abbey and hermitage windows. I would emphasize the paradox of a cloistered monk who commented on social issues and because of his fame influenced a surprisingly large public audience. The editor settled on the title *Thomas Merton—Social Critic*.

As I wrote and revised, as I studied and tried to explain Merton's perspective on contemporary events, I felt his guiding hand. He had not disappeared. I also realized that I was doing more than merely summarizing and analyzing his thought, that I was at the same time incorporating it into my own. What he had to say about racial justice and its social implications, what he had to say about war and its consequences, what he had to say about the obligation of religion to take bold and often controversial stands on these issues—all these became the framework for my own social conscience. No one could spend time with Merton's writings without seeing the world from his vantage point and becoming at least partially "Mertonian" in social philosophy.

The book brought me a small measure of fame, quite small as other books on Merton, most of them by Catholics, began to appear. Still, I was asked to write Merton articles and speak at Merton conferences. The time came when I had to decide whether to spend a career on Merton, as other scholars had done on religious and literary figures and historical figures, or abandon him to his fate with other scholars and go on to other topics. Wisely or not, I chose to go on. I found myself flitting from person to person, subject to subject, writing on Eric Hoffer, Jimmy Carter, Nat Turner, Andrew Carnegie, Abraham Lincoln, Eleanor Roosevelt, among many other people and topics; but I ever forgot Thomas Merton. I realize now that he was more influential on the development of my life and philosophy of life than any of the others.

I was not asked to write Merton's official biography. That commission went to someone far more gifted and appropriate than me, to John Howard Griffin, a Catholic convert like Merton, the author of the famous personal pilgrimage through the Deep South posing as an African American, *Black Like Me.* Yet I was briefly but memorably invited to participate in Griffin's work by having dinner with him at Merton's hermitage. Griffin flew up from Texas on regular occasions, rented a car, and spent time doing research at the hermitage cabin in the Gethsemani woods, all in order to get a feel for Merton's life. One night three of the brothers took me in a jeep up the rugged hillside to the hermitage where Griffin had prepared a sumptuous meal of roasted fish over an open fire. I wondered as we bounced along if this were the same jeep Merton drove so recklessly that he was forbidden ever to drive it again. Griffin, a bear of a man with a strong Texas drawl, was in delicate health but was vibrantly engaged in his research. He told us about reading Merton's meticulously kept diary while living as Merton did with only a fireplace for warmth. He laughed about how the night before he had been awakened suddenly by an exploding faggot. He was confident that he was capturing Merton's life and that the book he would write would be the most important achievement of his life. Unfortunately, he died before he completed it, and the assignment went to someone else.

During one of my two years as a Fulbright Senior Lecturer, both of them in Asia, I found myself on the program at a conference in Bangkok. While there I determined to see the place where Merton died. Merton was still well known in Thailand, and a local scholar knew where I should go and helped me hire a taxi driver, who for ten American dollars agreed to take me out to the retreat center, stay with me while I hunted, and drive me back. The retreat's director also remembered Merton and his accidental death and readily took me to the dormitory and the room where he had lived and died. A fan stood in the corner. My guide asked if I wanted to turn it on, and I declined. He touched it and got a shock. Whether it was the lethal weapon or not, this one too was defective. He laughed and pulled the plug out of the wall. He called out the window for a handyman to come up, and the last I saw of it, the man had it over his shoulder carrying it to a shop for repairs. I had escaped Merton's fate, barely, but I had once more walked in his steps.

One other time I got an eerie warning to be careful of dangerous electrical currents. I was leaving the Merton Study Center at Bellarmine College in Louisville with a colleague, the Kentucky Poet Laureate Jim Wayne Miller, after a day of searching through Merton material and listening to tapes of his talks. As we made our way to the restaurant where we would dine before leaving town, lightning struck an electric pole and sent a shower of sparks across the road ahead of us. I remembered that Merton had ended his autobiography by speaking of the Christ of the burnt men. I am not superstitious, but I do take omens seriously.

As a professor it had been my job, in addition to teaching, to do research and produce scholarly articles and books. I have fulfilled my academic obligations as faithfully as possible. On the other hand, I have always had a desire to do creative writing. This would mean novels and plays. In the decade after his death, still strongly under his influence, I decided to write a play about Merton's life. I took a phrase from the first line of his autobiography and titled it "Under the Sign of the Waterbearer." In it I tried to present in dramatic form many of the issues with which he wrestled during his brief but eventful life: the loss of both parents when he was quite young; the loss of his brother in the Second World War; the sometimes elusive search for his vocation, which took him into teaching and writing and finally to the monastic life, where he continued to teach and write; his inability to find and keep romantic love; and his quest to discover and explain in his writings what life on earth means.

The play was produced at several colleges and civic theatres, and I received notes from students and other viewers, all saying that they wanted to start reading Merton's books. His life seemed to have an impact on people who had not met him, many who had not known who he was, most of them young. They said that the agonies and ecstasies of his life were similar to their own and that they planned to use him as their example of how to deal with them. I also found that in writing a play I had myself once more met and spent time with Merton and that I could also apply the lessons of his life to my own: how to face the loss of parents, the loss of a brother, the search for vocation, the failure of romantic love, and the eternal quest for the meaning of life. So it was that Merton continued to appear and make his presence known to me.

The time came when I had published enough scholarly articles and books to become a full professor; the time came when I no longer had anything to prove to the academic world. I realized I could spend my intellectual energies wherever I wished. The desire to write creatively had never diminished, and so I began writing fiction. Merton had early on turned from fiction to serious topics. I would later turn from serious topics to fiction. Just as Merton had done in his fiction, I used chapters of my life as material and published books on my childhood, my education, my travels abroad, and my quest for lost parents and lost loves. Along the way I decided to create a monastic sleuth. Of course, he looked a lot like Merton.

The character I created is called Columba, and in addition to Merton, he is based in part on a man I met at a Benedictine priory located on the grounds of the old Shaker Village of South Union near Auburn, Kentucky. The priory ran a seminary for belated vocations, and since they ran it on a shoestring, I was asked to come over as a part-time and modestly paid teacher of Church History. The first story of Columba was based there, the second on the island of Iona, and then came stories set in Vienna, Rome, and even Nashville, Tennessee. All the time I was thinking what Merton would have done had he lived to be an elderly man, having completed all of his monastic obligations, being asked to solve murder mysteries. Crazy, I know, but oh such fun. Merton continued to live on in my mind and became in some sense my own version of Chesterton's Father Brown.

After I became a part-time teacher, filling in gaps at my university when needed, being paid by the course, referring to myself as Rent-a-Prof, I followed Merton's footsteps by forsaking the city to build a small cabin in a conifer forest and make it my hermitage. Remembering what Merton said about his own death, which proved not to be accurate but is nevertheless wonderfully poignant, I think the scenario of my own final act will be a quiet death in the woods, surrounded by concerned chipmunks. On the other hand, since one of my neighbors raises game cocks and another keeps two lions, and since I now travel abroad more regularly than ever, maybe my death will be more dramatic. I do plan on my journeys through the woods to avoid meeting angry roosters and hungry lions, and I do not take cover under trees in electrical storms. On my journeys abroad I avoid all electrical appliances. There are limits to how far I want to imitate Merton.

THOMAS MERTON AND THE INTEGRATED LIFE

Justin D. Klassen

> I close my eyes and instantly sink into the whole rainy world of which I am a part and the world goes on with me in it, for I am not alien to it.
>
> Thomas Merton, *Raids on the Unspeakable*

I. INTRODUCTION

As is true of any great religious writer, one should only read Thomas Merton with a readiness to be exposed, challenged, and changed. The subject on which I have found Merton's provocations most insistent and helpful over the years is that of Christianity's call to integration. Merton rebels against theological and other habits of alienation that would separate us from our true Source. He emphasizes that deep Christian faith, contemplative awareness of God in full measure, is the same thing as fullness of life. There is no distinction between what is manifestly good for us as creatures of this earth and what God wants for us, nothing inconsistent between God's creative delight and God's redemptive agenda. For Merton, God lifts us out of sin by teaching us to "sink into the whole rainy world" of which we are a part.

This may not seem all that significant at first, since it means only that Merton holds to a basic Christian premise. In the words of Rowan Williams, the former Archbishop of Canterbury, Christianity is fundamentally about the possibility of "*an integrated life*—not a life where some bits of us have to be covered up and swept under the carpet."[1] Williams' claim to this effect has to do with one of the main emphases of the Apostles' and Nicene Creeds; that God revealed in Jesus none other than the maker of "all things visible and invisible." This means that trusting Jesus as Lord relates to every aspect of creaturely life. To trust Jesus is not only to have confidence in his moral righteousness,

1. Rowan Williams, *Tokens of Trust: An Introduction to Christian Belief*. Louisville: Westminster John Knox, 2007, p. 54.

but to take refuge in the loving source of all that is real—everything from mountains and whales to galaxies and banana trees. The one whom Christians call Messiah reveals the movement and energy behind it all. Consequently, there is no sense in dividing our spiritual lives from our material experiences, our religious obligations from our concrete callings. In Christianity, there is no basis for a spirituality that alienates us from creaturely life, because in Christ, God has reconciled our alienated selves to God's own creative action, the very origin and abiding energy of all that is—including our bodies.

This may be a basic feature of the Christian kerygma, but in my experience, it is also one of the most easily forgotten. Some variants of modern Protestantism in particular make integration seem elusive, or even undesirable. Evangelicalism, for example, which provided some of my early faith formation, tends to suggest that faith in Christ's righteousness is an inner transaction that seals us for heaven, but bears no relationship to concrete moral transformation. This is how such Christians strive to maintain fidelity to the Protestant creed, "*Simul Iustus et Peccator.*" For other Protestant thinkers, including some theologians of my own Mennonite heritage, the characteristic separation between Evangelical faith and social ethics is so destructive as to demand our rejection of the inward or existential dimensions of faith entirely.[2] Both emphases make the relationship of faith to moral formation seem like a zero-sum game. Thomas Merton's theology became significant for me as soon as I realized that he held those seemingly opposite poles together. Thus his work helped me to integrate aspects of my Protestant formation between which I would have otherwise needed to choose.

A second apparent obstacle to integration in modern Protestant thought arises from its well-known penchant for iconoclasm. Only Christ, and no other creaturely form, is up to the task of mediating God's truth, say many dialectical and apocalyptic theologians, especially since the publication of Karl Barth's *The Epistle to the Romans*.[3] In the modern Protestant imagination, the revelation of God in Jesus Christ is held to be so "other" that it stands as negation of any would-be discernment of divine truth in the natural world. This obviously limits the possibility of a robust Protestant theology

2. See for example, John Howard Yoder, *The Politics of Jesus: Vicit Agnus Noster.* Grand Rapids: Eerdmans, 1994, p. 214.

3. Karl Barth, *The Epistle to the Romans*, trans. Edwyn C. Hoskins. Oxford: Oxford University Press, 1933

of creation, and walls off the Christian moral imagination from the realm of environmental responsibility. Again, here I have found in Merton a thinker who integrates—in this case, by affirming the interruptive character of the Christ event while maintaining the omnipresence and visibility of divine activity in nature, if we can only learn to see it.

In this article I will elaborate on both of these Protestant modes of disintegration and elucidate more fully how Merton allows us to recognize paradoxical relationships where we might otherwise only see contradictions.

II. THE PARADOX OF FREE OBEDIENCE

I first heard of Thomas Merton while I was an undergraduate student at Simon Fraser University in British Columbia. I had a professor in an introductory course on world religions who was perennially excited about the manifold ways in which the divine is sought and revealed in the world. Given that I had been raised in a Mennonite family living in an Evangelical Bible belt, this professor was someone my elders would have called a bit "new age-y." The inclusiveness of this enthusiasm was, at the very least, new to me. But we made a connection of sorts; and because I heard him mention a monk named Thomas Merton in class one day, I picked up a book by Merton that I came across in a bookstore soon after. It was Merton's *The New Man*. Looking at the volume now, years later, I can see from my margin notes that I was most taken with Merton's reflections on the paradoxical relationship between freedom and obedience.

As a child I learned the importance of obedience, and even its centrality to Christian life. I remember being told that as Mennonites we were bound to reject any conformity to worldly power, especially in the form of state violence, out of obedience to the crucified Christ. Yet I also grew up at a time when a kind of hyper-Protestant theology of grace, based on a substitutionary theory of atonement, was sweeping the land. It affected Mennonite congregations no less than any others. For many in my church circles, anything related to obedience began to smack of un-Christian legalism, against which we were to wield imputed righteousness as a weapon. Faith formation in a modern Protestant context outside the mainline churches often means inheriting this division—between the inward locus of faith and any outward requirements of moral formation.

I recall celebrating as a young person that God loved me exactly as I was (*Simul Iustus et Peccator*), but at the same time failing to understand how that love could be salvific if it was not also binding on my life and action. I would ask questions about this in church, and most often I was told that gratitude for the free gift of salvation was the driver of personal transformation. I could not say why at the time, but that always seemed fundamentally inadequate to me. I thought redemption, to be effective, should not leave me with only gratitude, but that it should impose upon me some obligatory *telos*, a goal toward which my life ought to tend. Yet "freedom in Christ" loomed above any such moral requirement, never mind that the worry over sliding into legalism made such freedom perpetually vague. It was as if God in Christ had restored in us only what political theorists call "negative liberty."

If works-righteousness is one's most feared sin, as it is for many Evangelical Protestants, the result is that faith gets seated squarely in the inner world of intellectual assent. Salvation becomes a matter of saying or thinking the right things—never, ever a matter of *doing* things. When I read *The New Man*, I was therefore especially fascinated by Merton's articulation of the relationship between human autonomy and conformity to the ways of God. For him, this was a paradox, not a contradiction. Sin is not a categorical distinction that God sharply obliterates by decree, but a destructive way of being, from which God wills to restore us. Merton explains that a human being "could not be entirely happy left to his own nature since, in concrete fact of his nature made in the image of God, cannot rest except in the perfect likeness of the Divine Word."[4] There is no true freedom apart from conformity to his likeness. The purpose of the incarnation for Merton is therefore not simply salvation as punishment-avoidance, but salvation in the sense of "salve," a healing balm. God heals us by making us fully ourselves, which does not conflict with our autonomy but gives it an orientation that allows it to flourish. "We cannot become sons of God by an obedience that is merely a blind renunciation of our own autonomy. On the contrary, spiritual freedom consecrates our autonomy to Christ and, in Christ, to the Father, so that we may love the Father with His own Spirit of freedom, or, so to speak,

4. Thomas Merton, *The New Man*. New York: Farrar, Straus and Giroux, 1961, p. 134

with His own autonomy."[5] For Merton, there is paradoxically no conflict between human freedom and divine action, for the human being is by nature a product of God's activity, and remains characterized by it. "We are most truly ourselves when our souls 'reflect as in a mirror the glory of the Lord.' And when a mirror is full of light, you do not see glass—you are blinded by the light."[6] On Merton's account, then, Christian faith does not liberate us from an obligatory transformation, but directs us to seek the object for which our freedom naturally longs: the infinitely loving heart of God. We are freer the more we come back to, and proceed from, our proper origin and goal.

This relates also to Merton's idea in *New Seeds of Contemplation* that "we are at liberty to be real or to be unreal."[7] We are free to be as we wish, and yet our freedom is limited by the fact that we are not our own creators. We may pretend to be self-authored, but our freedom does not include the power to make this pretension true, or truly life-giving. As Merton puts it, we may "wear one mask and now another, and never, if we so desire, appear with our own true face. But we cannot make these choices with impunity."[8] Merton, of course, agrees with Evangelical theology that the source of salvation is not our own efforts (these being the masks of the false self), but God. For Merton though, trusting in my own efforts of self-making does not simply accrue a debt in the heavenly banking system, but actually damages my life. Sin is pretending that my ego is "the fundamental reality of life to which everything else in the universe is ordered."[9] Living out of this falsehood causes me to "use up my life in the desire for pleasures and the thirst for experiences, for power, honor, knowledge, and love, to clothe this false self and construct its nothingness into something objectively real."[10] Because faith implies acknowledgement of the true Source of my life, it is therefore inseparable from a process of transformation, whereby I am empowered to become the person God created me to be. I will no longer "use up my life" in the pursuit of a false

5. *The New Man*, p. 180.

6. *The New Man*, p. 159.

7. Thomas Merton, *New Seeds of Contemplation.* New York: New Directions, 1962, p. 32.

8. *New Seeds*, p. 32.

9. *New Seeds,* p. 35.

10. *New Seeds,* p. 35.

self but instead will begin to discover and become "my true self."[11] Thus we might say that Merton offers modern Protestants a way of recognizing how trust in God's utterly gratuitous generosity is inseparable from transformation. As an acknowledgment of the truth of my own creatureliness, which sin is always busy denying, faith cannot but set me on a new path.

None of this is to say that my early experience with Merton nullified my Protestant formation; in fact it allowed me to understand the sources of my theology in a richer way. For example, after reading Merton, the person I encountered in Martin Luther's writings appeared more sensitive to the paradoxes of freedom and obedience than I had been led to believe in my grace-conscious church experience. In *The Freedom of a Christian*, one indeed finds the Luther of the *solus* when he writes, "To preach Christ means to feed the soul, make it righteous, set it free, and save it, provided it believes the preaching. Faith alone is the saving and efficacious use of the Word of God."[12] Luther clarifies what he means by "alone" when he claims that "it is clear that the inner man cannot be justified, freed, or saved by any outer work or action at all, and that these works, whatever their character, having nothing to do with the inner man."[13] And yet, thanks to the nuances of Merton's account of freedom and obedience, I started to see that when Luther talks about these "outer works," he does not, in fact, disparage obedience. Instead, he seems to mean by "outer works" something akin to what Merton means by the works of the false self. As Luther says, Christian faith "honors him whom it trusts with the most reverent and highest regard since it considers him truthful and trustworthy."[14] By honoring God in this way, he argues, faith itself is *obedience*. "Is not such a soul most obedient to God in all things by this faith? What commandment is there that such obedience has not completely fulfilled?"[15] Luther concludes by suggesting that "faith works truth and righteousness by giving God what belongs to him."[16] How, really, is this faith different from contemplation in Merton's sense, as the transformative awareness of our Source,

11. *New Seeds*, p. 31.

12. Martin Luther, *The Freedom of a Christian* in *Martin Luther: Selections from His Writings*. Ed. by John Dillenberger. New York: Anchor Books, 1962, p. 55.

13. Luther, *Freedom*, p. 56.

14. Luther, *Freedom,* p. 59.

15. Luther, *Freedom,* p. 59.

16. Luther, *Freedom*, p. 60.

beyond the illusions of the false self? Merton says contemplation is faith in the deepest sense, faith that engenders "a deep resonance in the inmost center of our spirit in which our very life loses its separate voice and re-sounds with the majesty and the mercy of the Hidden and Living One." [17] In this manner trust in God's utter generosity is integrated with the process of moral transformation. It was this integration that allowed me as a young theologian to read some of my Protestant sources in a different key, discovering a desire for the integration of freedom and obedience at the heart of many of their writings too.

Anabaptist theological critiques of the modern separation of salvation from external action also had a formative influence on my thinking. Mennonite sociality had been part of my upbringing, certainly, but in graduate school I was able for the first time to plumb the theological depths of that social vision. John Howard Yoder, whose work I first encountered in a master's seminar, is highly critical of what he calls "mainstream Christian ethics," which is built on the premise that salvation has an exclusively inner relevance. "The status of being just or righteous before God." Yoder writes that such theology, "is therefore radically disconnected from any objective or empirical achievement of goodness by the believer." [18] This view does not preclude the possibility of ethical Christians, to be sure, but for Yoder it does seriously obstruct the development of specifically *Christian* ethical principles. In Yoder's estimation, in fact, the alienation of faith as inwardness from social ethics is so profound in the Western Christian tradition that we ought to have no truck with faith's contemplative dimensions at all. Thus his critique reaches beyond modern Protestantism, to the entire "heritage of Augustine." [19] For Yoder, these two aspects of faith cannot be integrated, for the "existential" dimensions inevitably take center stage in a way that makes obedience to Jesus' example of nonviolence irrelevant to salvation.

This became the other pole in my Protestant formation: a deep skepticism of the inwardness of faith.[20] Here too though, I found

17. *New Seeds*, p. 3.

18. Yoder, *The Politics of Jesus*, p. 213.

19. Yoder, *The Politics of Jesus*, p. 214.

20. Though at this point I did push back and defend the existential dimensions of Christian faith against Yoder's wholesale dismissal. See, for example, Justin D; Klassen, "Augustinian Existentialism and Yoder's Messianic Politics: Revolutionary Implications of Augustine's Understanding of Right Worship,"

that Merton provided a way through the dilemma. If Yoder became my Protestant (radically reformed) skeptic of the typical modern Christian focus on inwardness, Merton was one of the thinkers who held that skepticism in check. For Merton, to deal with social ethics in a Christian way, and particularly with the problem of violence, inwardness is inescapable. This is because the problem of violence is about fear. "At the root of all war is fear: not so much the fear men have of one another as the fear they have of *everything*."[21] This is an inward problem, a problem stemming from how we relate to ourselves and to God. It is a matter of failing to trust my Source and therefore falling back on trusting myself, then finding myself not powerful enough on my own, so joining with others to better prove my power to myself—by identifying and destroying "enemies." How do we get out of this cycle of fear? "God's grace is sufficient" is a familiar Evangelical Christian trope. It implies that God's attribution of righteousness is enough for me to attain salvation, so I don't have to do anything myself to earn it. Rather than dismissing this inner gesture of faith in God's sufficient power for salvation, as Yoder does, Merton looks at it from a different angle. For him, finding God's grace to be sufficient is about finding God as the source of life, trustworthy to address all my fears. Absent this inner attitude of trust, Merton thinks it will not be possible for me to live without killing, since fear is the root of all war. In other words, without trusting that God's grace is enough, I won't be able to follow Jesus in discipleship. Unlike Yoder, then, who dismisses the whole "heritage of Augustine," Merton maintains that "only the man who has fully attained his own spiritual identity can live without the need to kill, and without the need of a doctrine that permits him to do so with a good conscience."[22] One needs this inner movement, this inner depth dimension of faith, in order to have hope of concrete transformation into the form of Christ. It is trust in God as one's true Source that brings resiliency in the face of death, the fear of which would otherwise drive one to violence. It is true that this inwardness is not identical with the hyper-grace-conscious Protestantism that makes works-righteousness our supreme enemy. But nor does it fear "the heritage of Augustine." Instead it hears

The Conrad Grebel Review 25 (3) pp. 52-67.

21. *New Seeds*, p. 112.

22. Thomas Merton, *Raids on the Unspeakable*. New York: New Directions, 1964, p. 22.

both dimensions of faith in a new key, thereby registering their harmony with one another.

III. THE SANCTITY OF CREATED FORMS

Another tension at the heart of modern Protestantism is that between religious truth and the world of God's making. Many Protestant traditions are known for their iconoclastic rigor, affirming Jesus Christ as the sole material deposit of divine truth, and judging all other creaturely forms harshly in terms of their capacity for mediating God's reality. Thus the typical Protestant suspicion of sacramentality and iconography. In the modern Protestant imagination, to locate God's truth in the world is always to risk dethroning Jesus. This view remains a source of the tragic Christian objections to environmental responsibility that one often encounters today.

With regard to iconoclasm, Protestantism today clearly bears the imprint of the "dialectical" theology of the early and mid-twentieth century. For example, one can see Karl Barth's lasting influence in a range of recent "apocalyptic" interpretations of the New Testament.[23] Many of these Protestant works continue in the vein of Barth's interpretation of Paul's letter to the Romans in the 1920s, a book I studied with enthusiasm when I first discovered it. Faced with a surge in historical-critical readings of the New Testament, Barth reaffirmed in dramatic fashion the abiding "otherness" of the substance of the gospel. "I have nothing whatever to say against historical criticism," Barth offers in one of his prefaces. "My complaint is that recent commentators confine themselves to an interpretation of the text which seems to me to be no commentary at all, but merely the first step towards a commentary."[24] A genuine commentary, Barth reflects, should not shy away from the notion that Paul, however he might be understood in relation to his historical context, also knew himself as the bearer of a message that was utterly transcendent of any such context. "However great and important a man Paul may have been, the essential theme

---

23. See, for example, Samuel V. Adams, *The Reality of God and Historical Method: Apocalyptic Theology in Conversation with N. T. Wright.* Downers Grove, IL: IVP Academic, 2015; Joshua B. Davis & Douglas Harink (eds.) *Apocalyptic and the Future of Theology: With and Beyond J. Louis Martyn.* Eugene, OR: Cascade Books, 2015; Nathan Kerr, *Christ, History, and Apocalyptic: The Politics of Christian Mission.* Eugene, OR: Cascade Books, 2008.

24. Barth, *The Epistle to the Romans,* p. 6.

of his mission is not within him but above him—unapproachably distant and unutterably strange."[25] This strangeness, for Barth, determines the identity of Paul qua apostle, the substance of his message being the "perpendicular" truth of God made manifest in the person of Jesus Christ.

In Christ, Barth argues, "two worlds meet and go apart, two planes intersect, the one known and the other unknown. The known plane is God's creation, fallen out of its union with Him, and therefore the world of the 'flesh' needing redemption, the world of men, and of time, and of things—our world."[26] No matter what moment we might apprehend it, the truth of God as revealed in Christ will always be interruptive, an unknown plane intersecting the known. This means that for Barth, the form of Christian truth is always shatteringly paradoxical, strange to the point of being a complete negation of the known world, the world we perceive and apprehend with our senses and with the tools of historical criticism. Salvific divine truth can be apprehended only in the mode of a faith Barth describes as "awe in the presence of the divine incognito; it is the love of God that is aware of the qualitative distinction between God and man and God and the world . . . and therefore it is the affirmation of the divine 'No' in Christ, of the shattering halt in the presence of God."[27] So it is that gospel truth, for Barth, becomes a synonym for alien truth. This remains one of the abiding features of some variants of Protestantism today, the emphasis on Christ as a shattering interruption of ordinary events, to such a degree that not only human sin but the world itself stands irrevocably accused. What is the perception of rain compared with this "shattering halt?" What is the supposed wisdom of an ecosystem compared with the creator's truth apprehended in all its shattering perpendicularity? Nothing, apparently.

I recall the first time I was asked to teach a course on religion and ecology. I learned that to look at the world through the lens of the natural sciences is to bear witness to a long and complicated story, and to be filled with wonder. But it also became clear to me how the magnitude of this story, the story of created nature, utterly dwarfs the dialectical Protestant understanding of where and when truth may enter the picture. If you have never seen it, go and search

25. Barth, *The Epistle to the Romans*, p. 27.
26. Barth, *The Epistle to the Romans,* p. 29.
27. Barth, *The Epistle to the Romans*, p. 39.

for "Carl Sagan's cosmic calendar" on the Internet and you will see what I mean. How can we possibly imagine that God would wait billions of years—until very recently, in fact—to introduce a blinding and somewhat contradictory (or at least, perpendicular) truth to the world that supposedly finds its origin in this same God? In 1967, the historian Lynn White, Jr. suggested that Christianity is largely responsible for our present ecological crises, given its human-centered view that the whole of our unimaginably large universe was really made only for the sake of staging a parochial little human drama.[28] One can see how it would be hard to argue with him, since Christians persist in claiming God's agenda is visible in Jesus but not in the rest of the cosmos.

It is true that later in his career Karl Barth seemed more open to apprehending God in the passions of creaturely life, not only in the definitional clarity of theological categories and "intersecting planes." This is precisely the Barth in whom Thomas Merton took a certain interest. Despite his reputation for emphasizing paradox and the "qualitative distinction" between God and humanity, Barth ended up discovering God in his enjoyment of Mozart, some of which had to be corporeal and thus continuous with other immanent delights. So Barth wrote about Mozart,[29] and Merton points out that "Barth perhaps is striving to admit that he will be saved more by the Mozart in himself than by his theology."[30] Of course, Merton himself emphasizes the interruptive character of the gospel, for example, when he writes that "in order to become oneself, one must die. That is to say, in order to become one's true self, the false self must die."[31] In this suggestion that the truth of God in Christ turns the ordinary world upside down, Merton aligns well with Barth, and even with *The Epistle to the Romans.* As Barth puts it there, "Those who take upon them the divine 'No' shall themselves be borne by the greater divine 'Yes' . . . . Those who do not shun the contradiction have been hidden in God."[32] Both Merton and Barth thus have a clear sense that the action of God in bringing about a

28. Lynn White, Jr., "The Historical Roots of Our Ecological Crisis," *Science* Vol. 155, Issue 3767, pp. 1203-1207.

29. See Karl Barth, *Wolfgang Amadeus Mozart*. Eugene, OR: Wipf & Stock, 2003.

30. *Conjectures*, p. 11.

31. Thomas Merton, *Essential Writings.* Ed. by Christine M. Bochen. Maryknoll NY: Orbis Books, 2000, p. 64.

32. Barth, *The Epistle to the Romans,* p. 41.

new creation in the human person is tantamount to the undoing of our own independent activity.

The difference, from my perspective, is that Merton places a lot of emphasis on how the action of God in making all things new is entirely consistent with God's action in making all things in the first place. For Barth and much of the Evangelical Protestantism he continues to inspire, one almost gets the impression that the redemptive action of God is directed not simply against sin but against the whole created world. By contrast, for Merton, God's unmaking of the false self brings about a new awareness of the ever-present action of God in creation. For Barth, the "known" world is the world of immanent reality, never up to the task of expressing the infinite truth of God, which therefore remains an "unknown" plane. For Merton, the unknown is the world of the false self, while the known is the world in its proper relation to God, the world as it is known by God.[33] This variation in emphasis allows Merton to recognize the redemptive will of God in the manifestation of God's creative will all around him. We might even say that it allows Merton to see the Word of God continuously breathed into the flesh of creation all throughout the history of the universe, making the Christ event an interruption of human consciousness but not of cosmic history, as it sometimes is in the Protestant imagination.

Take Merton's description of an evening spent listening to the rain. "I celebrate its gratuity and its meaninglessness," he writes, "and I listen because it reminds me once again and again that the whole world runs by rhythms I have not yet learned to recognize, rhythms that are not those of the engineer."[34] For Merton, the problem of sin is a problem of alienation from our true created form. It is not a problem of a de jure lack of access to some "other" world, as Barth sometimes implies. The world as God made it and continues to make it is right here before our eyes. The truth of the world, revealed in Christ, is also disclosed in the trees and the rain, which we usually ignore. But if we could just open ourselves to the world, get out of the city and its mindset for a while, we might see what Merton sees. "The trees I know, the night I know, the rain, I know. I close my eyes and instantly sink into the whole rainy world of which I am a part, and the world goes on with me in it, for I am

33. *New Seeds,* p. 34.
34. Merton, *Raids on the Unspeakable*, p. 9.

not alien to it."[35] Merton is clear that the problem of sin is not inherent in the world of creation itself, nor the world of time, but in the human presumption to be like gods. To pretend to divinity is to insist that everything in creation should have an explicable use, that nothing (least of all ourselves) should be contingent. It is to desire a world in which nothing is a gift and all is a possession. Ultimately, it is to construct "a world outside the world, against the world, a world of mechanical fictions which contemn nature and seek only to use it up, thus preventing it from renewing itself and man."[36] The jarring interruption of the action of God in Christ and in the Spirit is therefore not an interruption of the created order, but an interruption of humanity's distorted imagination of reality.

For Merton, our vision of reality is distorted when we have rejected creation's contingency. We have decided that a reality in which not every single element can be made explicable is not good. We decide that the weather, for example, "not being planned, not being fabricated, is an impertinence, a wen on the visage of progress."[37] We think that to be considered real, a thing should first give us its reason for being, and that our own reality should be similarly justifiable to the others involved with us in this fiction. "In order to experience yourself as real, you have to suppress the awareness of your contingency, your unreality, your state of radical need."[38] Christ interrupts our world, Merton suggests, not by being something paradoxically and unutterably other to creation, but by consenting to live without self-deception in creaturely form. And the good news is that "the gift of truth with which Christ dispelled the three kinds of illusion offered him in his temptation (security, reputation, and power) can become also our own truth, if we can only accept it."[39] It is difficult for us to accept a truth we have worked so hard to obscure from our own sight. But the consolation is that such truth is already present in the world around us, and has been from the beginning. Christ resounds in the world with the interruptive acceptance of creaturely contingency, the daring faith that contingency is precisely God's name "written in us, as our

35. Merton, *Raids on the Unspeakable*, p. 10
36. Merton, *Raids on the Unspeakable*, p. 11.
37. Merton, *Raids on the Unspeakable,* p. 12.
38. Merton, *Raids on the Unspeakable,* pp. 13-14.
39. Merton, *Raids on the Unspeakable*, p. 18.

poverty, as our indigence, as our dependence, as our sonship"[40] But so too, and already, "the valley resounds with the totally uninformative talk of creeks and wild water."[41] The created world, in its transcendence of our demand for reasons, speaks the Word of God with the breath of the Spirit.

This is why, in my most recent scholarly work on theology and nature, I continue to find Merton such an inspiration and a force for integration. While remaining sensitive to the radically interruptive character of God's action in Christ, Merton refuses to separate redemption from creation. He can think alongside Barth but he is always hearing the music too. He is untroubled by the thought of Mozart's theological acuity without being a theologian. This makes him unrepentant about ascribing holiness not only to the paradoxical form of the god-man, but to the inspired forms of all creatures:

> This leaf has its own texture and its own pattern of veins and its own holy shape, and the bass and trout hiding in the deep pools of the river are canonized by their beauty and their strength. The lakes hidden among the hills are saints, and the sea too is a saint who praises God without interruption in her majestic dance. The great, gashed, half-naked mountain is another of God's saints. There is no other like him. He is alone in his own character; nothing else in the world ever did or ever will imitate God in quite the same way. That is his sanctity.[42]

For Merton, we are shattered by the revelation of God in Christ, but God's work as creator is affirmed. It is finally allowed to appear in truth before the newly receptive gaze of transformed persons, in the process of becoming not only new but also true to their original created character.

IV. CONCLUSION: THE ONGOING FESTIVAL OF RAIN

It is for all these reasons that Merton has been for me a thinker of integration. He holds together many of the separated and potentially alienating poles of Christian faith.

When it comes to faith and moral formation, Merton offers a

---

40. Merton, *Conjectures*, p. 158.
41. Merton, *Raids on the Unspeakable*, p. 23.
42. Merton, *New Seeds*, pp. 30-31.

compelling way to see them as mutually inclusive and enhancing. For him, the contemplative and inner dimensions of faith are no mere matter of intellectual assent, but are the essential source of transformed and transforming action. Counting on God for one's salvation demands a subjective turn away from one's own power and toward the authority and authorship of God. And thus it involves a turn away from fear. It is the first step toward a life that is free from care. As Merton says, "A life that has nothing but a straight line towards the grave and a lot of little circular lines to forget the grave as you travel toward the grave is a life of care . . . and it is a life of futility."[43] By contrast, a life free from care is a life that rests, not in its power to avoid or forget the grave, but in God. Faith in this sense of trusting God is not only transactional but also genuinely transformative. Merton does not hereby nullify the protests of Protestantism, of course. But what he does is to allow contemporary Protestants to read their sources a little more closely, and to recognize in their work, too, this connection between faith and moral transformation.

Merton is productively skeptical of the Evangelical's tendency to detach faith from a binding process of transformation, but is also suspicious of some skeptics' total rejection of the inner dimensions of faith as if they inevitably obscure the call to discipleship. While Merton agrees with the critique of abstract faith that one finds in Yoder and other Christian ethicists, he also respects the turn inward, and shows how necessary it is for engendering peaceable action in the world. For Merton, the existential shift, what we might call the Kierkegaardian moment of faith, is crucial for living up to a pacifist ethic: "Only the man who has fully attained his own spiritual identity can live without the need to kill, and without the need of a doctrine that permits him to do so with a good conscience."[44] In ways I have found instructive and challenging, Merton is both for and against each of the poles of Protestant faith and ethics that were formative for me as a young Christian.

Finally, Merton is productively skeptical of the way Protestant iconoclasm can sometimes function. On the one hand, he agrees with the dialectical theologians that the gospel is shattering and interruptive. But he also ensures, as perhaps only a monastic and a hermit is able to do, that the divine "No" does not escape its bounds

43. Merton, *Essential Writings*, p. 68.
44. Merton, *Raids on the Unspeakable*, p. 22.

as a critique of sin, and become a condemnation of creatureliness as such. For Merton, God's Word is Jesus, but it is also the animating wisdom and sanctity of all creation. And this, finally, is Merton's most crucial reminder of integration—that God creates out of *love*, which means God both empowers and trusts what God has made, herein calling upon human beings to trust it too, beyond any measureable usefulness, and entirely in its gratuity. Thus, in the end, Merton reminds us that the God of redemption is still the God who sees that creation is very good—and would, in an act of redemptive love, enable us to see it too, that we might join the angels in singing God's praise, a song that is none other than the ongoing "festival of rain."[45]

---

45. Merton, *Raids on the Unspeakable,* p. 11.

BIBLIOGRAPHY

The following volumes were consulted in the research for Part One.

Books by Thomas Merton

Collected Poems. New York: New Directions, 1977

Conjectures of a Guilty Bystander. Garden City, NY: Doubleday, 1966

Contemplation in a World of Action. Garden City, NY: Doubleday, 1971.

Faith and Violence. Notre Dame, IN: University of Notre Dame Press, 1968.

Love and Living. Ed. by Patrick Hart and Naomi Burton Stone. New York: Bantam Books, 1965.

Mystics and Zen Masters. New York: Dell Publishing Co., 1961.

Seeds of Destruction. New York: Farrar, Straus and Giroux, 1961.

The Seven Storey Mountain. New York: Harcourt, 1948.

Journals of Thomas Merton

Run to the Mountain. Volume 1. Ed. by Patrick Hart. HarperSanFrancisco, 1995.

Entering the Silence. Volume 2. Ed. by Jonathan Montaldo. HarperSanFrancisco, 1996.

A Search for Solitude. Volume 3. Ed. by Lawrence Cunningham. HarperSanFrancisco, 1996.

Turning Toward the World. Volume 4. Ed. by Victor Kramer. HarperSanFrancisco, 1996.

Dancing in the Water of Life. Volume 5. Ed. by Robert E. Daggy. HarperSanFrancisco, 1997.

Learning to Love. Volume 6. Ed. by Christine M. Bochen. HarperSanFrancisco, 1997.

The Other Side of the Mountain. Volume 7. Ed. by Patrick Hart. HarperSanFrancisco, 1998.

LETTERS OF THOMAS MERTON

The Hidden Ground of Love. Ed. by William H. Shannon. New York: Farrar, Straus and Giroux, 1985.

The Road to Joy. Ed. by Robert E. Daggy. New York: Farrar, Straus and Giroux, 1989.

The School of Charity. Ed. by Patrick Hart, OCSO. New York: Farrar, Straus and Giroux, 1990.

The Courage for Truth. Ed. by Christine M. Bochen. New York: Farrar, Straus and Giroux, 1993.

Witness to Freedom. Ed. by William H. Shannon. New York: Farrar, Straus and Giroux, 1994.

COLLECTIONS WITH BOTH SIDES OF THE CORRESPONDENCE

A Catch of Anti-Letters by Thomas Merton and Robert Lax. Kansas City: Sheed and Ward, 1978.

A Meeting of Angels: The Correspondence of Thomas Merton and Edward Deming and Faith Andrews. Ed. by Paul M. Pearson. Frankfort, KY: Broadstone Books, 2008.

At Home in the World: The Letters of Thomas Merton and Rosemary Radford Ruether. Ed. by Mary Tardiff, OP. Maryknoll, NY: Orbis Books, 1995.

Encounter: Thomas Merton and D. T. Suzuki. Ed. by Robert E. Daggy. Monterey, KY: Larkspur Press, 1988.

The Letters of Robert Giroux and Thomas Merton. Ed. by Patrick Samway, SJ. Notre Dame, IN: University of Notre Dame Press, 2015.

Signs of Peace: The Interfaith Letters of Thomas Merton. Ed. by William Apel. Maryknoll, NY: Orbis Press, 2006.

Striving Towards Being: The Letters of Thomas Merton and Czeslaw Milosz. Ed. by Robert Faggen. New York: Farrar, Straus and Giroux, 1997.

Survival or Prophecy? The Letters of Thomas Merton and Jean

Leclercq. Ed. by Brother Patrick Hart, OCSO. New York: Farrar, Straus and Giroux, 2002.

Thomas Merton and James Laughlin: Selected Letters. Ed. by David D. Cooper. New York: W.W. Norton, 1997.

The Letters of Thomas Merton and Victor and Carolyn Hammer. Ed. by F. Douglas Scutchfield and Paul Evans Holbrook, Jr. Lexington, KY: University of Kentucky Press, 2014.

When Prophecy Still Had a Voice: The Letters of Thomas Merton and Robert Lax. Lexington, KY: University of Kentucky Press, 2001.

LIST OF CONTRIBUTORS

JAMES BAKER was a Professor of History at Western Kentucky University, a Fulbright Senior Lecturer which took him to Asia, a novelist, and the author of a play about Merton. While a campus minister and graduate student at Florida State University he wrote the first Ph.D. dissertation on Merton, consulting with Merton throughout the process. It was later published under the title *Thomas Merton—Social Critic.*

BRIAN L. COLE is the rector at Good Shepherd Episcopal Church in Lexington, Kentucky. He previously served as the Sub-Dean at the Cathedral of All Souls in Asheville, North Carolina and is now an Associate of the Order of the Holy Cross. He first visited Gethsemani as part of group of seminarians led by Dr. Bill Leonard, also a contributor to this volume. Father Cole has also served as an adjunct professor at Wake Forest University School of Divinity.

GARY HALL trains and teaches a range of courses in practical theology at the ecumenical Queen's Foundation in Birmingham, UK. A Methodist presbyter, he previously had pastoral responsibilities in diverse urban communities in Leeds and Leicester. He developed cross-cultural learning programs for the Methodist Church working with partners in India and Latin America. He is co-editor of *The Merton Journal,* and regularly leads conferences and retreats on Merton.

LIBBY FALK JONES is Professor of English and Chester D. Tripp Chair in Humanities at Berea College in Berea, Kentucky, where she teaches creative writing, autobiography, vocation, and contemplative writing and photography. She has published poems and creative nonfiction in regional and national journals including *The Merton Seasonal.* Her collection of poems, *Above the Treetops*, appeared in 2010 and she is coauthor of a 2015 poetry collection, *Balance of Five*. She received her Ph.D. from Stony Brook University in New York.

JUSTIN D. KLASSEN earned his M.A. and Ph.D. in religious studies at McMaster University in Hamilton, Ontario. He teaches and researches philosophical theology, Christian ethics, and ecotheology at Bellarmine University in Louisville, Kentucky. He is the author of *The Paradox of Hope* and co-editor of *Aspiring to Fullness in a Secular Age: Essays on Religion and Theology in the Work of Charles Taylor.*

ALAN KLOP holds the Baldwin Wallace University Chair in Faith and Life and is Professor of Religion, teaching historical and spiritual studies. His Ph.D. is from Harvard University. Formerly Professor and Dean at the Earlham School of Religion, he is the co-founder of the Center for Innovation and Growth at Baldwin Wallace. He currently serves on the Board of Directors of the International Thomas Merton Society.

BILL J. LEONARD was the founding Dean of the School of Divinity at Wake Forest University where he now serves as the James and Marilyn Dunn Professor of Baptist Studies and Professor of Church History. He is the author of twenty-five books. His Ph.D. is from Boston University. He has lectured widely in the United States and abroad.

STEPHANIE A. PAULSELL received her Ph.D. in Religion and Literature from the University of Chicago Divinity School. She is currently the Susan Shallcross Swartz Professor of the Practice of Christian Studies at Harvard Divinity School. She is the author of *Honoring the Body: Meditations on a Christian Practice* and, with Harvey Cox, author of *Lamentations and the Song of Songs.* She edited *The Scope of Our Art: The Vocation of the Theological Teacher,* and is a regular columnist for *The Christian Century.*

WILLIAM OLIVER PAULSELL is the President Emeritus of Lexington Theological Seminary. Prior to his service as Dean and later President of the seminary, he was Professor of Religion at Barton College in North Carolina. His Ph.D. in church history is from Vanderbilt University. His area of specialization is the history of Christian spirituality. He is the author of six books.

STEPHEN V. SPRINKLE is Director of Field Education and Professor of Practical Theology at Brite Divinity School in Fort Worth, Texas, and an ordained minister of the Alliance of Baptists. He graduated from seminary at Yale Divinity School and holds a Ph.D. from Duke University. He is the author of *Disciples and Theology: Understanding the Faith of a People in Covenant.*